BOB MCNESBY

OCEAN LIFEGUARD

Reflections from a Son of the Beach

ISBN: 1461015766

ISBN-13: 9781461015765

DEDICATION

This book is dedicated to all past, present and future life-guards of the Atlantic City Beach Patrol, but especially, and in remembrance of the following: Murph, Geza, Jackie, Jimmy, Roy, Boomer and Mike.

ACKNOWLEDGEMENTS

I'm indebted to the following people for committing to me what I consider their most valuable asset—time. In reading my book and giving me feedback, positive or not, they were gracious enough to interrupt their own lives and share their honest opinions. For that I am deeply grateful. They are: Susan Genova, Keith McNesby, Jim and Carolyn McHale, Bob Murphy, Jay Deitch, Marilyn Mendez, Gina Rogers, Gittan Manson, Regina Robinson and Sue Trottier.

I must include special thanks to my brother Mick, who has been my best friend my whole life. He encouraged and helped me more then I can say, by offering his valuable knowledge, and expertise in English grammar, and all things technical. His assistance was invaluable in helping me recall memories of our Atlantic City days, in which he played a major part. But mostly, for being my brother, who has always stood by and supported me throughout the years we have spent together.

And, to Juliana Ashe, my friend of many years, without whose help this book would never have been completed. Julie encouraged me, after I had all but abandoned this work. She inspired and pushed me to finish what I had started, and gave me confidence with her valuable input, as to why she thought I had something worthwhile to offer. Finally, a willingness to spend countless hours of her time, demonstrating her faith in me, by assisting in the editing process, resulted in the finished product. Julie is an angel.

TABLE OF CONTENTS

Chapters and Subsection Headings

CHAPTER 1

THE RESCUE

Of all the beach front motels I rented in winter, this was the best. Actually, it was only the second. The first was great in that it butted right up to the boardwalk and had an ocean view. Only problem, my room was on the side of the building so the ocean view wasn't exactly viewing me back.

But this place was different. It was located in Ventnor, N.J. a quiet city just down beach of Atlantic City. We had a second story apartment with sliding glass doors overlooking the boardwalk, beach and ocean. The rent was very reasonable because motel owners had a problem filling units during winter.

I had recently married and my new bride was at the end of a teaching contract she had to fulfill before we could move to her hometown in N.Y. State.

With the exception of a four year stint in the U.S. Navy and another four years at a Florida college I had lived in Atlantic City all my life. It hardly seemed like a winter had passed since I'd completed my fourteenth, and final year as a member of the Atlantic City Beach Patrol.

I walked out on our balcony and surveyed the scene before me. It was strange to overlook an empty boardwalk and beach but this was a cloudy overcast day in early June. A chilly wind came down from the north whipping the waves into an angry frenzy.

Ventnor Pier lay a short block away. As I focused on its skeletal frame I was reminded of a rescue my partner and I had alongside another pier years before. Of the hundreds of rescues I'd been involved in during my years on the beach patrol, this clearly remained the most challenging and dangerous. My mind drifted--once again I experienced the memory of that day when...

I walked across the boardwalk, and was greeted by an ocean bathed in brilliant sunshine; its reflective surface cast a shimmering glow. To the casual observer the day would seem ideal, and yet, an ominous feeling persisted that this would be no ordinary beach day.

One observation, not to be denied, was a dry nor'east current running swiftly down-beach toward Million Dollar Pier. The danger was further marked by a churning offset covering a two-block area from Michigan Avenue to the pier. These conditions were exacerbated by high waves and menacing winds, blowing from the north, that momentarily hid the sun and brought about an uneasy chill.

Even the locker room banter, as we changed into our uniforms, was not the same. It was subdued, without the usual good natured camaraderie that normally set the day's tone. No one engaged in the daily ball-busting ritual. Guys were uneasy, as if they felt a sense of foreboding. Where silence is sometimes thought to be golden, this was anything but.

"Murph," our captain, was pressing us to "make sure your boats and stands are down by the water's edge." He kept repeating, "This is a bad ocean," as if we didn't know. His five-year-old son, Stevie, whom we had to endure on a daily basis, was even more annoying than usual.

It was that kind of day.

We grabbed our oars, donuts, can buoys and proceeded to our stations, as if to say, "Let's get this day over with." My partner, Tommy and I turned the boat upright and rolled it to the water's edge. We went back, picked up the lifeguard stand and carried it down to its place by the boat.

Tommy put curtains up on the sides and back of the stand to shield the wind. He then laid a beach chair pad the length of the seat and stretched out with the morning paper. I opted for reclining in the boat which rested on its rollers. Lifeboats carried donuts in their bow and stern and like a comfortable potty were quite pleasant to sit on. We both wore our full uniforms consisting of tank top, trunks, sweat suit and jacket. Days like this could get chilly after being exposed to a cool wind blowing down beach for hours.

While Tommy read the paper, I kept an eye on the empty ocean. Apparently, the beach goers also had some reluctance about getting to the beach early. Somewhere around 11:00 A.M. we snapped out of our lethargy and sent our thirty something year old mascot, Kenny, for coffee.

Even though the wind had picked up the day began to warm and beach goers began to succumb to the allure of the salt sea air. As the more adventurous found their way to the 67-degree water we introduced them to the shrill blast of our whistles. It was necessary to keep the crowd herded uptown, away from the pier, and out of trouble. This was not difficult, since none had ventured out past their waists.

There was, however, still reason for concern. During a fast-running nor'east current, a bather who attempts to swim or float can be drawn swiftly into a dangerous situation. Before they realize the seriousness of their condition, it's sometimes too late. It was the same way along our entire stretch. All the guards were down by the water's edge directing bathers to stay clear of danger. Because of this necessity, and at our urging, beach goers moved their blankets and umbrellas from the area between Million Dollar Pier and our stand at Arkansas, closer to the safer ocean confines of Michigan Avenue. In so doing, they had less distance to travel from their beach location to the water.

We had been keeping tabs on some French Canadians, who'd come to the beach after we had moved the previous bathers closer to Michigan. They couldn't have missed our efforts to keep everyone up and away from the danger. However, they saw this expanse of empty beach and predictably planted themselves close to the pier. It was often our experience with French Canadians that they seemed to have an affinity for keeping to themselves. I don't know if it was because of the language barrier, or, if in this case they thought they'd found an open area away from the throngs.

The group consisted of two men and four women. Immediately they started breaking all beach conventions, throwing mud, not disposing of food wrappings and--as we strongly suspected--drinking.

We were just getting ready to go tell them to cut out the nonsense, and direct them to the safer area, when suddenly the four girls, yelling like banshees, broke and dashed for the ocean. They were heading straight for the danger area. We whistled to them but they either ignored us or didn't think the warning was for them.

Knowing we had to react quickly, we sprinted for the boat shedding our jackets and sweat suits as we ran. This was definitely trouble!

We launched the boat off its rollers and leaped in, me in the bow Tommy in the stern. We were rowing in seconds. As bathers heard the chilling staccato of our run whistles they scurried to get out of the way. Seconds later, we observed our backup crew of Geza and Jackie launching their boat in pursuit. It was comforting to know we weren't in this alone.

As we moved through the break we rowed at a dangerous angle, waves pounding us on the port side, while being soaked by the resulting spray. It was difficult keeping our bow into the wind. Every time we'd gain momentum, another wave would crash over us. We feared capsizing with every stroke.

I turned to assess the situation, it was already worse than I feared. Two of the girls had recklessly abandoned any caution and were moving headlong into the offset.

The waves mounted. Our adrenalin was pumping as we pulled with all our strength, while a powerful wave bore down on us. For a split second I didn't know whether to let it break first and then plow over it, or race for the crest before it swallowed us. As the bow man I opted for the latter.

I remember shouting, Tommy, give me some motor! It wasn't necessary for him to look. He dug in as we frantically picked up our stroke. We felt ourselves go straight up in the air, hang suspended for what seemed like five seconds, and come down with a mighty splat!

We gathered ourselves, now clear of the break, no longer subject to the crashing waves. Free of this impediment, we were able to move faster and better survey the situation. Suddenly, remembering the other two guards, I looked up just in time to see Geza and Jackie get broadsided by a huge wave filling their boat to the gunnels, and dashing them headlong to the beach. They grabbed can buoys from the sunken boat and took off down beach in another attempt to assist us.

Turning for another look, my worst fears were confirmed. The first two girls were now being controlled by the deadly offset. The second two were following the first duo into this vortex of danger, unaware of their plight. It didn't take long for all four to realize their predicament. They tried to swim against the set in a vain attempt to reach shore. The harder they swam the more exhausted they became. The merciless currents carried them inexorably toward the pier where rows of pilings with razor sharp barnacles awaited them

The two men had followed the girls but were not yet themselves in trouble. When they became aware of the girl's distress they raced to help. The two were good swimmers, but, as they would soon learn, no match for the wrath of this angry maelstrom.

Brave but foolhardy, the men swam into the set realizing quickly they were now part of the problem. We saw the panic in their body language, similar to a scene from *Jaws*. A look of panic came over their faces as they grasped the reality of their situation. The two realized they had made a big mistake and were floundering badly as the deadly offset took control. Tommy and I saw what was coming instantly. It played out before our eyes like a bad horror flick. We kept moving with the force and speed necessary to overtake them.

The set was now tossing the four girls wildly about. The choppy seas lapped their heads causing them to disappear beneath the surf, only to resurface arms and legs flailing frantically. We heard their cries of "Oh God, please help me!" Maneuvering as best we could, we battled the heavy surf, feeling the spray wash over the boat, soaking us with every stroke. Fatigue was setting in. We rowed as hard and fast as we could into this perilous situation.

Turning to take my last bearing I spotted the four panic-stricken victims whose repeated cries of "Oh God, oh God!" could still be heard above the high winds. The four were separated into pairs about forty feet apart.

We decided to go after the farthest two girls first because they were closest to the pier. As we closed within range, Tommy stood, braced himself, and threw the donut. They caught it and held on as he reeled them in. Locking on to the gunnel in a death grip the girls would not let go. Tommy, knowing our situation was getting desperate, reached down over the gunnel, grabbed the first girl by the seat of her bathing suit and hoisted her into the boat. He repeated this maneuver with the second girl.

As we turned to look for the other two girls, we realized their momentum was carrying them toward us. We intercepted them and in a moment they were alongside the boat. We'd hoped to maneuver them to the stern where the other two were already huddled in fear. Unfortunately, the first girl had grabbed the gunnel between the tholepins shutting down our ability to row. The second girl latched on to another part of the gunnel, close to the oars, further impeding our progress.

The two men who had tried to help were still upwind of us and closing fast. I abandoned my oars and moved quickly to the bow where there was another donut. This left the boat dangerously unattended and subject to the whims of the sea.

As the two men closed, I threw the donut almost ringing an outstretched arm. When I got them to the boat they grabbed onto the bow. Their combined weights had the effect of an anchor, impeding our ability to control the craft, placing us in further danger. There was no way I could get them into the bow, since the sides at that end are much higher and narrower than at the stern.

Tommy managed to get one of the second two girls to the stern. She was crying hysterically, holding on tightly to the gunnel, for fear of being washed back into the sea. Tommy moved to the girl who was now holding on between the oars. He tried to pry her hands loose to move her to the stern. She screamed in terror at the thought of losing her security. Her death grip was vise-like.

The two men hanging on to the bow started working their way toward the stern. They realized it would be easier to get in the boat at the lower end. As they got closer to the tholepins, they started tipping the boat at a dangerous angle. We tried to help them aboard but their combined weight caused the craft to list badly and we started taking on water. They quickly abandoned that plan.

We turned to see the hulking pier looming menacingly closer and realized we only had one choice; to sink the boat, and turn it over. [1]

Standing on the lower gunnel we rocked the boat and as water started pouring in, the vessel heaved upward. We reached for the upper gunnel to pull it over. The two men, who had been holding on to the lower gunnel,

---

1   The reason for this is twofold and part of our training. First: Piers have hundreds of pilings beneath them, further apart from side to side than front to back. This allows a lifeboat to be maneuvered through the openings. There are also huge groundswells below the pier running toward the beach, capable of lifting a boat like a cork and dashing it into the pilings. The pilings feature sharp barnacles that can cut like a razor. Second: When turned over, a boat becomes much heavier since the bulk of it is now underwater, thereby less affected by groundswells. However serious damage can still be inflicted by these dangerous conditions.

thrust themselves backwards to avoid getting hit by the overturning hull. The two girls on the other side let go when water started rushing in and grasped the craft's underbelly.

The pair in the stern, who may have thought they were secure, started screaming uncontrollably as they were thrown back into the sea. If any of the victims were able to have a rational moment they probably thought we had taken leave of our senses. But now, with the craft over and part of its belly exposed above the water, the six had something to cling to. Due to its heaviness, the vessel was not as easily moved by the current.

The girls continued screaming, sobbing and begging for God and their mothers to help them, while they held on for their lives. The men looked terrified.

We pointed our bow toward the pier and worked to get the victims moved to the seaward side of the boat to avoid the pilings.

I had moved one of the girls to the safer side of the craft and went back to the inside to see if others were in need. Instinctively I realized we were being carried under the pier. Just at that moment, a black cloud passed overhead blotting out the sun. Was this an omen?

The next instant unfolded like a slow motion picture. I saw the lifeboat being lifted by a groundswell and realized I was caught between it and some pilings. The boat descended upon me. At the last second, as it was about to crash into my head, I ducked beneath the surface and felt the concussion of its 500 plus pounds slam in to the piling, missing me by inches.

I had, however, gotten too close to the piling and as the sharp barnacles sliced me it was like hot coals searing my flesh. The burning sensation was compounded by the salt water. My back and legs were slashed and I saw the green water turn crimson. I started to surface with my arms held high above my head and came up under the vessel. Since an air pocket forms when a boat is turned over my training kicked in. I surfaced into the air pocket, took a breath, submerged, and came up safely on the seaward side of the boat.

This was not the end of our desperate saga.

One of the girls had slipped from the hull and grabbed a piling. Tommy swam to her but as he approached she made a wild lunge, catching him off guard. Bleeding profusely from the razor sharp barnacles she threw her arms around him in a death hold. Instead of resisting, Tommy grabbed her shoulders and dragged her under water. She let go immediately struggling for the surface. Tommy came up behind her, encircled her in a cross-chest carry, and draped her over the belly of the boat.

Geza and Jackie were now joined by two other guards who had decided it was fruitless to launch a boat. They made a dash for the piers underbelly. Their plan was to intercept us. A huge crowd, up beach, in hot pursuit, witnessed every moment of this human drama.

The boat, with our endangered victims, had gotten caught between two pilings. It was being perilously pummeled by large groundswells that threatened to swallow us.

As Tommy and I struggled to free the boat from its restraint we heard shouting and looked up to see the four guards racing to our rescue. A feeling of relief enveloped us. However the four guards were having difficulty making headway due to the heavy surf. Pounding seas kept tugging on their can buoys, pulling them back toward shore, as they struggled to negotiate each monstrous wave. We were still not out of danger as the heavy surf continued to wash over us.

Two of the four guards finally made it to our position; working with them, we were able to free the boat from its fetters. Once the boat was liberated, guiding it the rest of the way through the pier was much easier. We soothed our victims as the sun became visible and we drew closer to the other side.

I can only imagine what the Missouri Avenue guards thought as they saw us emerge from under the pier. There was no hesitation. They quickly launched two boats, followed by the two can men who hadn't been able to reach our position earlier.

The waves are smaller, the ocean floor shallower, on the downtown side of the pier. The reason for this was because on the Arkansas side the pier acted as a buffer to wind and currents on the Missouri side. This made the distance from the beach to our position much easier to cover. The guys were there in no time.

We helped get the victims in two vessels as they were swiftly transported to shore. The rest of us swam the sea filled boat toward the beach and as we reached shallow water were able to tip it and dump some of the water.

We repeated this maneuver until we were on the beach, the boat empty, and ready for more action.

Two more guards from the Missouri crew had launched another boat to pick up our equipment that was scattered over the ocean. Surprisingly, they recovered all six oars and both can buoys. The donuts with their long lines are always secured to the boat so they stayed with us. Normally you don't get all of those items until later, when they wash up on one of the beaches, sometimes miles away.

When we reached shore the crowd had gotten bigger, bolstered by a new contingent of people coming from the boardwalk, as well as beaches on the south side of the pier. A number of onlookers came to congratulate us saying what a good job we had done. A couple of concerned women advised me to get my barnacle cuts looked at. By now, they had mostly stopped bleeding as the blood congealed. I knew from past experience they looked worse than they were, though they burned like hell.

We chewed the fat with the Missouri guards for a few minutes, not daring to linger considering the conditions. We thanked them for getting to us so quickly and for retrieving our equipment. Even though our stations were just on the other side of the pier, we seldom saw these guys.

One of the unique things about the Missouri Avenue lifeguard crew was, they were all black. Atlantic City was still mostly segregated at that time. Blacks lived mainly on the city's North side. Years before, Missouri Avenue had been designated the "Negro" beach. It was still like that during the fifties and sixties, though blacks were starting to spread out to other beaches throughout the city.

As we made ready to go back to our station a large portion of the crowd still lingered. It was always the same after a dramatic rescue. The Canadians we had rescued were long gone. When the boats that carried them to safety reached shore the embarrassed six were helped out and disappeared faster than a magician's assistant. The crowd must have felt they'd been cheated. After witnessing this melodrama, and in some cases having followed it for a few blocks to its conclusion, they were not ready to have it end so abruptly. I always sensed they wanted us to address them with a critique of the rescue, putting aside the fact they had just watched the entire event for themselves. From our prospective, rescues were so common, that at times we probably exuded an air of indifference. Regardless, it always took the crowd a while to disperse

With the help of the Missouri guards, we picked up the boat by its inside braces and walked it back under the pier to our beach. This was much more efficient, and safer, than rowing it back out and around the end of the pier.

I left Tommy on the stand to watch the bathers while I went to the tent to have my cuts attended to. Each tent employed a medical student who served part of his residency for the beach patrol. They treated all comers including guards, beach goers, bathers, boardwalk strollers and anyone else who was in need of help.

During summers covering the 1950's and 60's, medical students along Atlantic City's beaches treated upwards of 60,000 people during a single season. This appointment was considered a plum position by future M.D.'s because of the experience it afforded them. Our guy was a handsome, personable kid named Ralph, who had married a Miss Atlantic City of that time.

After Ralph cleaned and sterilized my cuts I went back to the stand and resumed my duties. Tommy and I sat quietly and collected ourselves. Our reverie didn't last long. The weather began to deteriorate as the hours passed. The sky turned gray and the wind increased. The number of rescues accumulated along our stretch. We stayed busy herding bathers in small groups to prevent them from straying. Still, we had a fair number of runs, some routine others more serious. However nothing matched "The Canadians," as that rescue would come to be known.

Finally, the day ended.

The tent was abuzz, the adrenalin flowing, as it always did after multiple rescues. Murph was his old self again, busting our chops, saying what an easy day we'd had. His son Stevie, obnoxious as ever, stayed true to form. And the guys were commenting on who would score the best "chick" of the night.

That evening Tommy came over to my place where I was living with a few guys. We stretched out with a couple of beers.

Later in the evening we'd take a run uptown and check out the female situation.

Maybe we'd get lucky.

CHAPTER 2

DUCKTOWN DAYS

Ducktown, is a section of Atlantic City, New Jersey. It runs from Missouri Avenue to Texas Avenue. According to local legend the area was named for the many duck farms found along the bay before the turn of the century.

Although in recent times the district has become very diverse in its population; it was formally home to a large Italian American community.

As a boy, growing up in Ducktown, I remember pungent smelling cheeses hanging from ropes outside Italian grocery stores along Georgia and Mississippi Avenues. The women gathered on stoops outside their modest row homes. Ever vigilant, they stood out in their ubiquitous black dresses, brooms in hands, ready to whisk away any invasive bit of dirt marring their spotless sidewalks. Later, they would head up the street to St. Michaels Catholic Church to offer novenas and pray for us wayward sinners.

At mid-day we'd rush to Rando's Bakery to buy--hot out of the oven--a fresh square of tomato pie (forerunner of today's pizza) for a nickel. The old men of the neighborhood would congregate on a dirt road back by the bay and play Bocce Ball, while smoking their crooked foul-smelling stogies. Reminders of the neighborhoods past ethnicity can still be seen by the few Italian flags adorning its buildings.

For many years, Italian Mafia boss, **Little Nicky,** called Ducktown his home.

Ducktown, is also home to a number of Atlantic City attractions including **The White House Sub Shop,** on Mississippi and Arctic Avenues. The White house opened its doors in 1946 and is an Atlantic City institution. The subs are so good that Frank Sinatra use to have them flown to Las Vegas where he was performing. It has been family owned and operated for over 60 years.

Two other Atlantic City landmark restaurants located in Ducktown are **Angelo's Fairmount Tavern** located on Fairmount and Mississippi Avenues. It has been in the neighborhood since 1935. It is owned and operated by the Mancuso family and known for its Italian cuisine, as well as steaks and seafood. The other, **Dock's Oyster House** on Georgia and Atlantic Avenues is Atlantic City's oldest restaurant (circa 1897). Dock's, has for years been considered one of Atlantic City's finest seafood restaurants.

NEIGHBORHOOD CONNECTIONS

For ten of my first seventeen years I lived on Georgia Avenue in Ducktown.

Though Little Nicky's mother also resided on Georgia Avenue only a block away, we never knew her personally. Unfortunately, we wouldn't enjoy the same anonymity with Little Nicky.

Years later, in 1983, my brother Mick and I managed a restaurant/nightclub called The Flying Dutchman, where we would come face to face with Little Nicky.

We were hired, in part, to clean up and rid the place of some of the union employees who were stealing the place blind. Consequently, local union 54, controlled by Little Nicky, started sending their trained goons around to intimidate us. They told us to stop harassing their union employees. We ignored them until the day Nicky got out of prison. He came straight to the restaurant with five or six of his thugs to intimidate us.

He wasn't called Little Nicky without reason. Not much bigger'n a pissant at 5'6," he had a frightening presence, projecting danger. The group had lunch and sat around for a couple of hours. They never addressed us--they didn't have to--these guys were definitely scary.

One of Nicky's henchmen was his good friend and bodyguard, Salvatore. Salvi looked like he could have played linebacker in college. Clean cut and good looking, Sal did not fit the description of a Mafioso, though he'd been credited with fifteen murders. Regardless his body was found several months later in a ditch alongside the Atlantic City Expressway. He was the victim of a mob hit, through orders by none other than Nicky himself.

Shortly after Nicky's meeting at the Dutchman, we were told by the guys who fronted the place we'd better leave. We couldn't get away fast enough.

The White House Sub Shop, two blocks from where I lived was a favorite eating place. Many a night the family ordered subs from this landmark establishment. The place got so busy over the years it had to take its phone off the hook to avoid customers calling for pickups and deliveries.

On the walls of the White House, are photographs of every famous celebrity who ever came to Atlantic City. Very few of those ever left without having visited the popular eatery. Some included Frank Sinatra, Dean Martin and Jerry Lewis, The Beatles, Rocky Marciano, Robert Goulet and Mick Jagger, just to name a few.

Angelo's Fairmount Tavern, was a block from where we lived. It housed a small bar and separate dining room. My father used to call my mother from work occasionally and tell her to gather the kids and meet him at the restaurant. Although Angelo's was an Italian restaurant, it was unique in that it sold great steaks and seafood. The seafood was not of the Italian variety, normally found in Italian restaurants, but more like that of a typical New England seafood house.

My father spent about six months in a tuberculosis sanitarium as a young man during World War II. This forced my mother to seek employment, notwithstanding her daunting task of raising three young boys.

My mother was friendly with Ann Dougherty whose husband, Joe owned Doc's Oyster House. Joe was away in the service so it fell to Ann to manage the restaurant, a task she performed admirably.

Ann wanted to hire my mother but her husband was against it. His reason: my mother's brother George had dated Ann prior to the Dougherty's marriage. But because Ann had been so competent running the restaurant in his absence, Joe relented. My mother worked there several years and made more than an adequate income to care for us while my dad was away.

I didn't mention the world famous 500 Club in the description above as being in Ducktown, since it was destroyed by fire in 1973. Simply known as "The Five," it was, by far, the best known night club in the history of Atlantic City. It was located on Missouri Avenue, four and a half blocks from where I lived. The 500 Club was owned by Skinny D'Amato, who was well liked and respected by all important celebrities of the day.

Skinny teamed Dean Martin and Jerry Lewis for the first time at The Five where they literally became overnight sensations. He also helped Frank Sinatra revive his sagging career by booking him at the 'Club' every summer.

If gambling was your thing: no problem. A quick trip through The Five's back entrance and voilà your favorite game of chance awaited. Need a woman? Just say the word and a bevy of beauties was yours for the taking. As long as you possessed the requisite bankroll nothing was out of bounds.

All of this is wonderfully chronicled in Jonathan Van Meter's book *The Last Good Time*. For someone not from Atlantic City, I was shocked by how accurately Van Meter captured the essence of the city in the 40's, 50's and 60's. His book is a fascinating read.

THE VILLAGE

Toward the end of the depression my parents moved to a housing project called Pitney Village, named for Dr. Jonathan Pitney. During the 1800's Dr. Pitney had a dream of turning Atlantic City into a beach village resort. (This was long before the island was called Atlantic City). It and surrounding areas were known as Absecon Island. Pitney believed the ocean waters had a curative affect and people would flock to the resort for its restorative benefits. Later there were others who would turn his dream into reality, although not in the same way Pitney had envisioned.

The "Village," as we referred to it, was a great place to grow up. The beach was four short blocks away and the bay just two. There were so many kids in the project you could afford to be selective about your choice of friends. There was no need to adjust to another's personality. There were enough kids who held similar interests to your own.

Families in the village were considered poor by economic standards. I never remember anyone who thought of themselves that way, financially or otherwise. After all, we lived in the "World's Playground" with the ocean, beach, boardwalk and bay at our doorstep, and took full advantage of the pleasure they provided. Families in the village were very close. They felt they had a stake in the well being of the community. Some fathers were off to war while working mothers with kids were left to fend for themselves

Intact families would share these mother's burdens, especially in the area of child rearing. Fun nights were spent with dads who were ineligible for the draft and would arrange father-son baseball games. Night swimming in the bay, on warm summer evenings, was a popular activity enjoyed among families. Even silly things like hose fights, between neighbors, while watering their lawns, brought about a neighborly camaraderie.

Conoboy's saloon was across the street from our house. On occasion our parents would invite friends to come over with their kids. The adults would sit out on the porch and share pitchers of beer. They would discuss topics of the day which usually coalesced around the war. We would be treated to soda or ice cream. Afterwards, we'd toss around a football or play box-ball, a two person hand game similar to tennis. It was played within two sidewalk squares separated by a line between opponents.

This is not to suggest we were living in Utopia, or that we were a bunch of Little Lord Fauntleroy's. To the contrary, we found our share of trouble.

There were many bums who hung out around the Village. This was for a couple of reasons: 1) Snyder's Junk Shop was a block from our house. This was where the bums sought gainful employment in order to earn enough money for their nightly ration of Sneaky Pete. 2) The neighborhood was off the beaten path and no one bothered them--but us. Shamefully we'd seek them out to spring our latest traps.

Harry's Tire Shop was located a block away. A couple of their old service cars had recently given up the ghost and the owner abandoned them in an empty lot across from our house. They stripped everything but the upholstery, which wasn't any good to anyone, except the bums, who used them as sleeping quarters. These cars were small and in order to stretch out a tall person had to put his legs out the window.

One of the bum's was Les. Whenever he passed we'd ask, "How ya doin' Les?" His response was always the same, "I'm gettin' lesser and lesser every day."

Whenever Les or one of his buddies went on a toot they'd usually wind up sleeping it off in one of the junk cars. One day Les was snoring away peaccfully, with his legs dangling out the window. Someone had a pack of matches and we decided to give him a hotfoot. Les's shoes looked like clown's shoes. They were long and flat, made of cheap leather and had thin soles.

We were afraid to approach him but finally my partner in crime, Jackie and I, worked up the courage to proceed. He was snoring loudly as we stealthily crept toward the target. We were shaking at the thought of his waking but felt the element of surprise, plus a quart of Sneaky Pete, was on our side. Finally, we stood and placed the matches under his soles, gingerly at first, but then more aggressively as we saw how easily they slid in. When he didn't stir we decided to use the whole pack and lined them up one at a time.

We fired them up and ran behind a nearby building. We watched as Les slept peacefully. Without warning his foot twitched slightly, paused, and then shook more violently like someone trying to rid themselves of a pesky fly. Suddenly, like a Toon out of a scene from *Who Framed Roger Rabbit*, we heard YEOWWW!!!!

We got the hell out of there fast, running for our lives. We didn't stop to look back--we were too scared. After the incident I felt ashamed--and a little proud--but was afraid to tell my parents. They would have been very upset. My dad probably would have given me a knock upside the head--something I richly deserved.

Growing up in that environment had a lot of positives. It gave us an appreciation for the family unit and taught us socialization skills. Atlantic City is a small town and walking was a common means of transportation. The city held many attractions for kids that developed in us a measure of sophistication. I don't believe kids from other towns enjoyed the same benefits. We acquired an early sense of independence.

We became little entrepreneurs.

OUR OTHER EDUCATION

Goin' junkin' was an early means of employment we'd engage in after school and on weekends. Snyder's Junk Yard was a half block from my house. Old man Snyder would supply the junkin' carts necessary to transport our booty. If someone asked what we were doing that day, often the response was "goin junkin".

I lived on the north side of town but my kid brother Mick, who sometimes tagged along and best friend Jackie always did our junkin' on the south side. The reason for this was the neighborhood bums made up the majority of Snyder's work force. They always worked the north side, knew all the good spots, picked them clean before you could get there, and considered it their territory.

The south side was a good distance away, over by the boardwalk. It took significant effort pushing that heavy cart four blocks to get there, and once there, having to push it farther to reach our various working locations.

There was, however, logic behind our decision. The south side was the more affluent side of town. It was where hotels, rooming houses, bars, restaurants and wealthy residences were located. And where you had those types of locations, the trash pickins' wuz much better."

Besides all the scrap metal, bottles, papers, rubber, etc., we'd find working radios, repairable fans, toasters, all kinds of pots and pans, dishes, silverware and much more. These latter items brought more money. The trek back to Snyder's with a full cart was especially difficult. It took all three of us pushing, with rest stops along the way, to wend our way back to the north side.

We'd usually have to wait behind a couple of bums to unload our junk. We were considered, what today would be, second class citizens. However, the bum's loads weren't very big because as soon as they had collected enough to buy a bottle of Sneaky Pete their day was over. There was one guy named Newt, who after enough dips into his bottle, became nocturnal and later we'd catch him howling at the moon.

When we first started junkin' old man Snyder would take advantage of us. He'd cheat us out of money by manipulating the scale or short change us on some metal that was worth more money. It didn't take long to catch on to the tricky old bastard. We learned a few tricks of our own. Our favorite was stacking weighable newspapers in a box and loading the bottom quarter with beach sand. When he caught on he'd banish us for awhile, until his love of money overcame his love of integrity, which forced him to reinstate us--*but no sand*!

We sometimes made as much as two or three dollars a day--a lot of money. We received good early financial training at the junk yard and I swear, old man Snyder could have taught a business course at Wharton.

OF SOLDIERS AND SHOESHINES

Another one of our enterprises was shining shoes, financed of course, through our entrepreneurial junkin' skills.

All you needed were a couple of good rags, a sturdy brush (two if you wanted to be fancy), a black, brown and neutral polish and a box. We learned to make our own boxes since all it required was some wood, nails, saw, hammer and strip of canvas for a shoulder strap. Some kids used rope for this purpose--which was practical--but painful.

Atlantic City was an army convalescent and training center for the military, so designated for its many hotels and other desirable wartime attributes. Tourists were given the boot and soldiers returning from the war were housed in the hotels. Haddon Hall and Chalfont Haddon Hall were converted into England General Hospital where returning amputees were cared for.

The Convention Hall, boardwalk and beach were great places for marching and drilling. The troops used the ocean to practice assault landings. One night the local citizenry was invited to witness a mock invasion. We lined the boardwalk to observe this very realistic event.

Ships at sea sent assault landing craft to the beach filled with troops. I couldn't believe my eyes when ramps were lowered and all those soldiers came pouring out, screaming like banshees. It was scary as hell, but at the same time exciting. With shells bursting overhead the troops raced toward the boardwalk as if they were pursuing an actual enemy. Fighter planes flew overhead in mock support. We all got a pretty clear picture of what a landing invasion was like.

Now, instead of waiting nine months for the tourist season to arrive, the city was humming twenty four hours a day, three hundred sixty five days a year. Soldiers were everywhere. This outstanding bit of good luck was what launched my shoeshine career.

Servicemen were plentiful on the boardwalk, in the hotels, and along the avenues. The best pickins' however, were in the bars, of which Atlantic City had about 360 at the time--this in a town of only 64,000 residents.

We did good business throughout the city but the bars were the best. There was just one problem. Most of them wouldn't let kids in. We found ways to overcome these restrictions. We'd wait for someone to go in or come out the door so we could sneak a peek at the bartender's location. If his back was to the door we'd hustle in. Covering the distance to the bar with lighting speed was crucial.

Once safely hidden by the height of the bar we were out of the bartender's view. Also, the place was noisy as hell. We would quietly work our way along the stools tugging on a pant leg to see if one of the *boys* needed a shine. Usually everyone was feeling pretty good, so often guys would take a shine whether they needed one or not--just to give us the business.

If you were spotted and told to get out your customer would usually come to your aid. He'd say something like, "Leave the kid alone, he's just trying to make a buck." The military commanded a lot of respect and people didn't mess with them. Often a soldier would buy you a soda and silently dare the bartender to say something.

There was one place called Babette's Yacht Bar on Mississippi and Pacific Avenues, a block from the boardwalk. This place was always buzzin'. The bar was an actual replica of a yacht. It was said to offer gambling in the back room along with prostitution, which we found out later was true. Actually, most of the bigger clubs all offered these services.

There were always a lot of women in Babette's.

Most of the women were very attractive and liked being with servicemen because they spent their money freely. The girls wore open toed strapped shoes and often their soldier date would make them get a shine. If you got shoe polish on the girl's stockings, which happened often, they would mildly complain. We had a stock answer for everything. In that particular instance we'd say, "No charge for the extra polish ma'am." A few of them would think that was cute and muss your hair. They'd turn your face crimson by saying, "I'm going to wait for you to grow up." I'd leave with thoughts of what an interesting future I might be in for. Often I could rake in a buck or two from just one place like Babettes. This beat the hell out of junkin'.

MONEY BAGS

Two other means of income presented to us were carrying bags and selling bags. The train station was located one block from Atlantic Avenue, where the buses ran. When tourists, business people or travelers came to the city we'd be waiting outside the station. When the passengers came out on to the street many carried suitcases. We would try to choose among the most promising and offer to carry their bag(s). If they asked what we charged we would say, "Whatever you want to give." We felt since they had no idea what the service was worth they'd give us more. We were not above a little theatrics.

Usually with women, we'd shamelessly, through body language, fake like we were really struggling with the bag. The women would felt sorry for us and give us more than we'd normally get. Other times people would question our reason for doing this difficult work at such a young age. Our response was that our family needed the money. If my parents knew I was saying that I would have been drawn and quartered; most of the time we'd get a quarter. The trouble with carrying bags was a lot of waiting for trains without the requisite financial rewards.

Our other bag enterprise was selling shopping bags during the Christmas season. All the retail stores, 5&10's, and department stores, were located on Atlantic Avenue, generally between Ohio and South Carolina Avenues. This covered a span of seven blocks.

As soon as school let out my brother Mick and I would walk the eleven blocks to our destination. The first order of business was to purchase shopping bags from one of the 5 & 10's. The store's cost was two cents and we'd sell them for five.

Atlantic Avenue always had a festive holiday air during this season. The street was filled with frantic shoppers. All the stores had decorative window paintings and glittering Christmas trees. Multi-colored holiday lights were strung across a major section of Atlantic Avenue. The Salvation Army was at every block, some ringing bells and collecting money, others playing Christmas Carols. We were mesmerized by these sights and sounds. If it snowed, that brought a special bonus. Since we were there every night leading up to the big day, we felt a vital part of this magical holiday.

Choosing a good location was important. Being close to a 5 &10 was good strategy, in case it was necessary to load up with more bags. Calculating how many bags to buy wasn't easy. Some nights we'd start with ten, sell out, and have to get more. At other times that same ten would last the night and we'd be stuck with leftovers. Of course, the next evening we'd start out with a surplus and not have to buy as many.

It was always a mystery to us why people didn't just buy bags themselves. Possibly they didn't know the stores sold them, or they were in too big a hurry. For whatever reason, it provided us a thriving seasonal business.

Some shoppers would come out with the intention of just buying a few things. As their load got bigger they would search us out. Some would have their bags overloaded and need another bag. Others would come to us with torn bags. We would open a new bag for them, stack their gifts neatly, and send them happily on their way.

As with our other enterprises we had many little tricks. A favorite was, if someone only had a dime and looked particularly frantic, we would tell them we had no change but would be glad to get some. They would tell us to keep the dime and hurry on their way.

Although we always wore gloves, by the end of the night our hands were frozen. I never seemed to notice until I was about a block from home. The hot chocolate our mother had waiting was always welcome. The heat from the cup warmed our hands, as well as our stomachs. Still, it seemed an hour before they thawed. The downside of selling shopping bags–it was seasonal.

Another activity we engaged in, at night, outdoors, that was not entre-preneurial, but did bring about the same exhilarated feeling similar to that of the holidays was hooking cars. However there was one crucial element required for this activity–snow!

Hooking cars was a highly prized pastime since we were lucky if we got to do it three times a winter. During that time we'd pray for snow, but normally, even if we did get it, it didn't last because of the salt air. The city always bragged that they didn't have to buy snow removal equipment because Mother Nature provided it. But every so often, that same sweet lady would rear her sadistic head dumping up to a foot, or more, of the white stuff, leaving the city paralyzed. This was her gift to us and her cause of embarrassment to the politicians.

Unfortunately, this did not close our school since we were within walking distance. But happily, it reminded us that we were not immune from the wrath of winter's fickle mood swings.

In the evening after supper my brother Mick and I would announce to our parents that we were going sledding. My mother would caution us to stay out of the street, to which we dutifully agreed.

Fairmount Avenue, from my front door, was literally less than ten yards and though it was a main thoroughfare it produced little traffic. Realistically the best place to sled was in the street. Following a day of snow being tamped down by cars it became hard-packed, easy to run on, and fast. During our initial foray into this activity we were content to see, who, after a running start, could propel his sled the farthest. Guys got good at this activity and it became a fierce competition to see who could squeeze the last bit of movement from their Flexible Flyers.

As with all competitions we gave ourselves every advantage. The first order of business was waxing our runners for least resistance. Too much clothing slowed you down so we'd shed our heavy hooded mackinaws and sweaters. In no time we'd be down to pants, shirt and gaiters in twenty degree weather not feeling a trace of discomfort. There was even a method to laying your sled down to get maximum glide distance. If you flopped too hard you'd blunt your speed; lay it down easy and you'd effectuate a smooth takeoff.

But the night the first daredevil discovered hooking cars it put an end to our self- propelled pleasure and took us to greater heights of exhilaration.

No one could say who the first madcap to get the idea for hooking cars was, but it changed forever the concept of sledding in Pitney Village.

Unsuspecting drivers would stop for a red light at Georgia and Fairmount Avenues. Like soldiers crawling on their bellies under barbed wire, we'd stealthily make our way to the occupant's back bumper. Positioning was everything. Both ends of the bumper were prime spots, except for one small detail. On the side of the car with the exhaust pipe asphyxiation was a real possibility. The reason for those two location's desirability was that you could peel off easily in any situation. The guys in the middle were clumped together and subject to the whims of other guy's moves.

The best situation was when we made it to the car's bumper and the driver had no idea we were there. Some drivers would fly down the street at upwards of 30 mph. It was thrilling to go that fast, and we would have ridden to Albany Avenue (about twelve blocks), but usually dropped off after two or three blocks. The reason for this was that Fairmount Avenue was a back street away from the city's main streets. Although cars would occasionally use Fairmount to leave town, they seldom used it to enter. This meant, in most cases, we would have had to walk those twelve blocks back to our base.

Because some guys never ducked low enough we'd get caught by the driver. He'd get out and chase us. As soon as he was back behind the wheel we'd make another approach. Sometimes we'd be rewarded with a good ride. Other times he'd drive a short distance, get out again, a bit testier this time, telling us he'd get the cops. That usually did it.

After a few days of melting, bare spots would appear along the street. We weren't aware of it until we'd be flying along Fairmount Avenue, behind a car for half a block, and suddenly run out of snow. If you didn't know better, you'd think someone had a welding torch beneath you. The sparks from steel hitting asphalt lit up like the fourth of July. We sure as hell let go in a hurry.

The drivers we liked best were the crazies like us. They enjoyed being part of the fun. As soon as they knew we were on their cars they'd zig-zag from one side to the other trying to cause a whiplash to throw us off. Theirs was an exercise in futility. The more they zigged and zagged the better we liked it. If we could have saluted them after we dropped off we would have.

The guys we liked least were the sadistic ones. After several nights of melting snow icy slush puddles settled along the curves. As soon as the driver knew we were on his bumper, he'd make for the slush puddles. Timing it just right, he'd swerve, making sure we caught the full spray of the icy puddle. The effect was similar to today's victorious football coaches getting doused with Gatorade. It also produced a big negative. Coming home dripping from head to toe was not what mother had in mind when she let us out. It was necessary to have an excuse handy, so logically we used one involving a slush puddle. We told mom some mean guy swerved his car and purposely splashed water on us. Of course mom believed her little darlings.

THE BOARDWALK

We were still shining shoes and pulling in good money. And what did we do with those monetary windfalls? We spent em! I mean Atlantic City wasn't called the "Worlds Playground" for nothing. There were ten movie theatres on Atlantic Avenue alone. There was one for "Negro's" on the north side and another seven on the boardwalk, counting two on Steel Pier and one on Million Dollar Pier.

For kids living near the boardwalk, it was like having a fantasy land in your backyard. Starting with Steel Pier, "The Show Place of the Nation," you could spend the entire day for one low admission of about thirty five cents.

The thirty five cents entitled you to two movies, a stage show, a circus, trapeze artists and diving acts, including the Diving Horses. You could dance in the Marine Ballroom to the most popular bands of the day. They included: Glenn Miller, Tommy and Jimmy Dorsey, Benny Goodman, Vaughn Monroe and many others. Some of the big name stars that appeared were Al Jolson, Bing Crosby, Bob Hope, Perry Como, Frank Sinatra, Dean Martin, Eddie Fisher, the Beatles, as well as many from other eras.

There was the famous Diving Bell, a cylindrical contraption whose function was similar to that of a submarine. It was operated with cables and lowered to the depths of the ocean floor. Tourists were conned to take the plunge with the promise of viewing myriad sea creatures through portholes. Most of the time, they saw only murky water. Upon emergence, it would burst forth like an empty bottle being released from its watery constraints. This sudden unexpected discharge scared the hell out of its occupants. You could hear their squeals through topside loudspeakers as the Diving Bell burst above the waterline. This experience probably made the occupants forget about the creatures they were supposed to see. This thrilling experience cost about a dime.

Whereas Steel Pier was more conducive to an older crowd, Million Dollar Pier was strictly a fantasy world for kids. It was great fun to introduce a new kid to the pier. The first and most sadistic "amusement" you'd introduce him to would be the Haunted House.

This was a no nonsense scary place for young kids. The tunnel was so dark you had to hold hands to stay together. I had been through the Haunted

House many times and loved to see the reactions of a first timer. There were skeletons popping up at every turn. Another few steps and an eerie green light would come on behind a glass partition showing a headless man with blood oozing from every orifice.

There were witches, goblins and monsters of all sorts coming toward you at unexpected moments, followed by ungodly sounds from the dead. And from the crowds passing through came screams of horror. Usually the new kid you were escorting would latch on tightly, fearing to let go, lest he be spirited away. For some kids being fitted with a pair of diapers might not have been a bad idea.

What greeted one at the end of the tunnel was for males a bonanza, for females a humiliation. The walkway, upon leaving the tunnel, had air jets in the floor. As women passed over the jets a hidden operator would trigger a device blowing a stream of air up their dresses.

The pier had placed chairs in front of the walkway at the tunnel's exit. The chairs were always occupied by males where they could comfortably take in the sights. A few trips through the tunnel found us more attracted to spending lengthy periods occupying the chairs. As horrified as some people would be, upon hearing this today, it was not all that bad. Most women had been warned ahead of time and were prepared for this assault. So when they walked that gauntlet, they held on tightly to their skirts. Those who did get caught, screamed, got red faced, recovered quickly, were good sports—and laughed.

After the haunted house the fun really began. There was an amusement resembling a gigantic record. This was appropriately called "The Record." Kids would sit on it and the operator would spin it, slowly at first, gradually increasing its speed.

It was hilarious watching riders get unceremoniously dumped on their butts. They slid off, flying in all directions before slamming into a carpeted backstop. The person who held the center position stayed on because he experienced the dynamic of being met with equal force on all sides. Whoever that person was usually exited like a conquering hero while the others stared in awe. The only thing the winner did to receive those undeserved accolades was be the first to get his lucky but-tocks on the ride.

The Barrel was just that, a gigantic barrel. This was another ride that was great for having fun with novices. The idea was to walk through the spinning Barrel without falling. Once mastered, you achieved veteran status. Taking the new kid through was another form of sadism.

You could sense the novice's hesitancy as he watched the huge Barrel spinning around, afraid to take that first step. Finally, after much coaxing, he'd take the plunge. As soon as his foot touched the inside he was on his ass. We could have helped, but preferred watching how silly he looked. He would be partially carried up the barrel, only to come sliding down.

Each time this happened he'd grab for some imaginary handle to pull himself up. Even funnier were other veterans who stepped in and around him as if he didn't exist. At some point the operator would be called to save the day, though we could have easily helped the hapless victim. Once the bumbling one got the hang of it the system repeated itself. It was payback time and the victim became the veteran prankster.

Everyone's amusement of choice was the Giant Slide. Looking up from the floor, it seemed a mile high. This is where the showoffs really performed. The first time I walked up those endless stairs I looked down from the top on wobbly legs. My first thought was how I could weasel my way out of taking this death-defying plunge.

Just across from the giant slide was its clone, but much smaller. The Baby Slide, as it was referred to, had only a short one-level dip whereas the big one had two. The Baby Slide was for the younger kids, but a lot of older kids who didn't suffer embarrassment cut their teeth on it.

Not quite ready to enter into this foolhardy feat, I fearfully mounted the long flight of stairs as riders whizzed by. Most rode their carpets sitting in the upright position. The showoffs were another story. They rode down in different positions. A few rode backwards, some rode lying down, some on their bellies, others on their knees. They always had smug looks on their faces knowing the rest of us didn't have the stomach to engage in their daredevil tactics. *And,* they were always little guys.

Because of the chances they took they often fell off the rug. Once your butt, or any part of your anatomy, hit that bare hardwood you were in for some nasty burns. We reveled in watching the showoffs limp around crying in pain.

Finally, I worked up the nerve to send myself hurtling off into space. The feeling of exhilaration I experienced was breathtaking. When I hit that first dip I felt my heart go up in my throat, then again at the second dip. The only other things that ever gave me that same rush were surfing, skiing (snow) and shooting seas with a lifeboat. Once I got that first ride under my belt I couldn't get back to the top fast enough.

There were a few other minor un-amusements like the Maze. This was a series of what were deemed intricate labyrinths, supposedly difficult to find your way through. It wasn't. It was boring, and after a time or two I never went back. Also, advertised as a big deal was the Deep Sea Net Haul. This took place every day at 3:00 P.M. at the end of the pier. The tourists loved it. Why?–I have no idea–I guess because, to them it was a novelty. There were assorted crabs, jellyfish, sand sharks, balloon fish, clams, oysters, and other sea matter. We saw the same things wash up on the beaches regularly.

The theatre showed B movies, where, even at our age we had a little more sophistication than to waste our time on those turkeys. But, it also featured stage shows, so it was a different story when we heard Sally Rand was coming to the pier. Sally was a stripper billed as "Sally Rand and her Fan Dance." It would be difficult to state how excited we were about seeing our first nude woman. Her show was "off limits to minors," but that statement was like telling us not to pee in the ocean. We knew every nook and cranny of that pier. We were like little Houdini's–there was no place we couldn't crack.

The theatre was among the easiest.

Finally, the day arrived. We negotiated our way into the theatre and went immediately to the balcony. Normally, that section was closed. Now it was packed with a crush of tongue-panting horny guys. We had to sit through some crummy acts and a lousy movie before Sally appeared.

Our little package of testosterone had been raging for days. Finally she appeared, holding two large ostrich feathers. As she danced around the stage she manipulated them in a very sensuous way. Taking one away, she instantly replaced it with the other creating a split-second illusion of seeing a nude body. This teasing continued throughout her act causing us to get hornier with each feathered move.

We were told that by the end of her act she opened her feathers to reveal all. As the finale approached we were almost beside ourselves with ecstasy.

And then, the climax (no pun intended). The feathers opened and my heart sank There stood Sally, in all her glory, covered in a body stocking, instead of a birthday suit. What a fake! If I'd paid admission I would have demanded my money back. I resolved to tell all the kids how great it was. I didn't tell them she wasn't naked. Like her, I just told them enough to fire up their imaginations. I made a few enemies with that little ploy.

So those two amusement castles by the sea, Steel Pier and Million Dollar Pier were where many of us enjoyed a misspent youth. I'd spend the entire day at the piers from opening bell until dinner bell, and still not take in all they had to offer.

There were three other piers, Steeplechase, an all amusement pier with Ferris wheel, bumper cars, and various and other sundry amusements. This pier was very popular with smaller kids.

The other two were Garden Pier and Heinz Pier.

Garden Pier stood apart from the other piers in Atlantic City. These were not amusement piers and I don't think I was on either one more than twice. Opened in 1913, its uptown location placed it away from the frenzied activity of the downtown boardwalk. The Spanish Renaissance architecture of the buildings and the beautifully landscaped gardens gave the pier a formal appearance which attracted an upscale crowd. The centerpiece of Garden Pier was the stately B.F. Keith's Theater, which for many years rivaled any of those on Broadway. Here, Tobacco Road and George White's Scandals premiered. It housed one of the city's largest ballrooms. A young Rudolph Valentino worked as a dance instructor and large conventions met before the Atlantic City Auditorium was built.

The other one, Heinz Pier (originally Iron Pier), was basically an advertisement for its 57 varieties. Visitors to Heinz Pier got to taste Heinz products, especially pickles, and were given a souvenir of an ugly green, worm-like looking, Heinz pickle pin. The Pier held daily organ recitals, and it included a museum which featured displays of "Kitchens from the Past," present, and other countries. Heinz Pier was destroyed by a hurricane in 1944.

But the wooden way had a lot more to offer. Running from the boardwalk to Pacific Avenue, along Georgia Avenue to the south and Mississippi Avenue to the north, Convention Hall covered a city block. Built in 1929, and hailed as a modern marvel, it was the largest unobstructed room in the world, having no pillars or roof posts. It took six years to build at a cost of $15 million dollars.

As a publicity stunt one year, Miss America was flown around inside the Hall in a helicopter. This was also where the final night of judging for the Miss America Pageant was held. Miss Atlantic City was not eligible to compete in the Miss America Contest but was always a special guest on pageant night. Years later, as a member of the beach patrol and friendly with the girl who'd been crowned Miss Atlantic City, I was invited to escort her to the pageant. This was one of those rare times when I didn't feel the need to sneak in.

During the winter, an ice skating rink was laid down inside the hall for the public to enjoy. The town also had its own semi-pro hockey team, the Atlantic City Seagulls. Kid's hockey leagues were organized, and my brother Mick played for Kiwanis, who were co-champions in their first season. When the Harlem Globetrotters came to town a wooden basketball court was laid over the ice rink. People would flock to see this unique event.

Convention Hall was big enough to lay down a regulation football field with seating accommodations for 12,000 fans. In 1968 I had the pleasure of watching my former high school team, Holy Spirit, beat our old nemesis Atlantic City High School. That was the first time we'd won since 1935.

Throughout the summer, the Ice Capades performed at Convention Hall for a period of about six weeks. I would go every year with a buddy. We never considered subjecting ourselves to the indignity of paying admission, and, would once again call on our Houdini skills to sneak in. For the first few years the Ice Capades were a novelty and truly lived up to its billing—"Magic on Ice."

Audiences were treated to an array of theatrics: ballet routines, classical figure skating, operettas, daredevil antics, choreographed plays, and comedic skits. My favorites were two clowns, one of whom, because of some intended sleight would grab a bucket of water and chase the other around the rink. As soon as they got close to the railing, and for the most part an unsuspecting audience, the one with the bucket would let fly. Of course the other clown would duck. The screaming audience thinking they were being doused with, water, were showered with nothing more than silver confetti. People would vie for those seats, hoping to be the hittee, thus assuring themselves a nightly dose of attention.

One of the acts was called "The Old Smoothies." To my young way of thinking, all this couple did was come on the ice and do this really saccharine waltz. They were probably in their forties and had some extra pounds, but wore very colorfully tailored costumes to deflect scrutiny. The adults loved them but we thought they were corny. We'd take this opportunity to leave our perch in the balcony to find better seats at ground level. There we could get a close-up of all the attractive showgirls. We carefully avoided security, wary we looked like sneak-in types, which of course we did—and were.

Later during the 1960's we would seek the Ice Capades girls out. There were a few bars on both avenues next to Convention Hall where the skaters hung out. Often the girls were accompanied by boys, most of who seemed to be named Bruce. They acted as the girl's protectors and told them to, "Stay away from those nasty, one-track-minded lifeguards." In retrospect, they were right.

After a few summers, the Ice Capades became old news and I stopped going.

Although on occasion, when I was really bored (which was rare) and had nothing to do, I'd check it out. Only the costumes and themes changed over the years, never the routines. The Ice Capades came to Atlantic City each summer for 40 years, from 1941-1981.

All day rains that kept me from the beach made the two piers a welcome diversion. I got pretty good at detecting when the rain wasn't going to last all day. On those days, instead of committing to the piers for the day, I'd hit the penny arcades. For the most part the games, as advertised were a penny. With just a quarter, you could kill some serious time waiting for the sun to come out.

Most popular were pinball machines, similar to slots in a casino, and they dominated the room. Just as you entered, there was the fortune teller machine (similar to the one in the movie *Big*. You'd drop in a penny and the fortune teller would execute some turns, deal from a deck and spit out a card with your fortune on it. To my knowledge no kid ever turned into an adult.

There were electric rifles you fired at lights. One was at a bear, who, when you hit his light would rear up and turn around. Having been pretty good with a bb gun I could usually make that sucker turn with every shot.

Most annoying was the car with the big steering wheel you had to keep on a cylindrical rolling highway. I must have gotten killed a hundred times trying not to veer into the wrong lane. Most exciting, were machines with turn handles that flipped cards at a rapid pace showing naked women dancing and cavorting. The quality of the pictures was awful! Still, they were played so often you had to look for machines that worked. It pissed me off that management never fix the broken ones. Such were the tribulations of a pubescent boy.

Just taking a stroll on the boardwalk was fun. It was jammed with tourists during the summer. The wonderful mixture of food smells combined with the sea air was indescribable.

The boardwalk was both honky-tonk and classy. It seemed every other store sold some kind of food. Almost all offered hot dogs, hamburgers and french fries. But in addition, you would find corn on the cob, pork roll, pizza, stromboli, popcorn, peanuts, birch beer, fresh squeezed orange juice, cotton candy, salt-water taffy, ice cream, corn dogs, etc.

There were junk stores that offered any souvenir you could think of, as long as Atlantic City, N.J. could be printed on it. This included hats, shirts, pennants, ashtrays, pens, banners, balls, etc.

The boardwalk stores that fronted the hotels were a different story. They consisted of fur salons, leather shops, jewelry stores, men's and women's high-priced clothing stores, and expensive Persian rug stores. If you didn't enjoy traveling by shoe leather express you could always rent a rolling chair. These were just what the name inferred, a covered wicker chair on wheels. It seated two or three and was pushed by a rolling chair company employee. The price was determined by the distance you traveled. The hotels that dotted the boardwalk were not for the "common people." You had to be in the high-middle to upper income group to afford staying at one of those pricey behemoths.

THE BEACH

Upon arriving in Atlantic City, if you didn't know it was a resort, aside from the unmistakable smell of salt sea air, you might take it for just another brick and mortar city. The beach and ocean were hidden from a visitor's view by the many buildings and hotels. Only by glancing down one of the avenues could you catch a glimpse of the boardwalk.

I lived four short blocks from the beach. During summer I was there almost every waking hour, except for times when I was at the bay. Because of how I described Atlantic City as a brick and mortar town, I never felt it conformed to the traditional concept of a beach and ocean resort. I always imagined the city, and beach and ocean, as two distinct entities.

My four block trek to the beach took me past stately rooming houses with expansive verandas with rocking chairs placed there for guests. The four, four cornered blocks I passed were made up of eclectic businesses. All had a bar, one a restaurant and one a liquor store. The rest included a Laundromat, drug store, tire shop, barber shop, piano store, meat market, and Convention Hall. The latter took up the entire block, from Pacific Avenue to the boardwalk, and from Georgia to Mississippi Avenues.

Anticipation would build whenever I was within a block of the beach. It never failed when I reached the top of the boardwalk ramp. There before me stretched a panorama of glistening white sand and green white-capped waves. The contrast between these Atlantic City's was unique, and to me, what made the town special. In later years I realized others were drawn by this magnetic quality as well. College kids, vacationers, and the just curious came to town in June and many never left. Or if they did leave, they returned every summer. Maybe it was because they found their own home towns dull after a magical summer in the Worlds Playground.

I was so connected to the beach I seldom wore a shirt and never took a towel. Bare feet were also the order of the day. Kids who wore footwear to the beach were considered sissies. If you wore them in the ocean you were considered a lost cause. Once my feet touched the hot sand I'd run all the way to the water. My momentum didn't stop at the water's edge; I kept going until that first wave approached and I took the plunge. Disappearing beneath the fold I resurfaced immediately due to the shock to my body (the ocean temperature in June was usually in the high fifties to low sixties—cold!). But it was customary to keep going in order to show your metal. By the time I negotiated the waves and cleared the break, the water temperature was no longer a factor. I was over my head, away from the crowd, swimming to sea.

At times, when the lifeguards thought I was out too far they'd whistle me in. As I swam toward shore and got closer to the break I'd look for a good wave. Waves ran in sets, the later ones being the biggest. To the seasoned body surfer catching the right wave was a mastered art form.

The largest wave might be forming while I was still out over my head. At times, when it had not yet crested enough for me to catch, I'd swim like hell in order to stay with it, until it peaked. Once I felt myself teetering at the top, knowing I had it, I'd tuck my arms to my sides and let it take me.

As the wave broke evenly it felt like I was coming down a long flight of gradual steps at pulse-pounding speed. My body was in a cannonball position; my head in front of the wave. I was able to see everything in front of me and avoid any bathers in my path. Sometimes I'd ride a wave a hundred yards, not stopping until my belly hit the sand. There is no way to describe the thrill I derived from this experience.

Along with my beach buddies we'd stay in the water until shortly before hypothermia set in. That's an exaggeration of course, but at times our lips did turn blue. We'd remedy that by dropping to the hot sand, basking in its comforting warmth. Tourists would stare quizzically, trying to figure out how anyone could stand being covered with sand from head to foot. I never understood until years later why anyone brought blankets or beach towels to the shore. To me it was just some burdensome non-necessity.

One of the not-so-neat things about the beach, were days when debris would wash up on shore. This was brought about as a result of how the tides were running. So on any given day jelly fish would blight the shore. Another day it was king crabs, and not in any order, oil slick dumped from ships, sand sharks, seaweed, stuff that looked like straw and clam shells of varying sizes. None of this was of any interest except maybe to curiosity-seekers, marine biologists or shoobies (day trippers who took the train from Camden and packed their lunch in shoeboxes).

Actually, the clam shells were useful. The ones that washed up were much larger than a cherrystone. Whereas good clams reside in a soft muck these were buried in sand. They were tough as shoe leather and locals referred to them as "surf turkeys." Fisherman used the meat for bait and I was told some people used them to make chowder (ugh).

Since playing ball wasn't allowed on the beach we found other ways to amuse ourselves. We made up our own version of horseshoes by getting a couple of surf turkeys, splitting them in half and taking out the meat. Then we'd dig two holes about thirty feet apart in the hard sand near the water's edge. Holding the shell hollow side under we'd toss it in the same manner you would a Frisbee. Scoring was the same as horseshoes, one for closest to the hole, three if you holed out.

Georgia Avenue beach was not considered dangerous, nor were the two beaches to the north, Mississippi and Missouri Avenues. The latter was located just to the right, or south of Million Dollar Pier. On the other side of the pier to the north was Arkansas Avenue, or as the locals pronounce it, Are-Can'-Zis. At times this was not a safe swimming beach. Due to northeast storms, whose swift currents raced toward the pier, holes were formed in the oceans floor causing dangerous offsets. In fact, the beaches to the north or uptown side of the piers were generally more dangerous than beaches to the south. I often took long walks uptown, usually as far as Steel Pier, some fourteen blocks. Over the years I saw many more rescues on Arkansas Avenue than on Georgia Avenue. When one considers I was on the beach practically all day at Georgia, and only as a passing observer along Arkansas, the safety factor between the two beaches was striking.

Witnessing a rescue on Georgia Avenue, then, was rare. Normally, this would occur after several days of a shitty ocean. Storms would stir things up and the sea would not be receptive to intruders. As always, that never deterred the foolhardy but, surprisingly, where the ocean was concerned, foolhardy was something we kids were not. Being aware of mother ocean's occasional lapses that brought about one of her temper tantrums, we had great respect and didn't tempt her.

Watching the guard's launch the boat, blowing run whistles, and challenging the huge surf was thrilling. At times they looked like they'd be swamped, and sometimes were. But one or more backup crews were always there to take up the slack and complete the rescue.

Unless the rescued bather swallowed too much sea water, and had to be resuscitated, he would scramble from the boat and get lost in the crowd. Later, some would come back and make a point of thanking the guards. Sometimes they came bearing gifts. For the most part, these gifts were in the form of salt water taffy. Since we'd act as mascots for the guards whenever they needed something, they'd usually reward us with the taffy.

One of the reasons mascots were an important part of the Atlantic City Beach Patrol is because guards were basically confined to their stations. They were not in any way employees of the A.C.B.P. Each team of guards was responsible for finding their own little gofer. There are three characteristics to look for in a mascot, 1) a strong attraction to the glamorous and sometimes dangerous life of a guard, 2) undying love for the beach 3) a solid sense of responsibility.

Mascots performed services such as running for coffee, pastry, sandwiches, etc. They delivered messages to other stands, or to headquarters. At times they helped to whistle bathers away from dangerous areas. But most important, tell a girl you'd spot at a distance you wanted to talk to her.

Later, when I became a guard and our mascot ran an errand we'd include him in the treat. We took him out in the boat during layout and taught him how to row and throw a donut. When the surf was big, we'd let them dive off the stern, catch a wave and ride it to the beach. We had a tradition of the tent crew going to dinner on payday. We'd each throw our mascots a few bucks for spending money, occasionally inviting them to join us for dinner.

Probably, what mascots liked most about the job was that they got to wear the uniform. We were issued new uniforms every year and would give them a used tank top, pair of trunks and whistle. They would have their mother, or someone, alter it for them. The first day they wore it to the beach you could tell how proud they were. They would strut around like little peacocks projecting an exaggerated sense of self-importance. Come to think of it, they acted just like—us.

Being a mascot when I was a kid was not quite the tradition it would become. Still, we would act in this capacity for the guards if they needed something from the store. Because of the expense, and because it was not easy to find someone to go to the boardwalk, it was customary for guards to pack a lunch. But once in a while they would opt to treat themselves to a soda and hamburger.

A group of us gathered every day taking turns as mascots. There was one kid named Larry who constantly interjected himself into our conversations with corny jokes. We all considered him a pain in the ass but he'd do almost anything to hang out with us. So whenever the opportunity presented itself, we'd enlist him as our designated sucker.

On one of those rare days when they needed a mascot a guard asked me to go to the store. It was very hot and humid and I wasn't up for it, still, I agreed. When I went back to the soft sand where all the guys were gathered Larry had joined them. I immediately saw a way out. I told Larry I was going to the store for one of the guards, but if he wanted to get in good with them he could go in my place. He turned me down saying I was just trying to use him for a sucker. I said ok, but he would probably never be allowed a ride in the lifeboat. That got his attention and after saying I'd put in a good word for him he relented.

The sand was blazing hot so he used a trick we all knew. He tore up the beach until he came to someone's umbrella, where he stood in the shady edge, to cool his feet. People usually understood and wouldn't say anything. Then he'd take off again, repeating this routine, until he reached the boardwalk.

His trip back carrying sodas was worse. Because he had first refused going to the store, as he came within earshot, we all stood up and in unison hollered, "SUCKER!" That was it he said, he'd never go again. Then we'd say we were just foolin' around and tell him what a good kid he was.

One of our favorite pastimes was burying each other in mud. We'd go close to the water where one of us would lie down and let the others pile mud over him. Everything would be covered but your face. After a while the mud got quite heavy, but, because it was wet, there was no problem getting free.

We always timed these burials with the incoming tide. The person buried was, in our fantasy world, a superhero. As the tide grew higher, we evil mudders would leave our protagonist to his fate. As the tide drew closer to the high water mark, the idea was for the buried one to drown. Just as the first waves approached the victim's coffin, he would, with much exaggeration, begin to break free, first one arm, than the other. Once he was free he'd chase the evildoers up the beach with the remnants of mud still dripping from his body.

One day Larry was watching and asked if he could play. We said not only could he play but he could be the superhero. He was thrilled. He lay down by the water as we proceeded to bury him. As soon as we had a good covering of mud one of the guys went and filled a bucket with soft dry sand. We mixed the dry sand with the mud.

Larry asked what we were doing. We told him we were making a new kind of tomb. Actually, when you mix dry sand with mud it gets very hard, and heavy, and there is *no* breaking out. We watched as the tide came in and Larry started yelling for us to get him out. Sadistically, we left and went on up the beach. We knew some bather would free him, as indeed someone did.

As Larry walked up the beach avoiding us we couldn't help shouting our inimitable refrain, yep, you guessed it–SUCKER!!!

We were always able to get Larry to trust us again after a period of schmoozing (think Charlie Brown kicking the football), but I'd be ashamed to say how many times we pulled the same stunts.

Significant time was also spent on the beach in winter, since horseback riding was very popular. I always had a thing about the west and was a big cowboy and horse lover. However horseback riding on the beach was mostly for the benefit of hotel guests who had the means to afford it. The first time I ever saw beach horses I was playing baseball on Missouri Avenue, about two blocks from my house. I heard what I thought were horses and looked up to see a group of them coming toward me. They were all mounted by black kids since blacks lived on the North side where the stables were located. One exception was a white kid, older than the rest, who was leading the pack. He was in semi-western dress and sat his horse like John Wayne. I was impressed.

Later that day, I ran to the beach and found the horses headquartered on Arkansas Avenue. They had some spirited looking steeds, as well as the requisite nags. One of the neatest things was a little cart and pony ride for children. I could imagine that being so appealing to kids.

All my working endeavors now went to support my latest addiction–riding. It didn't take long to find out all the best horses were reserved for hotel guests. We got the leftovers. There was no skill involved in getting on one of those has-beens. My biggest struggle was to keep the horse I was riding heading up beach. The horse's biggest concern was heading back to the hitching rail to join his buddies. I often wondered if mounting the horse backwards would trick him into thinking he was always heading back to his home base.

Trying to get one of those plugs to run was futile. They had been ridden for so long, that from their perspective, they were retired. The other thing was, I didn't like spending my money to ride English saddle. Being a kid who watched cowboy movies every week I wanted to ride western. The only horse with a western saddle was the one the John Wayne kid rode. They certainly weren't going to put *me* on *him*.

A fortunate event took place not long after my riding debut. Behind the aforementioned Snyder's Junkshop were stables I hadn't been aware of. One day as I was passing by, I recognized the distinct smell of hay and straw. I peered in to see a short muscular kid tending a beautiful pinto. We struck up a conversation. His name was Sammy—his horse—Butch.

Sammy and I became fast friends, not in small measure, because of my willingness to clean horseshit. I would have done anything to be around horses. Sammy taught me to ride and soon I was galloping bareback along a dirt road that led to the bay.

As I became a more proficient horseman, Sammy and I, riding double, would take Butch to the beach. There, we would take turns galloping him along the shallow surf. It was thrilling to watch Butches hooves pound the ocean and see the water spray up in a silver circle around him.

Later I would buy my own horse riding him for hours on the beach. I became a proficient horseman.

On overcast days when the beach was unappealing I'd visit that other body of water...

THE BAY

Considering the number of kids who lived in the village it seems only a handful of us had an attraction for the bay. Neither one of my brothers was a bay rat. They, like most other kids, were more interested in playing sports, which included anything that involved a ball. I believe my buddy Jackie and

I were always considered somewhat peculiar because of our Tom and Huck preferred lifestyle.

To us the bay held a particular fascination. It was only two blocks from my house. Once we left the rows of project homes behind, we entered a different world.

Our surrounding environment was now composed of dirt and weeds. The first sites we passed were an oil company to our left and a gravel and train yard to our right. Moving on, we followed a narrow path that eventually led to the bay. From there, we encountered docks where human bay rats kept their boats. This is where I kept my sneak-box, a one man duck hunting boat for which I'd paid five dollars.

The docks were rented primarily by those with rowboats. Some few had cabin boats and one or two, living on a fixed income, had houseboats. These docks were old and not very sturdy and subject to being wiped out by a good size storm. Unbeknownst to me, the event that would usher in that destruction was just around the bend.

In September of 1944, the great Atlantic Hurricane swept over Atlantic City, leaving devastation in its wake. I was 11 years old when this catastrophe occurred. We had been dismissed from school early due to reports of the storm.

On the way home I realized the sky was growing dark. It appeared somewhat threatening, but, otherwise, a typical overcast day. Arriving home I quickly changed and headed for the bay.

My dad worked at the American Ice Company, loading blocks of ice onto trucks. My mom was a waitress at a boardwalk restaurant called Chateau Renault. My dad got off around 5:00 P.M. My mom worked the dinner shift late into the evening.

I had a few good hours to spend at the bay before going home for dinner. Being out in my boat always gave me a feeling of peace and independence. This day reinforced that feeling, due to its unusual calm. The smell of salt air made me appreciate my good fortune–being brought up in a seashore resort.

Taking the southerly route I rowed a mile to the Albany Avenue Bridge. This is where traffic entered the city from the resort's downtown end.

Atlantic City airport sat within close proximity to the bridge. At times during my travels I would row to the other side of the bay, pull my boat to shore, and watch the planes take off and land. Generally, as I rowed to the bridge, I would examine the myriad pilings along the way in search of crabs. This was automatic since crabbing was a favorite pastime and another way to make money. There was a swimming dock with a diving board close to the bridge. If the tide was high I'd sometimes tie up my boat and join in the fun with the rest of the kids. The tide was high now, higher than usual, but there were no kids. I thought that strange.

It was getting late so I didn't dally. For most of my row back it was eerily calm—the bay like glass. As I got closer to my destination the wind started picking up. When I reached the dock and secured my boat I noticed the water level, marking the pilings, was higher than I'd ever seen it. As I retraced my steps home it started raining. It came slowly at first, then as a torrent with fierce intensity. By the time I got to my house I was drenched.

When I walked through the door, my father looking very concerned said, "Where've you been?" I told him I had been out in my boat. "Out in your boat, didn't you know there was a hurricane on the way?" I said we had been told about it in school but thought it wasn't due until later that night.

He told me he and my brother Jim, who was fourteen, were going to bring my mother home from the restaurant. I was to stay with my brother Mick who was only eight. If anything happened, I was to call dad's brother and wife who lived next door and go to their house. That scared the hell out of me. It was the first I realized how serious the storm was. Little did we know at the time what a harrowing adventure would befall my parents and brother.

My brother and I wanted to call our uncle right away but were afraid our three cousins would think us sissies. Finally, the excuse came that we needed. The wind had grown much worse and was now blowing at gale force. At some point we heard a loud crack and saw a tree had snapped in two, missing our living room window by inches. That was all either of us needed. Miraculously the phone was still working. I called my Uncle Joe and told him what happened. He said he'd be right over. Instead, my Aunt Katherine (Kate) showed up. She was one tough bird and wore the pants in the family. Her maternal instincts had probably ruled the day. She huddled us under a large raincoat as we battled the elements to get to their house, about sixty feet away. I couldn't believe the force of the wind. Luckily it was at our backs so it practically blew us to their house.

My cousins were no less insecure then we were. The sounds from the storm were getting louder and all of us were becoming increasingly uneasy. Our thoughts turned to our parents and brother. Earlier reports had been urging everyone to stay at home and batten down the hatches. My dad and brother had to cover eleven blocks to and from the restaurant. Realizing how serious the situation was, we all started fearing for their safety.

About an hour and a half later the door opened and in came my father soaked to the bone. We were all so thankful to see him. Aunt Kate wanted to get towels but he declined. My mother and Jim were at our house alone. The three of us struggled the short distance back.

It was then we found out what happened.

As dad and Jim made their way from the house they found shelter from the wind where ever they could, mostly in doorways. They decided to take Atlantic Avenue, because that's where most of the businesses were. They knew they could find shelter in the doorways of the many retail stores.

When they reached Arkansas Avenue, they looked up to see that a roof-top billboard had snapped and was swinging perilously in the wind. As they were struggling to make headway the wind ripped the sign from its mooring. My dad later said, as it came toward them, it seemed to be moving in slow motion.

The next thing they knew, the sign slammed into the building just above them. It missed them by just a few feet. Finally, they made their way to Illinois Avenue which left them two blocks from the boardwalk. They battled their way to the boardwalk.

When they finally climbed the walk they encountered a truly frightening sight. The waves were monstrous, as far as the eye could see. They made their way toward the boardwalk, at times, seeing cascades of seawater crash over it. The restaurant was halfway between Illinois and Kentucky Avenue–a distance of half a block.

While they were making their way, my dad turned to see my brother being blown down the boardwalk. Dad started after him, but miraculously, as they described it, a huge man who was huddled in a doorway grabbed Jim, shielding him from the wind.

My dad and brother then traversed the final distance to the restaurant. When they encountered my mother she first had a look of fear, then relief. The manager wanted my dad and brother to rest briefly but my dad informed him that my brother and I were home alone. My mother also expressed concern.

The return trip was no better. My parents and brother clung to each other and fought the fierce winds all the way back.

Seeing them safe at home brought a great sense of relief to Mick and me. We all watched the storm through the windows as the water approached the second step of our three-step-porch. This meant the bay and ocean had met and our house was in danger of flooding. It was now a matter of just how high the water was going to go.

Fortunately that evening the rain stopped and the water began to recede. The moon burst through the clouds and we all went out to witness what turned out to be a spectacular night. What a relief!

The next morning I was up bright and early. All the schools were closed giving me a chance to check out the damage. I was also concerned about my boat. The first thing that caught my eye was the debris-filled streets. There was dirt, driftwood and weeds throughout the city. Trees were uprooted everywhere. I couldn't believe the devastation. Later we heard the section of boardwalk running through Margate and Longport had been washed away. Much of the walk in Ventnor was damaged, as well as that in the lower end of Atlantic City. My heart sank as I turned my attention toward my boat. I ran all the way to the bay. When I got to where the docks should have been my worst fears were confirmed. The docks were gone—washed away—and with them my boat. I wondered if the folks on houseboats had sought safety. If so, what would they do when they found their homes had disappeared? I'd never know.

For the next three or four days I searched the banks of the bay looking for my little sneak-box to no avail. Even if it wasn't destroyed and someone had found it, whoever that was, would have no way of knowing who it belonged to. And yet, it's funny how a personal tragedy can turn into a triumph of sorts.

My friend Jackie was also searching. The same day my boat disappeared he was scanning the bay for anything of interest. While surveying the water, he spotted a Garvey (stable, flat bottom duck boat), floating by itself with no occupant. He quickly stripped to his shorts and swam to the boat. He later told me it had no oars and he had to paddle to shore using his hands.

We were best friends and he had always been welcome to use my boat. Now the same courtesy applied to me. Whereas a sneak-box is a one-man boat, and limiting; a Garvey is much larger. This expanded our horizons. Since two could occupy the boat we were now able to explore the curiosities of the bay in more detail.

We started exploring the back-bay and salt marshes. There were narrow channels of water we'd follow until they ended. Along the way we would see various forms of crabs and other bay creatures. Garvey's are practical for exploring shallow water because their flat-bottoms have a wide raised bow and make no wake. They're excellent for crabbing.

Crabbing and swimming were our favorite bay activities. Some days we'd grab our BB guns, nets and baskets and head for the boat. There were separate bridges for trolleys and trains, each of which served Atlantic City. The trolleys came from nearby Pleasantville and the trains from Philadelphia.

Both bridges featured rows of pilings. These were a favorite nesting place for crabs. The pilings were so close together it wasn't necessary to use oars. We hand pulled the boat from one piling to another. On good days crabs were plentiful and we'd scoop them with nets and deposit them in our baskets. At times we'd even snag a couple of soft-shells. As soon as we had a significant haul, we'd take them to Angelo's Restaurant and sell them. The hard shells brought ten to fifteen cents; the soft shells thirty five.

Most days we went swimming in the bay and never bothered to bring bathing suits. There was a dock by the trolley bridge where others seldom ventured. We would strip off our clothes and dive in the bay. Whenever a trolley crossed on its way to Atlantic City, we would duck under, offering up our butts, and toss the passengers a full moon. We were definitely ahead of our time.

One day my brother Mick, Jackie and some other kids were at the docks. We were having a good time except for Mick who didn't know how to swim. Eventually Jackie and I started urging him to jump in. He was very reluctant and after awhile we left him alone and forgot about it. Unfortunately he hadn't.

Without warning his body came hurtling off the dock. Mick had failed to inform us he'd finally gotten up his nerve. I was totally taken by surprise. Jackie was still up on the dock while I was in the water. As soon as Mick hit the water he started going under. He was thrashing about wildly and I was already sorry we had badgered him.

As I reached him, he grabbed hold and started taking me under in an effort to stay above water. I tried to get away but to no avail. Finally, he let go but as he did I felt his feet on my shoulders, then my head. I was running out of air, starting to panic, thinking how my mother would kill me, if anything happened to her baby. Suddenly, the weight was off and I surfaced like a cork that had been held under water too long. Fresh air had never tasted so–fresh!

Luckily some guy working nearby heard the cries for help. He scrambled down the ladder grabbed Mick and pulled him to safety. Later I wondered why Jackie didn't do that, especially being the bay rat he was and a terrific swimmer to boot. Possibly it was a reaction from his little brother having drowned at Lake Lenape a year earlier.

That incident scared the living hell out of me, knowing I could have caused the death of my own brother. Whenever I thought of it, I'd shutter. We offered Mick every bribe we could not to tell mom. Bless his good little heart I don't think she heard about it until years later. Even then, she still read me the riot act.

Well, that's about the way it went until I was seventeen except somewhere during those years I became more interested in organized sports. I started playing Kiwanis baseball and organized football for a team called the Wimberg Bears. We won the junior league championship in our first year. My Mark Twain inspired days had come to an end.

My seventeenth year was significant. It was the year we moved out of the village. In truth, we didn't go by choice–we were kicked out. It seems my parents were making more money than low income village people were allowed. As usual, politics played a role. There were residents making much more than my parents. These cheaters were hiding income, lying about their circumstances and sucking up to the sleazy projects manager.

We only moved two blocks away to Atlantic Avenue.

I was attending Holy Spirit High School, where I was a member of the swimming team. My coach's name was John Daley, who was a marvelous swimmer. Though I'd always been a good swimmer he played a big role in refining my technique. What I found more interesting was, during the summer, John was a lifeguard.

I started asking him questions like: How long he'd been a guard? How old you had to be? What was the test like? Not only did he answer my questions, he encouraged me to take the test. This really excited me. One day he asked me if I'd ever rowed a boat. I told him of my bay experiences and how I'd been rowing boats since I was a young kid. He said rowing a lifeguard boat was quite different but knowing the basics would still give me a big advantage.

That did it. I decided, no matter how long it took I was going to become a member of the Atlantic City Beach Patrol. The idea had always been in the back of my mind. All I'd needed was a little encouragement. There were only two months until the beach opened.

I would get ready for the test!

CHAPTER 3

THE TEST

Taking the test to become a member of the Atlantic City Beach Patrol was not as simple as just taking the test. In order to understand that statement you have to have some understanding of Atlantic City's cultural underpinnings.

From the time Atlantic City was incorporated it never operated as an official city government. Although it had a sheriff, judges and made other pretenses at legality it was totally corrupt. It was a *Boss* town virtually controlled by one man. This was a town rooted in the promotion of "booze, broads and gambling."

Louis Kuehnle, commonly known as the "Commodore" (he served as chairman for the Atlantic City Yacht Club), was Atlantic City's first big-time boss. Though corrupt, Kuehnle, and Nucky Johnson, who succeeded him, were both generous men who took good care of the city's residents and generously included themselves. A fascinating book by Nelson Johnson (no relation to Nucky) titled *Boardwalk Empire*, details the lives of these men, as well as a history of the city.

Blue collared workers came to the city for the weekend and a chance to get away from their dreary existence and seek a little excitement. The bosses realized this kept Atlantic City humming and willingly provided visitors the pleasures they craved.

The rest of the state of New Jersey operated within legal boundaries, not Atlantic City. Whereas other towns had laws against bars opening on Sunday, the resort simply ignored them. The city was wide open, 24 hours a day, 7 days a week and the more upscale clubs provided whatever illegal activities were desired.

Atlantic City was not lacking for reformers who wanted to clean it up. The problem was the bosses who controlled the Republican Party, were able to buy the black vote. Blacks, who came after the civil war, were beholden to the bosses for providing them with work at the city's many hotels. These were service jobs but still afforded a better life than what they'd previously known. When the city slowed during the off season the boss made sure blacks were taken care of, where needed, by providing food, clothing and shelter.

When Election Day rolled around blacks were given two dollars for each time they voted. A Republican poll worker would be stationed outside the polling place. As each voter came out he would be given a different name and sent back in to vote again. It's been estimated that in the election of 1910, 3000 fraudulent votes were cast. The hotels generally supported the reformers. The boarding houses, which numbered many more, supported the bosses. Most citizens either didn't know or didn't care what was going on. For them, Atlantic City was simply the place to be.

So it was not far removed from this environment in 1950 that I decided to take the lifeguard test.

The city had undergone some serious cleansing due to investigative groups such as the Kefauver Committee. On August 1st 1941, the incomparable Nucky Johnson, age 58, was sentenced to ten years in jail.

Was this the end of Atlantic City as we knew it? Not quite.

Two new characters, a State Senator we'll call Frank, and a front man, Stumpy, the power broker emerged. And though things were not quite as they once were, not much had changed.

This was my introduction to Atlantic City politics, though it took some time to catch on to how the game was played.

WHAT DO POLITICS HAVE TO DO WITH LIFEGUARDING?

My first step in becoming a lifeguard was to get an application from City Hall. Fair enough. Upon completing the application I was to take it to my Precinct Captain for his signature.

My Precinct Captain turned out to be an older gentleman, not particularly impressive. He had probably been thrown a political bone for his party loyalty. In time, I'd find the machine took care of its own for toeing the political line. These loyalists probably came in for a certain share of the col-lected graft to help supplement other income.

Mr. P.C. lectured me on the benefits of being a Republican and how the party took care of its own. I listened and nodded feigning interest. I was mindful that one negative word from this guy could sink me (no pun intended). Finally, he finished, signed my application, and told me to see the Ward Leader. As he gave me directions I wondered where the glad-handing ended.

The Ward Leader turned out to be a nice guy, who was more impressive. He didn't seem to care whether I was a Republican, and didn't lecture me with the same bullshit. He was more interested in why I wanted to be a lifeguard. I told him I'd practically grown up on the beach and spent a good deal of time at the bay. I related conversations with my swim coach and said how he encouraged my interest and built my confidence. I stated my theory on the two Atlantic City's, the brick and mortar component and the beach and ocean version. He nodded with approval when I said I could never envision myself working in the steamy city while only two blocks away the ocean breezes were beckoning. He signed my application, shook my hand, and wished me luck.

My last hurdle was the ever humorless and intimidating head of the County Freeholder Board and leader of the powerful Fourth Ward of which I was a resident. Jimmy had an innate, unfriendly demeanor and I was immediately out of place in his presence.

He talked about the Republican Party and all it did for the citizens of Atlantic City. I was thinking, yeah, so what? What's this have to do with being a lifeguard? Boy, was I naïve. He kept pressing the issue like he knew I, as a good Republican, wanted to support the party (my family were all Democrats).

He kept up this mantra, referring to me as a Republican, and finally said, "You are a Republican aren't you?" Well, I was a pretty dumb kid, but not that dumb. I wanted to say, Jimmy, I'll be whatever the hell you want me to be even though I can't vote for four years. Just let me take the test to become a lifeguard. Instead I said, yes sir I sure am. He was pleased and asked if I'd like to become a member of the Republican County Committee.

Not knowing what that was, or what it entailed, without hesitation I agreed. I was afraid not to.

He was trying to smile but it looked more like a grimace. He signed my application, for which I thanked him profusely, and offered me a limp handshake, as if he was stuffing a hundred dollar bill in my mitt; though I'm sure he was used to it being the other way around. Through his not so subtle body language I was made aware that our conversation was over. It came none too soon for me.

Mercifully that ordeal was over. What kept bothering me was why I had to join the Republican County Committee. I would find out soon enough.

PRACTICE BEGINS

The Atlantic City beach officially opens the weekend of Memorial Day.

All the equipment is kept at the boat yard during the winter months. There, it is worked on by a crew of guards who hold beach patrol positions year round. They are also members of the local Painters-Carpenters Union. These are considered plum positions for members who plan to make the beach a year round job.

Guards who have seniority are hired a few weeks before Memorial Day to move boats and stands to the beach. A large flatbed truck is used to move one boat and stand at a time. Although all the boats and stands are brought to the beach, there is only one working crew for each tent on Memorial Day. The rest of the beaches open each week thereafter, until July 4 when a full complement of guards is in place.

But, what was most important to us was that the workers also brought a few old water-logged boats to the beach. These were what we would use to practice for the test.

After Memorial Day, we were allowed to start using the practice boats. I was surprised and gratified not to see more contestants the first day. It gave me the opportunity to get in more practices with the boat. The boats were dropped off at South Caroline Avenue, the site of Beach Patrol Headquarters.

Two captains, Dutch and Eddie were assigned to help with our training. These men were excellent oarsman, having won the annual A.C.B.P. boat race as a crew. Eddie, in addition, was also a great swimmer, having won the annual swimming race seven times.

Lifeguard boats were normally manned by two guards. During practice and during the test you were required to get the boat out and in by yourself. This was no easy task. The practice boats, having been water logged from so much use over the years, were much heavier, weighing about six hundred pounds. Though still seaworthy, they sat low in the water and were difficult to get moving. Unlike the newer boats that took the waves with graceful ease, these proud old ladies could only crash their way through the rugged surf.

The water wasn't very rough that day and the waves not very big. However, they were of the hollow back, or dumping variety. This type of wave builds very fast and breaks even faster. It is one whose base can no longer support its top causing it to collapse. Whether large or small, these waves are quite powerful, and scary. They're more common during a prevailing westerly wind.

Though I was by no means a Charles Atlas at 5'11 and 150 lbs, the first kid to go out couldn't have been more than 5'7 and 130 pounds. He was a cocky little guy who seemed to have no fear. As he climbed in the boat Dutch gave him some whispered advice. Then both captains, behind a running start, pushed him out into the break.

As soon as he took his first stroke I could see he didn't know how to row. He was wind-milling (raising his oars back and forth in large circles). This keeps the oars out of the water longer than practical, not allowing the rower to pick up momentum.

He made it over the first few seas, ran into a temporary calm, and was able to pick up speed from the wave's backwash. This helpful momentum can be deceptive and was in his case. A small fast dumper came from nowhere, crashing over his bow, knocking him under the stern seat. Both oars were gone and the boat was turned side-to. He pulled himself up and peer over the gunnel ala *Kilroy*.

He didn't have long to assess his predicament. Another wave was close behind the first, and a little bigger. This one crashed over the gunnels sinking him on the spot. A lump formed in my throat. He abandoned ship as the two captains went to retrieve the boat. They were only in chest deep water and the three of them towed it in. This scene would've been funny if it hadn't been so frightening.

The next kid was taller than the first with a stocky powerful build. He jumped in the boat like he knew what he was doing and got the complimentary push. He was a pretty good oarsman. Because of his skill he had the boat moving quickly and took the first couple of waves without incident. Then he hit a nice lull and made it through the break with no further problems.

After clearing the break, you are required to row about a hundred yards further and turn a flag, toward the windward side–*only*! Upon returning you must demonstrate seamanship on the way in. Just before reaching the break you have to turn and push in with your oars. This is done to simulate an actual rescue and also has a practical application.

During a rescue if you pick up a victim and attempt to bring him ashore with your bow pointed toward the beach you are sacrificing both control and safety. When a wave approaches a boat from its stern the crew is at its mercy. As the wave passes underneath, the craft is picked up and propelled at a high rate of speed. This can cause the boat to shear (peel) off and flip over, further endangering the victim(s), as well as the bathers. By bringing the boat in stern first, pushing with your oars allows you to pull back into a wave as it approaches. This takes a crew longer to reach shore, but, is a much safer technique.

The stocky kid made a nice turn just before the break and pushed in without incident. When he hit the beach the captains congratulated him.

The next kid to follow was big but not in the right way. He was bordering on fat and not athletic. As soon as he was in the boat and rowing we knew this was a disaster in the making. This guy had no clue what he was doing. He was not able to coordinate his oars that were moving in opposite directions. It was painful to watch.

It didn't take long before he rowed into the hollow of a dumper. Like the first kid, the sea crashed over his bow, hitting him in the back, knocking him to the floor, sending his oars flying. As he laid there, his hands gripping the gunnels, the wave bounced him to the shore at an alarming speed. It looked like a scene out of the Keystone Cops. Even though I was next it was difficult not to laugh. As soon as he exited the boat he put on his shirt, and, ignoring encouragement from Dutch and Eddie, disappeared. That was the last we saw of him.

I was nervous as I bounced into the boat. I knew now that this was a lot different than rowing in the bay. As the guys pushed me into the break I pulled with all the strength I could muster. The boat was unbelievably heavy and felt as though I was rowing one of those old cast iron claw foot bathtubs.

As a kid I'd watched how guards picked their way through the surf. That's what I did now. If I saw a wave cresting, I would wait for it to break and race to get over it. I did fine until just before I cleared the break. A wave made up very fast. Pulling to try and beat it the wave broke over me. It dumped some water in the boat, making it even heavier, but I was already beyond the break. I rowed to the flag, executed my turn, returned to the break, made my second turn, and pushed in without incident. Even though it might not *be* the same I gave silent thanks for all those years of rowing in the bay.

One thing I noticed was that my arms were incredibly tired. I asked one of the captains if this was normal. He told me I had to advance from the rowboat stage and stop bending my arms. He jumped in one of the boats sitting on the beach and demonstrated the proper technique. He told me to keep my arms straight and use them as fulcrums. Continuing, he said, "All the power comes from your legs and upper body. Brace your feet on the stern seat and drive with your legs. As you reach forward, keep the arms straight until your oars catch water. With your arms still straight lean back with your upper torso and drive with your legs. Only bend your arms on the recovery." This advice made perfect sense and took little time to put into practice.

I was able to get three more practices in that day wiping out only once. The one that got me was a sneaky little bastard that crashed over my bow, knocked me off my seat and sent me plummeting to shore. It was good to get that first wipeout, now I knew what it felt like.

Even though I have always been a very good swimmer, I wasn't going to take a chance of not being in shape for the swim. The ocean temperature ranged in the high 50's to low 60's but I had swum in those temperatures many times. Whereas most of the contestants didn't bother to practice, I was in the water daily.

I would start from shore and charge through the waves. On rough days this was a challenge as the waves would impede your progress, driving you back toward the beach. If you weren't in shape, by the time you made it through the break you were already exhausted.

The chief of the beach patrol always waited for the roughest day to give the test. We'd had about two and a half weeks of practice when the ocean turned rough from an off shore storm. Dutch and Eddie announced the test was being held the following day.

READY, GET SET, TEST!

Test day was overcast and chilly. The ocean was rough with large, uneven, angry waves.

The final number taking the test was thirty three. The total number of those hired would be fourteen. Out of that number, eleven would start July 4th weekend. The other three would be alternates, put to work if needed. Otherwise they'd start the following year.

Several beach patrol members were picked to judge the contest. These were veterans selected from both officers and working guards. They sat on stands, observing the races, marking their scores separately. Later they would compile the results and post them inside the tent.

The test began with the swim. This was a race covering about 400 yards around a flag and back. The top finishers in the swim who had a good boat test were considered to have the best chance of making the list. Unfortunately, this was not always the case. If you had a prominent father, or other relative, who was plugged into Atlantic City politics, even with a bad finish, your chances were significantly elevated.

There were to be three eleven man heats. I was in the second heat. The race started from the beach and required you to swim with a can buoy. Can buoys impeded your progress, by acting as a drag, when you went through or under a wave. The idea of the can buoy was to simulate conditions of an actual swim rescue.

The first eleven swimmers lined up in a crouched position. The starter fired his gun and the group galloped toward the ocean. The crowd's roar was palpable and stayed that way until the swimmers cleared the break. Some swimmers got lucky, hitting a calm and getting out in a hurry. Once the swimmers cleared the break, the crowd settled down to await the finish.

The finish was more exciting than the start. Three guys were in a dead heat for first place. The din of the crowd was deafening. They swam neck and neck for about twenty yards when a big wave approached. The three swam frantically to get on top of it. One of the swimmers fell off but the other two caught it. When it broke, there was so much white water the two disappeared from sight for a few seconds.

When they emerged, they were still neck and neck. The wave propelled them headlong toward the beach. As they approached knee deep water they stood and sprinted for the finish. One of the swimmers, suffering from exhaustion, had to settle for second place.

Now it was my turn. I walked over to Eddie and asked him if he had any last- minute advice. His only counsel was: "Get out in front kid–and stay there." I hoped it was as simple as that.

I lined up and looked to see who was to my left; no one very imposing. To my right was a different story. A tall black guy about 6'4 looked down at me with a smile. Later I'd get to know Teroy, and we'd remain friendly throughout the years. I nodded and moved into position.

When the gun went off Teroy took off like *The Streak*. He hit the water almost before the rest of us got started (I found out later he ran track). Uh oh I thought, ain't no way you're going to get out in front of this guy and stay there. As Teroy approached the waves he took them in a single bound. He was already swimming before the rest of us were barely up to our knees.

When the water was deep enough to swim I turned on the after burners. Since Teroy was on my right, and I breathed from my left, I had no idea of his position. Finally, I took a peek to see how far ahead he was. To my surprise he was nowhere in sight. I looked behind to see him struggling, no longer a factor.

That was the only time I looked around for anyone. My focus was on swimming as hard as I could, for as long as I could. I pushed on with one thought in mind; *get to the flag first*. I was growing tired from the constant buffeting of the waves. Finally, I looked up to see the flag directly in front of me. I executed a quick turn and immediately felt the swells propelling me inward. This gave me a second wind and I turned on a burst of speed. Half way in I heard the crowd noise, faint at first but growing louder, as I closed the distance to the beach.

Drawing closer to shore I caught a small wave that had already broken. Still, the short distance it carried me gave me great relief. As I stood up in knee deep water, and looked around, the closest guy to me was fifteen yards behind. As I ran toward the finish line I saw Eddie. With a knowing expression, he smiled giving me a wink and a nod. What a great feeling.

All I had to do now was pass the boat test.

The boat test was the same distance as the swim, 400 yards. It was more difficult, much trickier, and carried a long standing tradition that was etched in stone. **You had to pass the boat test.** This meant making it out through the break and back in, without losing oars, turning over, filling up with water, washing in or demonstrating poor boatmanship. Any of these missteps would disqualify you immediately–period!

The ideal initiate had a good to excellent boat test and finished his swimming heat in the top five.

The actual scenario was that you could have a mediocre-to-good boat test, do crappy in the swim, and voilá, somehow you still made it. If daddy or relative made a call to their favorite political hack the wheels of city corruption could be made to turn in your favor. I always felt bad for kids who trained hard, only to get unfairly beaten out by some no-talent daddy's boy. Eventually, I would experience this political favoritism first hand.

As if the day wasn't nerve racking enough with a lot of veteran guards observing us, there were spectators on the boardwalk and beach, as well as family and friends. I was praying no one would see me if I were to get unceremoniously catapulted from the boat as the result of an unsuspected wave.

We drew numbers hoping to get an early pick so as to get this part of the test behind us. I drew somewhere in the top third. That was not bad since we would be using three test boats and turns would come quickly.

Four out of the first nine guys ran into trouble and were disqualified. The others, either because of skill, luck or both negotiated the course successfully.

Two of the oarsmen who wiped out did so in spectacular fashion. The first caught a lull with just a few small waves to get over. It looked like he was going to breeze through the surf and clear the break easily. Instead, a large swell that was making up started to crest. He hesitated then started rowing toward it, then stopped to wait for it to break. Again he changed his mind and made for it, but too late. As he pulled into the wave which had reached its apex, the bow shot straight up and continued over. It catapulted him like a giant slingshot. With oars still in hands, as though shot from cannon, he hurled through space. The boat pitch-poled hitting the water upside down, its hump backed hull resembling a giant white tortoise. There was no need for words. He collected his things and vanished.

The second kid had trouble from the start. As soon as he got underway a series of broken waves hit him, impeding his progress. He was not able to get up a head of steam. Just when it looked like he was making some headway a huge sea made up. He tried to pull through it but it slammed into him, knocking him from his seat, turning him broadside. He lost both oars and took a half boat load of water.

As the next wave approached all he could do was hold on to the thole pins and await his fate. He didn't wait long. A huge wave hammered him as he was enveloped in white water that drove him careening toward shore. The next time we glimpsed him, he was still holding on to the thole pins, sitting in a boat full of ocean. At least he had the guts to ride it out. Others just abandoned ship. That ended his dreams for the year.

My turn came and my heart skipped a beat as I hopped in the boat. The only thing Dutch said just before pushing me was, "Use your head." Then I was on my own. My first obstacles were a couple of waves that had already broken. As I took them they slowed me down a little, nothing serious.

I hit a lull, but waited to see what was coming. A good size wave was developing. I thought I could make it over, but hesitated as it gathered steam. It broke quickly and I was glad I'd waited. Just as I made it over the first one another bigger one was making up. This one kept building. If I remained stationary I was a sitting duck. I pushed forward with my oars, moving away from it, giving it time to break.

When it broke, I took a few quick strokes and felt my bow lift high in the air above the white water. There followed a nice series of innocuous looking swells. I pulled so hard my ass was coming off the seat. Once I got past the break I settled down and struck a rhythm. My turn at the flag was crisp. I welcomed the ground swells pushing me toward shore, easing my fatigue.

I estimated where the break would start and executed my turn. It was right on the money.

I turned to see a wave bearing down on me and pulled into it. The boat lifted high in the air and came down with a splat. That was close. Each time a wave approached I pulled into it so as not to get swamped. Generally it is easy to ride a wave in stern first steering with your oars. This is considered a sign of good boatmanship, but the judges weren't looking for that right now. They wanted to see how you handled the boat on the way out and in under rough sea conditions.

Touching shore I pulled in my oars and bounced from the boat. After confirming my identity with the judges I rejoined my group.

Unfortunately for guys in the latter part of the pack the sea turned nastier as the day wore on. We saw a few more spectacular wipeouts but most of the guys made it without disqualifying.

After the test we were told to come back in a few hours when the judges would post the results. A few of us who'd become friendly bundled up against the deteriorating weather and headed for the boardwalk. We had all been soaked from waves crashing over the boat and resultant sixty degree ocean spray. We were in need of some warmth and nourishment.

Besides having great pork roll, Taylor's served wonderful hamburgers and hotdogs, was indoors and warm. The smell of the place made you weak with hunger. It was almost mandatory to get their birch beer with whatever food item you ordered. We stuffed ourselves and hung around, killing time, talking to the waitresses. They were college girls down for the summer. We eventually got around to telling them why we were there. They told us what beach they went to (Kentucky Avenue). We said we'd look them up.

When we returned to the beach some of the guys were playing touch football and we joined in. Finally, enough time had passed and we moved toward Beach Patrol Headquarters—with much trepidation.

The lists were up and we clamored to see the scores. I was toward the back and not close enough to make out the results. Suddenly, one of the guys said, "Christ McNesby! You came in first." I pushed my way to the front and, sure enough, there it was: 1) Robert McNesby. To say I was shocked would be an understatement. I thought I'd made it but had no idea I'd finished first.

The rest of the guys who'd made it were jumping around congratulating each other. Others were disappointed since they thought they'd passed, and in truth a couple had, only to be done in by politics. Some knew they hadn't but were hopeful anyway. One kid took it really hard and broke down. We tried to console him, saying there was always next year. It didn't help.

After things settled down those of us who'd passed were called upstairs. (Beach Patrol Headquarters has a second level with offices reserved for the chief and assistant chief). We were ushered in to the Chief's office. He congratulated us and said we'd be going to work on Saturday, Memorial Day Weekend.

From there, I was walking on clouds. When I got home and told my mom I made it, and finished first, she was thrilled and started calling relatives. My dad took the news more stoically. He never showed much emotion. But my mom told me later he couldn't stop talking about it. Both Jim and Mick were excited. Having a family member on the Atlantic City Beach Patrol was/is a big deal.

UNDER THEIR WING

I didn't need a wake-up call on Saturday, I'd hardly slept. It reminded me of being a kid again, waiting for Christmas Day.

Dressing quickly I ate breakfast, packed a lunch and said goodbye to my parents. I ran to Pacific Avenue and caught a jitney to South Carolina. (We referred to all beach avenues minus the word *avenue* and I will do so with exceptions throughout).

We had been told the day before to get to the beach at 8:00A.M.to attend the first of three days of lifeguard school. The school would be conducted under the tutelage of Captain's Eddie and Dutch.

Our first order of business was to swim around Steel Pier, a distance of about 600 yards in ocean temperatures hovering in the upper fifties to low sixties. Captain Eddie, who had won his share of swimming races, was to be our guide. We had gotten used to cold water, somewhat, after all our training. However, at this time of the morning it seemed a little excessive, like an exercise in sadism, or masochism, depending on one's perspective.

As soon as my feet hit the water I felt certain body parts retreat into more secure confines of my anatomy. It seemed like I was at the quarter mark before I realized my limbs were moving and I still had blood. If hypothermia did not set in before this ordeal was over—it never would. Incredibly, a little further out, the cold became less of a factor and I was able to complete the rest of the swim without glaciating.

The rest of school consisted of mock rescues, taking the boat out, turning it over and learning about the potential lifesaving air pocket underneath. We learned about deadly offsets and how to spot them, the proper execution of a can buoy rescue and how to administer C.P.R (Cardiac Pulmonary Resuscitation). There were other instructions, like what to do with lost children, and quelling disturbances on the beach etc.

We had a full morning of classes at A.C. B. P. U.

When we returned to the South Carolina tent the place was buzzing with veterans checking out the *rookies*—as we arrived. We were directed to the medical room to pick up uniforms. Each guard was given two tank suits, two sets of trunks, a sweat suit and jacket. We were required to buy our own whistles.

We changed in the lifeguard's locker room. As soon as we came out we were greeted with catcalls. "Oh, check out the news (short for newbies), how pretty they look in their new red and blue uniforms." We did stand out from the veterans whose uniforms had been weathered by the sun and salt water.

The assistant chief called us out on the porch to issue our assignments. Most of us kept our fingers crossed, hoping we'd get on a front beach (beaches facing east toward the ocean). The beaches from States Avenue, located on the uptown side of Steel Pier, to Arkansas Avenue on the uptown side of Million Dollar Pier (covering about fourteen blocks), were considered prime beaches. The reason: that was where the action was.

Most of the hotels and rooming houses were located within these parameters. The rooming houses were where the girls stayed, the hotels where they worked and girls were one of the main reasons for being a lifeguard. Additionally, because of piers and jetties located along this expanse of beach, the ocean was more dangerous and rescues more frequent. Unless you were looking to retire to the easier beaches for the summer, and some guys were, this was the stretch of beach you wanted to be.

Beaches above States were not desirable to most guards. Farther up, the beach turned at the inlet where the ocean and bay met. This stretch of beach was known as the *channel* and the guards stationed there, affectionately, as channel rats. An assignment to the channel was something I hoped to avoid at all costs.

Below Million Dollar Pier, as you moved toward the Chelsea section, beaches were referred to as *the desert* and farther on down as *the leper colony*. They were also not very appealing as you can probably tell by their names.

Where you finished in the test had a lot to do with where you were stationed. I breathed a sigh of relief when the chief announced, McNesby, Mansion! Mansion Avenue was a half street, between North Carolina and Pennsylvania. These two beaches, along with South Carolina, site of beach patrol headquarters, were designated college beaches because this is where the co-eds hung out. This area was also the hub of Atlantic City activity. Most of the restaurants bars and some major hotels were located here which provided summer employment for the college crowd and a bonanza for business own-ers. So Mansion Avenue, besides being a working beach, which meant lots of rescues, also meant—lots of girls.

My assignment was as third man on the stand. My partners were Eddie and Walter, two seasoned veterans, and lucky for me, two nice guys. Being a third man and rookie for most seasoned vets, was a crappy experience. The majority felt rookies should undergo an initiation and would go out of their way to make life difficult.

Third men were not allowed to sit in the stand, which meant you stood in the hot sun most of the day. When the boat and stand had to be moved, which was about every half hour, you were the designated mover. Normally, two guys performed this feat but unless you wanted to undergo further harassment you learned to perform this feat solo. If it was necessary to whis-tle people away from danger, the veterans would have you doing it for hours. Some guys made you wade into waist deep water and tell bathers to stay clear of jetties or piers. That could get chilly after a sustained period. When it was time for layout they'd do half hour shifts, making you do the full hour.

New guys, being totally naïve, would be sent on an errand to the next stand for 20 feet of shore-line. Of course being a rookie you'd dutifully obey. The guards at the next stand, who were totally familiar with this ruse would say they didn't have any shore line and to "try the next stand." The rookie, in his ignorance, would repeat this process being directed to "try the next stand," until he'd walked for blocks, before catching on. You thought they wanted rope but they actually meant the *shoreline.* Even though they'd get a big kick out of their little trick, you daren't say anything—that would only make things worse. It wasn't that I didn't get my share of rookie ball busting. It was just that my partners were never excessive.

Eddie and Walter were educated guys and took the job seriously. (Eddie later became a doctor and Medical Chief of the A.C.B.P.). The first thing they taught me was how to watch the ocean for trouble spots. They pointed out offsets, explaining what caused them. They instilled in me the importance of never taking my eyes off the water no matter what was happening around me. Girls who came to the stand to talk would sometimes complain that I never looked at them. Being able to focus and concentrate on the ocean for hours took a lot of discipline and often separated the good guards from the ordinary.

They would have me practice boat rescues. When it was Walter, he rowed bow so I'd row stern. When it was Eddie, we'd reverse the order. This constant repetition gave me the advantage of being able to handle either bow or stern efficiently.

Besides backing up North Carolina and Pennsylvania on runs, we had our own share of rescues. The first time we went on a rescue, Eddie pointed it out to me. "See that guy trying to swim against the set?" I had no idea what the hell he was looking at. The next thing I heard was, "Let's go." I grabbed a can buoy from the side of the stand, looped the rope over my shoulder, ran behind them to the boat and helped them launch. As soon as they were in the boat I pushed them until they were underway. I started to run alongside to get to deeper water where I could swim. They pulled away from me like I was standing still.

I still didn't see anyone in trouble, but soon enough Eddie shipped his oars and threw the donut. The bather grabbed it and Eddie pulled him to the side of the stern. Then Walter leaned to the side Eddie was on so the boat tipped toward the bather. Eddie got the victim's arms and one leg on the gunnel. Walter yelled ok as they both hit the high side of the boat easily flipping the bather into the stern seat.

Witnessing all this from my vantage point in the water really impressed me. I couldn't wait to go on my first boat rescue. Eddie and Walter pushed the boat in stern first as I swam alongside. When they touched shore they helped the guy out of the boat. He was an older gentleman and expressed his appreciation to the guys.

We had quite a few rescues over the following days as the ocean turned rough. I didn't get to go on any boat rescues but I dutifully followed with my can buoy. Not once did I beat my partners to a victim. Usually, the only time a can-man would beat a crew was if the boat capsized. On the plus side, my uniform was not that of a pretty-boy anymore.

I hadn't realized how good I had it with Eddie and Walter, until a day when some out of town officials from another beach patrol came to assess our rescue techniques. Atlantic City has always been considered cutting edge in this area, so it wasn't uncommon for us to have these types of visitors.

Our chief set up some mock rescues to show them our system. Being a rookie, I was told to play the victim. The two guards working South Carolina were the designated boat crew. I knew these guys, and, like others, wasn't very fond of them. They were, arguably, the two best lifeguards on the beach and they knew it. They were arrogant and condescending and also major ball-busters, especially toward rookies. I wasn't looking forward to being their victim.

I swam beyond the break and when they gave me the signal, I waved my arms like I was drowning. The pair got to me quickly, threw the donut, and reeled me in. As the stern man pulled me in he was being unnecessarily rough banging my arms and legs on the gunnel. I thought he was overdoing it because I was a rookie. I told him to take it easy, I was one of them, but he ignored me. The rescue went well, and the chief congratulated us, but during my years on the beach I never had positive feelings for those guys. I also vowed to treat my fellow guards with more respect.

SHIPPED TO THE CHANNEL

Things were going well. I was enjoying my time at Mansion with Eddie and Walter. I had been there about two and a half weeks, when, after work one night while changing, the captain told me to stop and see him as soon as I was dressed. When I walked into his office he hurriedly said, "You're being transferred to Adriatic, you have to report tomorrow." I was dumbfounded. Everyone told me what a good job I was doing. I asked him why. He said, "Orders from the chief."

I was being transferred to the inlet, the channel, my worst nightmare.

Having been assigned to a front beach I thought my station was secure for the summer. Being transferred to the channel was more like being a lifeguard at a lake than at the ocean.

Adriatic Avenue was the first beach in Atlantic City. Whereas the boardwalk runs behind the ocean along the front beaches, in the inlet it runs over the ocean (or channel). What you're left guarding is a glorified kiddie pool. Most of our bathers were families with lots of kids. My summer went from one of total excitement to one of crushing boredom.

My partner, another Bob who I grew up and went to school with became my partner at Adriatic. We both bemoaned the fact that we were sent to the inlet. We kept asking each other why? This was further proof of our ongoing naivete.

A week or so later I was talking to a veteran, a guard of many years. I told him about my disappointment over being transferred. He said, "Don't you know why that happened?" When I expressed ignorance, he said, "The guy you replaced talked to his uncle, who has political pull, and had you two switched."

To say I was pissed off would be putting it mildly. I was furious. I had been dumb enough to think we would be treated fairly. This even more so from an organization with a reputation for being, arguably, the world's finest beach patrol.

Memory fails me as to why Bob was sent there because he also finished high in the test and I know that wasn't his first assignment station.

It was also around this time we found out why we were asked to join the Republican club. It gave the corrupt politicians permission to take dues out of our pay. These they funneled to the Republican County Committee. This was their legalized method of extortion.

We were an arm of the Public Safety Department. I still viewed the Beach Patrol in a positive light since they weren't directly responsible for the corruption that was going on. After all, our main purpose for being was a lofty one. It was important not to lose sight of our stated goal.

Bob and I swallowed our pride. I finished out the boring summer, all the while feeling I wasn't contributing. The real action seemed like it was taking place in another dimension.

School began and with the advent of football practice I quickly put summer behind me. I was going into my junior year and hoping to make the squad. High school held no particular interest for me and I was not a student who applied himself. My only interest was sports.

Except for football season the winter passed slowly. I had played in some games but did not make the starting squad. There was always next year.

Finally, Easter Sunday dawned, ushering in the advent of a new spring, and just beyond–summer.

School let out the middle of June. In two weeks I would be back on the beach. I felt confident I would be stationed on a front beach.

As with the previous summer I reported to the captain at South to pick up a new uniform and be given my assignment. Bob had arrived before me. We kept our fingers crossed, and then came the dreaded word, "McDonough and McNesby, Adriatic." I believe we audibly groaned. What a disappointment, another summer in la la land.

We dutifully fulfilled our obligation, wiling away the summer, watching mothers play with their inner-tube-encircled kiddies.

There were some positives; Bob and I did a lot of rowing. This was a great upper body workout to get us ready for the upcoming football season. We also did wind-sprints in the soft sand which was terrific for building endurance and leg strength. This conditioning served us well for the few rescues we did have.

The Inlet was referred to as the channel for a reason. It was a deep wide chasm just outside the boardwalk running east and west. During certain tide conditions the channels current was extremely swift. Regardless of how good a swimmer one was, once caught, the ability to negotiate this fearsome rapid was beyond daunting.

Bathers were not allowed to swim beyond the boardwalk during these dangerous tides. Since Adriatic was composed of mostly mothers with children, we never encountered reckless bathers. Drexel Avenue, a block to our east, was another story. Though it was very close to us, Drexel was made up of an entirely different type of beachgoer. For one thing, it was where the beach patrol tent was located. Tent beaches always drew a variety of people. The second reason was a hamburger and hot dog stand located right on the beach which appealed to stomachs of all ages. And, directly across Maine Avenue from the Drexel Beach tent was Cal's bar. Cal's, was a raucous neighborhood bar where beachgoers would go to partake of liquid refreshments, and then forget to bring back their brains.

These three factors contributed to a more diversified crowd at Drexel. Consequently, bathers at that beach were more what you might consider–risk takers. This was especially true if a good part of the day for the Cal's crowd, had been spent sipping cocktails.

Drexel and Adriatic were separated by a wooden jetty that extended out in the water to the boardwalk. This structure impeded our line of vision and obstructed our ability to see bathers at Drexel. If someone went out beyond the boardwalk at Drexel and got caught in the channel, we wouldn't see them until they were swept past the jetty and into our view. This gave us scant reaction time.

The first time this occurred Bob and I were caught by surprise. We looked out to see a bather trying to swim against the channel, getting nowhere fast. He was rapidly losing ground and would soon be lost to our sight. We launched the boat quickly, having to negotiate our way through the boardwalk pilings. It was necessary to pull our oars in so as not to hit the pilings with them.

Once through, we found ourselves in a race. A few blocks past our beach lay a huge rock jetty. We had to catch the bather before he was carried to the point where he'd be dashed into the treacherous rocks. Fortunately, our oars propelled the boat faster than the bather was moving.

When we reach him, we passed close enough for Bob to drop a donut. As Bob pulled the man into the stern we were getting dangerously close to the rocks. I quickly spun the boat around and started back. As soon as Bob had the man safely secure he manned his oars. As if it wasn't hard enough rowing against the swift current, having the added weight of the man made it even more difficult.

We were surprised at how hard we had to row to get back to our station. By the time we made it to the beach we were exhausted.

Fortunately, because conditions had to be just right for the channel to run that fast, we only experienced a few more rescues of that nature over the remainder of the season.

As with the previous summer, time passed and we found ourselves back in school. It was necessary to get an insurance waver signed by our parents to play football. I had a great chance to start that year. But when all the insurance notices came back I was declared ineligible. I had repeated my freshman year, and was only allowed four years of eligibility, whether I played all four years or not.

That did it for me. After a month or so I quit school and signed up for a four year hitch in the U.S. Navy. My parents were extremely upset but I was very headstrong telling them I'd had enough of school.

That was probably one of the best decisions I ever made. Four years in the Navy gave me the maturity I was sadly lacking, and would never have found, had I remained in high school.

CHAPTER 4

MICHIGAN AND MURPH

RETURN TO CIVILIAN LIFE

Having served four years on a Navy destroyer, the bulk of which was spent at sea, my discharge in January came as a welcomed event. It was odd finding oneself permanently back on terra firma. At times, I swore I could still feel that rolling deck beneath me.

The chief petty officer I had worked under urged me to re-enlist. I told him that was out of the question. The Navy had provided me a valuable learning experience but it was time to move on. Order and discipline had been programmed into my life and I was ready to make use of them.

During my stint, I realized without an education I was bound for nowhere. I was determined to make use of the G.I. Bill and get an education. The G.E.D. test had been made available to all military personnel, which I completed successfully.

My release came in early January, 1956. My parents assumed I would move back with them, which I did, temporarily. I told them of my plans to attend college. They greeted this news with little enthusiasm. Who could blame them after knowing what a screw up I'd been?

Undaunted, I applied to different colleges in Pennsylvania. It didn't take long to receive the negative replies. Not one of them accepted the G.E.D test for admission. Besides, I was told my grades had been so bad in high school I didn't come close to meeting their standards. I didn't view this as a deterrent, only a temporary setback.

I was faced with the prospect of getting a job. This was no easy task during the employment depressed Atlantic City winters.

A friend from the beach patrol worked at the Employment Office, commonly referred to as "The Unemployment Office." This was due to the fact that the office gave out many more checks than jobs.

My friend found an opening for me with a wholesale food distributor that needed office help. The position entailed taking orders over the phone, as well as making up and coordinating invoices with delivery drivers. The pay was not very good, the job stimulation even less. At that time however it afforded me enough to pay my parents rent and left some for entertainment.

The winter passed uneventfully, except for re-establishing old friendships. Some good times were shared at many of Atlantic City's vast array of bars and night clubs. Some of my lifeguard buddies asked if I was going back on the beach. I told them my first priority was getting accepted to college, but going back on the beach was something I hadn't ruled out.

BACK TO HIGH SCHOOL–AGE TWENTY THREE

Since my G.E.D. wasn't going to get me admitted to college, I decided on another plan. I paid a visit to my former high school, Holy Spirit. The same nun, Sister Mary Jane, was still the principal. She welcomed me into her office and I explained my dilemma. She called for my records. After looking them over she told me I had to make up four subjects in order to earn my diploma.

Sister Mary Jane was gracious enough to let me make up my senior year. I was told, by maintaining an eighty five average, I'd be exempt from final examinations and finished school by the first week in May. That was a challenge I was more than willing to accept.

Going back to high school at 23 was a little more than embarrassing. The kids tried not to stare but I felt their eyes every time I walked into class. They were uncomfortable talking to me and I had nothing in common with them. There was one girl named Lois who was very mature. She had a natural open personality and was comfortable with everyone with whom she came in contact. I always felt at ease in Lois's company and was able to communicate with her on an adult level.

Lois took away some of my uneasiness and I welcomed times I spent with her. If there was something going on in class I was unfamiliar with, she would bring me up to speed and go out of her way to help. Lois was a special person.

I applied myself like never before. It was amazing how easy the courses were when you kept up with the work. There were days when I wanted to kick myself for not having taken school more seriously.

I'd also had enough of working as an order-taking shipping clerk. Since college would occupy my next four years it made sense to go back on the beach patrol. I figured I could work a second job at night, driving a taxi, and put some money away in order to supplement my G. I. bill.

During the winter I met Jack, a high school friend of my brother Mick. He and some other guys from Atlantic City were attending the University of Miami. He told me he'd first attended Temple, and Philadelphia Museum's College of Art in Pennsylvania. On a day he was freezing his ass off in Philly he received a call from a buddy at Miami. This guy told Jack he was stretched out on the beach with girls parading by him like they were auditioning for a beauty contest. That did it, Jack transferred shortly after.

Now it was his turn to sell me on the University and the glamorous campus life. Jack spoke of Friday night football games, hanging out at the beach, meeting girls at campus watering holes, Fort Lauderdale during Easter break, etc. Moreover, these activities were comfortably enjoyed wearing the uniform of the day, Bermudas, tee shirt and flip flops, or bathing trunks. He said going from resort to resort, not having to experience the cold northeastern winters, was a natural for us. I only interrupted him long enough to find out where to sign up. The next day I sent for an application.

By the time May arrived I had easily maintained an above 85% average. Sister Mary Jane issued me my diploma and I now possessed the necessary credentials to apply for college admission.

Toward the end of May, I received a nice reply from Miami saying they would accept me on a probationary basis and I would have to maintain a C average.

REUNION WITH THE BEACH PATROL

My next order of business was to see the chief of the beach patrol. I was determined not to return to the inlet, or Adriatic Avenue. I had a plan to do a selling job on the chief that would ensure my placement on a front beach.

The chief frequented a seafood restaurant and bar called Magee's. As fortune would have it I accidentally, on purpose, ran into him there one night. Some of the captain's also hung out at Magee's, probably hoping to catch the chief and score some brownie points.

The chief had just finished dinner and retired to the bar when I approached him. He greeted me with a warm welcome and asked about my military status. I told him I'd completed my hitch and was looking forward to coming back on the beach. He was delighted. He told me I would get credit for my four years of service and be starting my seventh year. This would elevate my status regarding salary and seniority.

I told him that since I'd seen action in Korea (true), I was still carrying an edge from the war (not true). I made clear, being stationed in the inlet would be too boring and probably something I couldn't deal with. I said I would prefer a beach with some action, but especially one in between the two piers.

By the time he left I knew I wouldn't be going back to the inlet. The chief told me to report for duty on the 15th of May, three days hence. He was going to put me to work early, hauling equipment to the beach from the city's boatyard.

We hauled boats and stands up until Memorial Day weekend when all equipment was in place. The next day we reported to the assistant chief to pick up our uniforms and station assignments. Though I felt confident I wouldn't be returning to the channel, there was that moment of doubt.

We were called to the chief's office where the assistant chief, Harry, read the assignments. I kept my fingers crossed until he called out, "McNesby, Michigan Avenue." I breathed a huge sigh of relief.

Michigan Avenue was a block north of Arkansas, which was right next to Million Dollar Pier and definitely an action beach. Michigan Avenue had three major hotels to either side of it, the Shelburne, Dennis and Marlborough Blenheim.

I'd heard of my new captain known to everyone as "Murph," though he was partly Jewish. He was raised in the Inlet in a mostly Irish Catholic neighborhood with the likes of McCabe's, McCullough's, Sykes, Quigley's, etc. These guys were all athletes, as was Murph and they refused to have a kid with the name Bernie on the team; hence the nickname.

Murph was known for being tough but fair, which I could appreciate. That couldn't be said for the majority of Captains. He had an enviable reputation as a lifeguard and was considered one of the best on the beach patrol. An excellent swimmer and great oarsman, he competed in local and national lifeguard competitions, having won on several occasions. Murph was the very essence of a man's man.

I headed for my assignment, covering the seven blocks from South to Michigan via the boardwalk. Michigan was the only stretch that didn't have a tent. The owner of the Dennis Hotel a man named George, thought having one in front of his hotel and cabanas would be an eyesore. The hotel owners wielded significant power and the city dared not cross them.

George did provide Captain Murph a large cabaña by the boardwalk. This was to serve as Murph's tent, which ironically is what it was. When I arrived, there stood Murph talking on the phone. He nodded, smiled and indicated he would be with me in a moment.

I sized him up quickly. If you were looking for an individual to fit the profile of *lifeguard*, then Murph was your man. He stood 6'1," was broad-shouldered, powerfully built, somewhere in his mid thirties, squared jawed, handsome and prematurely bald. He hung up the phone, seized my hand in a vise like grip and welcomed me to the stretch. He told me this was his first year as captain and he was looking forward to the summer.

Because we didn't have our own quarters, Murph told me I would have to change in the hotel. There were stairs next to the cabaña leading down to the hotel guest's locker room and showers. I went below and changed into my uniform.

By the time I got back upstairs there was another guard talking to Murph. It turned out to be my partner. His name was Dick. Dick, because of his 6'3" slender frame was stork like in build. He was in his early twenties, had a winning smile and was not far behind Murph in sparseness of hair.

After he changed, we moved our boat and stand down to the water's edge. There were few people on the beach as it was still early June. We had to protect a stretch of beach from Arkansas Avenue to Indiana Avenue, a distance of four blocks.

Indiana had a wooden jetty that ran about 100 yards into the ocean. The ocean floor, alongside it, had deep holes that during high tide created some nasty offsets. The water temperature was in the mid fifties. Few ventured into the ocean and if so not for long, and, usually not beyond their knees, except for kids, who are immune to cold water.

FIRST RESCUE OF THE SUMMER

That first day and several beyond were uneventful but I was sure happy to be back on a front beach. Murph, apprehensive because of the distance we had to cover constantly scanned the ocean with binoculars. This prompted us to remark that he must have gotten nervous in the service or we'd refer to him as Nervous Norvis.

He'd had some pretty horrific experiences from his many years on the beach, which made him extremely conscientious. Now, during these early empty days it was hard to concentrate on the ocean all day, especially with the few bathers who braved the cold surf. We came to appreciate Murph's extra pair of eyes. This proved especially significant shortly thereafter.

Dick and I were sitting on the stand at Michigan when suddenly we heard a whistle behind us. We turned to see Murph heading our way pointing toward the Indiana jetty. Without seeing where he was pointing, we grabbed can buoys and ran toward the jetty.

Getting closer, we saw a man and young boy caught in a swirling offset, being buffeted against the jetty. We dashed into the water with Murph on our heels. Although the adrenalin was flowing it didn't mitigate the icy ocean conditions. The victims were about fifty yards out but we got to them quickly. The boy was screaming, holding on to his father and in a panic. The father wasn't much better off having swallowed a lot of sea water. Dick put the kid on his can buoy and holding him with one arm used the jetty to work his way in. I put the father, who was a big man on my can buoy and Murph helped me get him back to the beach. Other than being shaken both were fine. The father thanked us profusely. He said he thought they were both goners and was surprised to see us come from, seemingly, nowhere.

We took turns going back to the hotel to get showered and changed. This was a luxury. During the season, on days when there were a lot of swimming rescues, you sat around in a wet uniform all day. As I descended the stairs to the showers I felt my legs go weak and thought I was going to collapse. I grabbed the railing to steady myself. Though a cold ocean had never affected me before, a touch of hypothermia was the only reason I could think of for this reaction. A nice hot shower took care of that.

As July 4th approached crews were added each week until a full complement of guards was in place. Dick and I were displaced at Michigan by two veterans who had worked that station for several years. Before the other crews arrived, Murph asked if we had a choice between Arkansas, Ohio, or Indiana.

Since we wanted to be where the action was we chose Arkansas. There was a reason why Arkansas had so many rescues. Because it was located next to a pier with a vast array of pilings deep holes had been created on the ocean's floor. These were especially dangerous during the mid to high tide period and occasional nor'east storms. The swirling offsets that formed were especially treacherous for children.

SCRAMBLE

Michigan and Ohio could experience these same conditions, although not as frequent and not subject to the dangers of the pier. When they did, because of the difference in ocean conditions, rescues occurred farther out and were of a more sensational nature. One *spectacular* I remember in particular happened on a balmy sunny afternoon.

In order to fully grasp the details surrounding this rescue it is necessary to introduce the reader to Assistant Chief Harry, who, during the time of this rescue was a captain.

When Murph was a young guard he worked under Captain Harry out of States Avenue. The captain was immensely admired by members of the patrol. He was a legend on the beach, having won seven Atlantic City doubles boat racing championships with his son Charles. He won another four dou-bles with different partners and three more in the singles category

Whenever Murph spoke of Captain Harry, it was always with respect sometimes bordering on reverence. I suspect Murph looked upon him as a surrogate father. Captain Harry's feelings toward Murph were entirely mutual, though neither man was prone to expressing sentimentality.

One attribute guards admired about both men was they never put them-selves above the rest of the patrol. They were still lifeguards at heart.

Some guards, upon making captain, thought it beneath them to take part in rescues. They felt they'd paid their dues and it was their time to hang in the tent enjoying the benefits of command.

Anyway, back to the day in question. Every so often captains would get called to headquarters for various reasons, mostly concerning policy. They were required to pass the directives they received on to their crews. On this day Murph had spent most of the morning at South.

Captain Harry was now in his mid fifties, had been promoted years before to assistant chief and was stationed at South Carolina Avenue Headquarters. He wasn't big on hanging around the tent, and spent a good part of each day walking the beach, visiting with captains and guards. Much of his time he spent with Murph.

When Murph was finished at South and heading back to Michigan, Chief Harry, as he often did—joined him.

Though this day, as I described it, was beautiful with lots of bathers, a storm had passed through two days earlier. It had created a gigantic offset between Ohio and Michigan. The guards stationed there had been involved in several rescues already, mostly kids.

It was barely past noon.

Dick and I, besides watching our own bathers, kept an eye on the trouble spot up beach of us.

The guards at Michigan, Ohio and Indiana had been blowing their whistles steadily, keeping bathers away from the treacherous offset. This was proving to be an exercise in futility. There were so many ocean-goers enjoying the balmy day, warm ocean temperatures, and perfect rolling waves, some-thing seemed bound to get out of control.

This scenario was ripe for a major calamity.

We didn't have long to wait.

Two teenagers, both good swimmers had swum out off Indiana, a good distance beyond the break. This was a block up beach from the trouble area and they faced no risk at this point. But the longer they stayed out beyond the break the more they drifted down towards Ohio. When they finally decided to make their way back to the beach they swam directly into the path of the offset—and danger.

All stations immediately recognized the situation. Looking further up beach we spotted Murph and the chief. They had stopped at the Indiana stand to assess the unfolding drama.

Guards whistled at the two swimmers in an effort to get them to change course. The two swam with good technique, had their heads in the water and couldn't hear the whistles.

Curious bathers, alerted by the shrill whistles, started heading toward the direction of the swimmers, not realizing *they* were about to drop off the sandbar into the deep swirling offset.

As the boys approach the set Ohio launched its boat as a matter of precaution. One crew seemed enough at this point. Just as the guards got underway the swimmers reached the set. They were not prepared for the turbulence that greeted them and panicked. In an effort to continue to shore, they felt themselves being jostled and pulled by the powerful set. They tried swimming against this force but soon found they were in the grip of its power.

It was then that all hell broke loose. Observers who had wanted a closer look kept moving toward the dangerous vortex. Suddenly, like lemmings going over a cliff, the chain reaction started. As bathers dropped into the offset they took others with them. Some jumped in with the intention of helping and soon became part of the melee.

Simultaneously, Dick and I plus the crew at Indiana launched boats and headed for this precarious site. Michigan couldn't launch, because one of the guards, Geza, had gone to the tent to make a phone call. Jackie, his partner, took off running up beach, foolishly, without a can buoy.

Sprinting toward the victims, with the boat moving parallel to the waves, we were in danger of being broadsided. I saw Murph and the chief streaking through the surf into the turbulence. Even with all the excitement I was impressed with Chief Harry, who, in his fifties was dashing through the waves like a rookie.

We all converged about the same time upon a scene that would make the word turmoil seem insufficient. People caught in the offset were everywhere flailing about. Women were holding onto men, taking them under water. Kids were struggling to stay above the surface. Others were yelling, "Help" and "Save me," at the top of their lungs.

We started throwing donuts from the bow and stern for victims to grab, leaving the boat untended for the moment. We were even throwing spare oars to people. This at least was something to hold on to and give the victim a false sense of security until someone got to them. As we reeled bathers in, Murph and the chief helped them in the boat.

Jackie, the guard who had taken off without a can buoy almost became a victim himself. As he cross body carried a bather to another boat, a woman in trouble got close and grabbed him around the neck. All three started going under. One of the guards from another vessel dove in and wrested the lady from Jack's neck. The two were maneuvered to the boat and pulled aboard. Jackie went back to help more of those in trouble.

Just as our three boats were becoming dangerously overloaded another one launched from Illinois, the station above Indiana. Geza, the guard making the phone call recruited one of the black guards from Missouri and they launched the Michigan boat. Also more guards had come running over from Kentucky Avenue, the stretch above ours.

With this additional support, we were able to take people to the beach and safely unload them. Murph, the chief and Jackie (who we'll meet again) were helping load panic-stricken bathers into the newly arrived boats. By the time we rowed back out the situation had been brought under control. Except for those who swallowed water, and those who thought they'd spent their last day on earth, everyone was okay.

When we were back on the beach the chief came over and congratulated us on a job well done. We looked at each other as if to say, "Holy shit, are you kidding? We're young and do this all the time. You're the one who should be congratulated." We were all pretty much in awe of the chief.

We knew this scramble had involved a lot of people but didn't know how many. A few of the mascots settled that. They had been observing from the beach and all three counted sixteen. We had taken four, Ohio had four. The other three boats had three, three and two.

The rest of the day stayed relatively calm. Hundreds of people along the boardwalk and beach had witnessed this rescue. It became unnecessary to keep moving bathers away from the trouble spot. Though it's a tired cliché, in this case it was quite apropos. "One picture is (definitely) worth a thousand words."

Besides his other duties, Murph had those of a father to keep him busy.

Murph had married an Irish Catholic girl named Jeanne. Jeanne worked as a supervisor for the telephone company. They had a five year old son, Steve, who Murph would bring to the beach five days a week. Jeanne would take over that duty on weekends, giving Murph a much needed break, which mercifully also included us.

Before I came to know Steve, I saw him in a photograph with Murph. Murph had won the singles boat race the summer before. Someone had snapped a picture of the two at the finish line with Stevie posing on Murph's lap. It was a great likeness of both. Murph had a big smile on his face. A cute, somewhat bewildered-looking Steve, even at the tender age of four, looked like a chip off the old block. We would soon discover our perception was not reality–at least not for a while.

DEAN MARTIN TO THE RESCUE

Dick and I were having our share of rescues at Arkansas. There were quite a few nor'east storms that summer creating some serious holes off our beach. Bathers would enter the surf at Michigan, and, at times, get carried by the current into our offset. We always saw this condition developing. It became S.O.P. to launch the boat in anticipation of danger and get to the bather just about the time they realized they were in trouble.

Most of these rescues were routine. The reason for this was although the offsets were dangerous, the overall ocean conditions weren't critical. The waves were not threatening, the wind not fierce and the currents running toward the pier not that strong. During routine rescues we thought of ourselves as a shuttle service for ferrying bathers to safety.

It was on a day like this that we met Dean Martin. He and Jerry Lewis were appearing at the previously mentioned 500 Club. The Five, as it was called, was located two and a half blocks from our beach. Previously, Dean and Jerry had been booked as solo acts, not having much success. The owner, Skinny D'Amato, a celebrity in his own right decided to team the pair. The rest is history. To show their appreciation and loyalty to Skinny they appeared at the club almost every summer thereafter. People mobbed the place to see them.

On this particular day, there was a bothersome little offset right in front of our stand. As the tide came in, kids were getting off the sandbar and making their way to shore. We discovered quickly who among them couldn't swim, as some found trouble immediately.

The set was small enough so as not to need a boat. Dick and I were swimming out and making can buoy rescues. In some instances, where small kids were in over their heads we were only in chest-deep water. In those instances we merely laid kids over the can and walked them to shore.

As Dick and I sat in the stand in our wet uniforms we heard a familiar voice from the side of the stand say, "You guys need help?" It was Dean Martin, looking every bit the celebrity he was. As pictured, he was tallish, handsome, tanned, well built, with a dazzling smile. He exuded none of the phony airs often associated with famous people.

We thanked him for the offer and told him we were fine. He said he had been watching us from where he sat on the beach and was surprised to see how many rescues we were having. We explained it had to do with ocean conditions and this was one of those days, although this day was fairly mild.

He stayed and we shot the breeze for awhile but it wasn't long before a large crowd started gathering around the stand. This became somewhat uncomfortable for us. We needn't have worried. Dean instantly recognized the problem and said, "I'd better let you guys get back to work. If you were to have a rescue you wouldn't be able to get off the stand." We turned to watch him go and saw Jerry farther up the beach entertaining a large group of tourists.

MURPH'S WRATH

Dick and I had been on the lookout for a mascot, with little success. Most of the kids who came to *our* beach were with their tourist parents and only down for a day, a week, or on rare occasions, two weeks.

We had about given up on the idea, when one day a kid sauntered down from Michigan and asked if we needed a mascot. We just about threw a rope around him. His name was Jimmy. He was ten and hoped to be a mascot at Michigan, since he lived on that street. His problem was that Michigan already had a mascot. We became his second choice.

Jimmy was a bright kid, so bright in fact I dubbed him the professor which ultimately evolved into pro'-fes-sorio. Just about every day he came down he had words of wisdom to bestow upon us. When he was finished he'd stare up at Dick and me with this half shit-eating superior grin to see if we'd got it. He could be irritating, but what the hell, a mascot was a mascot.

Jimmy liked looking at girls, regardless of age. To counter his annoying habit of trying to educate us, when I caught him ogling a girl I'd ask if that was his girlfriend. Being shy and embarrassed because he'd gotten caught, his face would turn bright red. He'd stare up at me with one squinting eye for an uncomfortable period, his lip curled in a half sneer half grin.

Overall, Jimmy was a good kid. He was there every day, and mostly willing to help with our needs. We got him a uniform, whistle, taught him how to row and included him in treats when he'd go to the store for us.

I was experiencing a great summer, enjoying working out of Michigan tent and having Murph as my captain. We got along great. I knew he liked me and had a high regard for me as a lifeguard. I felt the same about him and realized I couldn't ask for a better mentor.

The biggest complaint guys had about Murph was, they thought him inflexible. Their beef was that he saw everything in black and white, with no shades of gray. Later I would come to see that as consistency. For now, I wanted to be given a little slack too, so I joined their thinking, and at times resented him for his intractable demands. I even labeled him with the nickname, Reggie Regimentation.

He insisted we be down at our boats and stands on the dot of 9:30 A.M. There was to be no hanging around the tent, even though there were virtually no bathers at that time. Even if it was an overcast day the same rule applied. Only if it was raining did he entertain the idea of letting you goof off a little. He wanted boats and stands at the water's edge at all times. On a chilly rainy day it seemed silly to have the equipment right by the water when there were no bathers.

Later I would find out through Murph, and by my own experience, that rescues happened when you least expected them.

Following is an illustration of Murph's penchant for discipline. One overcast day Dick and I were experiencing a period of laziness, and a little rebellion. Our boat was not as close to the water's edge as Murph would have liked.

Professorio had just gotten in and was hanging around the tent. Murph asked him to go down and tell us to move our boat closer to the water's edge. Because I somewhat resented the order I said to the professor something like, tell him to hold his horses, or tell him to relax. The professor dutifully reported my responses—verbatim.

In a matter of minutes Murph was at our station. Without a word he grabbed one of my legs and with great force, pulled me completely out of the stand. I landed on my back with a thud. Being possessed of a pretty wicked temper I got up and almost threw a punch at him (luckily for me I didn't).

What stopped me was the immediate look of surprise and concern on his face, like he was stunned by this act of violence. He realized he could have seriously hurt me. At the same time we both realized the comical aspect of the situation and started laughing. The blowup was instantly defused and I learned a lesson. Though I might not agree with certain of Murph's standards through the years, I never disrespected his orders again.

SUICIDE MAN

Back to the point of how rescues can occur when least expected, was one we experienced on just such a drizzly overcast day.

We worked two different shifts, alternating each week. One was 9:30 A M -5:30 P.M., the other 10:30 A.M. 6:30 P.M. This latter shift had come about as the beaches became more crowded over the years. Because bathers were allowed to be on the beach until 10:00 P.M., there was no reason for them to leave when the lifeguards went off duty. Consequently, more deaths by drowning occurred after 5:30 P.M.

On this day Dick and I were on the 10:30-6:30 shift. Michigan and Indiana were the two early stations being manned. Most of the guards were taking shelter up in the tent. One of the guards, Roy, had gone out to take a walk and scavenge along the beach. On his way back to the tent he looked up and saw a man out toward the end of the pier. The man had climbed over the railing and looked as though he was preparing to jump.

Roy sprinted toward the boardwalk to get to the pier's entrance. He was hoping to dissuade the man from what appeared to be a suicide attempt. As he ran, he blew a run whistle alerting us in the tent. We recognized the situation immediately. Two crews made for the boats.

The people in the admissions booth must have thought Roy crazy as he dashed by them heedless of their shouts for him to stop.

Just as the crews launched, the man spotted them and jumped. It was about a 200 yard sprint for the boats to get to where he plunged into the water. There was a good chance he would drown before the guys got to him. Fortunately, when he hit the water and saw he was going to get sucked under the pier it must have terrified him. He quickly grabbed a piling and this gave the crews time to reach him.

As the guards approached, they were careful not to get too close to the pilings. The stern man threw the victim a donut while the bowman kept the boat at a safe distance from the pier. Unfortunately, this guy was not about to leave the secure confines of his barnacle laden piling to take the donut.

The stern man dove from the boat, grabbing the donut and swam it to him. He talked calmly to the guy and said he would hold him on the donut until they reached the boat. This convinced the man and he let go of the piling. There was blood all over as a result of the razor sharp barnacles. Clothes offered no protection. The guys hauled him aboard and headed for shore.

Roy had gotten to where the guy had jumped. He'd left his shoes and wallet on the pier. Roy retrieved them and on the way back to the tent explained to the admissions people what had happened. The word had gotten out fast—they already knew.

Because it was still early in the season, we had no student medical doctor. They didn't come on until 4th of July weekend.

Murph called the Atlantic City Medical center which was a block away. The man just sat on a chair with his head in his hands. It appeared he was mentally disturbed and in need of professional help. When the ambulance arrived medics did what they could for the man's barnacle cuts. Roy turned over the man's wallet and shoes to the driver. We never found out what happened to him.

MURPH NEGOTIATES OUR HOME

Murph wasn't a happy camper, having to operate out of a cabaña provided by the Dennis Hotel. It was somewhat demeaning when all the other captains were provided a tent. We weren't exactly thrilled either, having to change and take showers in the damp touristy bowels of the hotel. Aging elitist guests would stare at us questioningly as to why we were allowed to use *their* showers—for nothing! We were like a modern day version of *The Man Without A Country.*

Our captain wasn't the kind of guy who took things lying down. Murph was determined to find a way for Michigan to have its own tent.

The wealthier guests who could afford it included a cabaña rental as part of their vacation package. The cabañas were located just in front of the boardwalk, close to the hotel. This enabled the guest's seclusion from the locals, or tourists, who laid their beach chairs, blankets or towels down closer to the ocean.

The guests were provided with cabaña boys who saw to their every need, right down to the act of spreading suntan lotion on female guests, married or not. The boys were usually the offspring of wealthy families and attended elitist northeastern colleges (sort of like Benjamin Braddock in *The Graduate*). They were very adept at schmoozing, and knew how to pour on the charm (not to mention the lotion). They made excellent tips.

Actually, the tent where Murph conducted his business was the same one the boys operated from. It was much larger than the guest's cabañas, located at the top of the stairs of the hotel from where the guests emerged. At times, it could get hectic with Murph dealing with us and the cabana boys dealing with the guests.

As guests became familiar with Murph, they came to recognize him for the heroic figure he was. They were captivated by his friendly manner, wit and charm, punctuated by a charismatic smile and open fun-loving nature. If one didn't know better, and Murph didn't wear a uniform, guests might have mistaken him for the hotel's owner.

Murph's burgeoning popularity with the guests did not escape the attention of George, the hotel's owner. George often spent time with the guests at their cabañas. He was very engaging and popular. As summer progressed he and Murph would build a solid, enduring friendship.

As the two men's admiration grew, Murph became comfortable about asking George what his objections were to having the city erect a lifeguard tent. This was a subject the city was not willing to take up with George. If he said no the city fathers accepted the decision not wanting to create waves (no pun intended). Not so with Murph, he made the construction of a tent his cause cèlébre.

George offered various reasons for his resistance to the tent. His main objection was his concern it would create an eyesore. Murph countered with suggestions for why he thought it would be more of an asset than a liability.

George's respect for Murph grew as he recognized the Captains leadership qualities. One day while George was at the beach he suggested Murph and Jeanne join him at the hotel for dinner. He told Murph he wanted to discuss, in more detail, the possibility of building a tent. On the day of the event we wished Murph luck, sensing this might be a do or die decision. We were impressed at how far the captain had already advanced his cause.

The next morning when we arrived, it was with heightened anticipation. Murph's first response was to flash that infectious smile telling us all we needed to know. The evening had been a stunning success. George was delighted meeting Jeanne and probably impressed with her Doris Day like features. She was at the height of womanhood, beautifully blond, tanned, freckled, with a personality complimenting Murph's.

Murph told us after enjoying a dinner fit for a king he and George got down to business. Murph gave George all the reasons he felt having a tent would be an asset. As far as being an eyesore, he assured him, the tent would not be in front of The Dennis, but right in line with Michigan Avenue. This would put it directly between the Shelburne and Dennis and not in any way offensive to either hotel's guests.

Furthermore, it would be closer to the ocean and away from the hotels. Another advantage was the city had just created a new and modern tent design and we would be one of the first to benefit from this attractive structure. Murph also posited the idea that neither guests nor guards were comfortable with the present locker room arrangements.

He sensed the guests felt, because they paid premium hotel rates, they should not go to support the needs of lifeguards. The guards, on the other hand, did not like dealing with some of the guest's snootiness. His final point was that there would be a beach patrol medical student on hand. Not only would this future doctor take care of the regular beach-goers' needs, but also of George's guests and their families.

George being a practical man, and after hearing Murph's logical reasoning, endorsed the project. Murph said he and Jeanne were floating on cloud nine on the way home. Now he could bring Stevie to the beach without worrying about him getting under the guest's skin—no such luck for us.

We were thrilled. Now we'd have a real beach home.

Construction would start in October and the tent would be ready to move into by the following Memorial Day.

The city fathers, and others, were somewhat in awe and probably a little more than embarrassed. Murph had achieved single-handedly what they couldn't collectively.

RESCUING A DEAD MAN

At times when I arrived to the beach early Murph would already be there. We'd sit on the porch and he'd relate stories of his days as a young guard under then Captain Harry. I always loved listening to these tales. Most of them had to do with rescues he'd had at States Avenue, considered far and away the most dangerous part of the ocean. What made States so dangerous were several prevailing conditions.

First, as with our beach at Arkansas, States was also next to a major pier, just to the north. This was the previously mentioned world renowned Steel Pier. Having a pier next to you causes waves to break in a different way than they do in other areas of the ocean. At States, because the shoreline dropped off suddenly it caused waves to crest quickly. These waves broke in a very swift and powerful motion.

Compounding this problem, a few blocks north of the pier at New Hampshire was a large jetty. The vortex between the pier and jetty created holes in the oceans floor which in turn created treacherous offsets, much more dangerous than those of other beaches.

Negotiating a boat through the surf at States, in a bad ocean, was extremely hazardous. It is difficult to relate how quickly one of these powerful waves can take you out. The surf breaks so close to the shore you may not get more than a couple of strokes in before a wave crashes over your bow. This can cause you to pitch-pole or sink on the spot.

The guys who worked States should have gotten hazardous duty pay. That's how bad it was. There was a certain type of personality who flirted with the danger of this erratic section of ocean. Some of the guys volunteered to work there, and those who did loved it. But few spent their entire career at States. It was a place where sooner or later your luck was bound to run out.

Murph related an incident about a rescue he and his partner Joe had that could have cost him his life. It happened on a day when the ocean was almost terrifyingly rough and the waves monstrous. A bather could be in the water up to his waist and in an instant, backwash from the huge surf could carry him out into a deep offset.

This is what happened to a bather that day.

Murph and Joe launched their boat as soon as they saw the man in trouble. Moving quickly, they rowed furiously to get beyond the break thinking they'd be pummeled at any moment. Unfortunately, their thought became reality.

They were no more than halfway to the victim when Murph turned and saw a huge hollow back bearing down on them. He hollered for Joe to give him everything he had, but to no avail. The wave crashed over them with such ferocity that the entire stern sheet was ripped off in the blink of an eye. Joe's feet were still on what was left of the deck floor but beyond that, there was nothing but ocean.

Murph's well trained instincts kicked in. He grabbed a can buoy, secured it over his shoulder and took off toward the victim. Murph battled his way through the obstructionist waves and churning offset. Joe, being smaller than Murph and not as powerful was unable to negotiate his way through the break. Murph finally reached the man, who had been in a life and death struggle, trying to remain above the surface.

The man was splashing about in such a way that Murph knew getting too close spelled danger. If the victim was able to grab him it could mean disaster for both. Murph took the rope from his shoulder and shoved the can toward the man who wrapped his arms around it in a death hold. Murph dove beneath the water surfacing behind him. He wrapped his arms around the victim cushioning the man's body between his and the can buoy's.

Meanwhile they were being carried swiftly toward the pier. Going under Steel Pier was the same as going under Million Dollar Pier. However, Steel Pier was more dangerous because the pilings were closer together the ground swells bigger and capable of dashing you into a piling with tremendous force.

As they started under Murph braced himself.

The waves immediately dashed them against the barnacle covered, razor sharp pilings. Murph used the can buoy as a buffer between he and the man to minimize damage from the barnacles.

Besides having to deal with the pilings the constant pounding of waves were taking their toll. Murph was used to being buffeted about by waves but the same could not be said for the victim. Whenever he could, Murph shouted words of encouragement to the man. There was no response.

Finally, when they were almost through the pier, Murph saw lifeboats approaching. As soon as the guards reached them and pulled in the bleeding and unconscious man Murph told them to work on him. The guards laid him face down over the stern sheet and administered C.P.R. There was no movement. Murph climbed into one of the other boats and lay down on the stern sheet, bleeding and exhausted.

When they reached shore the beach patrol ambulance was waiting to take the man to the hospital.

A couple of hours later Captain Harry called the hospital to inquire about the man's condition. The captain was put on hold until the attending physician picked up and told him the man had died. "He simply swallowed too much sea water and drowned."

Murph was shaken over the man's death as he faced the awful feeling that he had not been able to save him. His feeling of guilt was somewhat assuaged however knowing the pummeling they took from the waves and pilings was not something that could be avoided.

That story had a lasting effect on the way I viewed the responsibility of being a lifeguard. An experience like that is the ultimate test of how you'll react in a life and death situation. Murph faced that danger with only himself, his skills and a can buoy, pitted against the fearsome forces of nature. How many others in that same situation would have survived?

Working out of Michigan was a great experience. We were having our share of rescues that made for an interesting work environment and there was no shortage of females, who, we either met on the beach during the day or in bars at night. There was a lot of fun-loving camaraderie among the guys in our stretch. Every two weeks when we'd get paid, Murph, Jeanne and the rest of us would go out for dinner to a seafood restaurant called Oyster Creek Inn.

This gathering was so much fun, that at times we'd invite friends who were non-members of the beach patrol to join us. My brother Mick was one who joined us several times. Whenever we reminisced about Oyster Creek, it was always with fond memories.

My overall feeling was, life couldn't get much better.

I was about to find out differently.

Chapter 5

MICKEY

PRELUDE

It is difficult to express the wonder I felt at being back on the beach. To walk across the boardwalk every morning and see the expansive panorama open before me was like entering a fantasyland. This feeling, stemming from my childhood had never wavered.

As I crossed the boardwalk everything changed. People strolling the wooden way sparked an energy that brought the walk to life. Sounds of calliope music coming from Million Dollar Pier filled the air, creating a carnival-like atmosphere. Provocative smells from the myriad food joints prepared for the crush of strollers who would soon be sampling their tantalizing offerings.

The sun was still rising over the ocean, bathing it in brilliant sunlight. Whitecaps from the breaking waves gave them a majestic appearance as they rushed toward shore. The beach, empty and pristine, looked ready to take on the crowds that would later fill her up.

As I crossed the beach the soft glittering sand underfoot gave me an indescribable sense of pleasure. I experienced a total feeling of freedom.

Atlantic City's environment exudes a pleasant seashore aroma, brought on by soft breezes drifting in from the ocean. These breezes, combined with the smells of the beach, boardwalk, piers, marine life, etc., exert a strong positive impression on visitors. Perhaps it was part of the reason why many stayed at summers end.

These were the sights, sounds and sensations that greeted me each day I reported to work. Who wouldn't like being in this enviable position?

As soon as we changed into our uniforms we'd grab our equipment and head for our stations. Each night at quitting time it was procedure to carry the boats and stands five to seven yards beyond the high water mark. We would take all the equipment out of the boat and turn it over on top of its rollers which we strategically placed at the bow and stern. We laid the stand down to protect it from high winds that might arise during the night.

It was necessary to transport this equipment back and forth each day. In earlier times this paraphernalia had been left in the boats. However, over the years, some adventurous types, or possibly drunks, would turn a boat over drag it down to the shoreline and put to sea.

They'd launch the boat not knowing what they were doing. Without getting far they'd be dumped on shore in quick fashion by swift running waves. Boats were sometimes found blocks away. Others, set adrift by high tides, were damaged by piers and jetties.

In the morning after we turned the boats over and righted the stands, we would move them to the water's edge. If the tide was high little effort was required to move the equipment. When the tide was low, we had to place rollers under the boat alternating them as we rolled it down to the water's edge.

The stand, at ten feet, was both heavy and top heavy. One of us would grab the front foot-brace, the other the back cross-braces. At low tide, we would literally run it to the water's edge over the hard sand to avoid having the braces edges cut into our hands. We wanted to reach our destination as quickly as possible.

Not many people came to the beach early. Although some diehards, who didn't relish crowds, would come down get in a dip and some early morning exercise.

After everything was set up and we checked ocean conditions it was time for coffee. On days when our mascot didn't arrive early we had to scrounge around looking for a substitute to go to the store. We'd search for an early female arrival. About nine times out of ten, after relating our sad tale of woe, one would agree to help us out. She'd even don an A.C.B.P. sweatshirt in order for us to get our lifeguard discount.

The other one percent usually didn't beat around the bush. They essentially told us to "kiss their ass." Perhaps they were a small percentage of females to have fallen victim to a brother guard.

Around 10:30 A.M., people would start drifting down, many opting for space close to the ocean. Mothers, especially, made this a practice since they could keep a watchful eye on their children. By about 12:30 P.M., the crowds were in place. We became more focused on the activity around us. Mainly, we kept our eyes on the ocean watching for trouble spots.

But there were other distractions. A popular activity among kids was throwing mud. This was a definite no no, because at times they would hit adults or get it in another kid's eyes.

But worse were the football jocks where the guy with the ball would send out a couple of receivers. These guys had no consideration for others. In turning their heads to look for the ball they would bowl over an innocent bystander, or plow into a kid. These guys were one of our biggest headaches. Being macho, they often challenged our authority when we told them to knock it off. At times, it came close to being physical.

A more pleasant distraction, were the many people who walked the beach. This was a popular activity. Some did so to take in the sights along the four mile stretch. Others, like Burt Parks, emcee for the Miss America Pageant did it for the exercise. Frequently, a bather would pass with a fixed smile of wonder on their face, seemingly at nothing. It struck us as both silly and endearing. We assumed it was because they were so joyful at being away for a fun filled weekend.

Our most popular strollers were the girls who came to work in the hotels and restaurants over the summer. Most of them were coeds, but there were a smattering of girls from other walks of life, looking for a break from the status quo. It was from this latter group I'd meet someone who would change my life.

I don't believe many of the girls who walked the beach did so out of a love for sightseeing or exercise. Like us, they were interested in meeting members of the opposite sex.

Even if the girls at South Carolina beach weren't avid ocean goers, they still liked to get their feet wet. This meant being scrutinized by guards, who considered them a captive audience, as they made their way to the surf. The usual case history was solicited, such as where they were from, what college they attended, where they worked, etc. It didn't take the girls long to figure out, in looking north or south, that there were lifeguard stands as far as the eye could see—and beyond. As they became aware there were guards at every block, walking the beach became a more desirable pastime. This gave them maximum exposure to examine more of what was in the cookie jar.

Unless guards were married or had girlfriends, and maybe not even then, it was unlikely an attractive girl(s) could pass by a stand without being called over. But the girls knew how to play the game too. They would make an instant evaluation of their solicitor and if there was no interest, simply continue on their way. It was a game of chance. If a girl found you or your partner attractive, for the most part, she wouldn't hesitate to stop. Some girls stopped at a station only to encounter a crude guard who was immediately ready to pop the 64,000 dollar question. This was not considered a highly successful approach.

MEETING MICKEY

It was under these circumstances, kinda, that I met Mickey.

My brother Mick worked the beach as an ice cream vendor. This job required the procurement of a city license, was restricted in number to 100, and only open to veterans. There was a lot of money to be made but it was grueling, backbreaking, work. A fully loaded box with various ice cream treats could weigh anywhere from 75 to 100 pounds.

The vast majority of beachgoers spread their blankets on the soft hot sand, a short distance from the ocean, and this is where most guys peddled their goodies. Because they carried heavy boxes, it was necessary to put padding under the straps to protect their shoulders. One guy, everyone knew as Muscles carried two boxes.

The vendors wore army boots to protect their feet from the blazing sand. Not only were weather conditions hot, they were humid, causing these guys to sweat buckets.

All day long people were peppered with cries of "get your fudgie wudgie here," or "take your tongue for a sleigh ride." As soon as their box was empty, they would hurry back to the "drop" (reloading station) for another load.

There were also the less ambitious, who would peddle their product down on the hard sand. Not many beachgoers parked in that area but carrying the heavy box was less fatiguing. These guys weren't regarded with much respect by the soft sand guys and they made a helluva lot less money.

Brother Mick usually stayed uptown and concentrated on the busiest beaches, those being, New York, Tennessee, South Carolina, North Carolina and sometimes Pennsylvania and States. He once told me, every time the guards went on a rescue the vendors had to drop their ice cream boxes and wait for more sales, until their customers finished taking in the action. He said it was like watching people chase fire engines–only wet.

Every so often Mick would saunter down to my station some seven blocks away. At times, there were not many ice cream vendors in our section, but too many in his. He'd stop long enough to shoot the breeze and force a free ice cream on us (not that he'd meet with much resistance).

I often thought how ironic it was that both our summer jobs were on the beach, but in vastly different capacities. What our work did have in common was, we were each working to save for college.

I knew many of the guys who sold ice cream since a lot of us had gone into the service at the same time. One in particular was Don, who had been a year ahead of me in high school. We were never particularly close, but always friendly. Others were not so friendly toward him. Don was a very bright student, who, when expressing himself, used a large vocabulary, that offended some and intimidated others. Having always been a reader myself I enjoyed vocabulary. If he used a word I wasn't familiar with, I'd look it up.

Don was a slight person with a pale complexion and never looked particularly healthy. However he had a lot of moxie, and was ready to lace-em-up with any bully. He eventually joined the military and instead of picking an easier branch of service, joined the Marines and I believe served in Korea. I admired his guts.

Don and I had not seen each other over the years but now that we were both working the beach would run into each other occasionally. Like Mick, he mostly hawked ice cream on the uptown beaches. Also like Mick, he would work our stretch once in a while.

It was such a day when he stopped by our stand. I thought he was there for the usual reason, to take a break and chew the fat. But this day was different. He told me he had met this beautiful girl on Kentucky Avenue who was down for the summer. He said she was from Manhattan and on his next swing down would bring her by.

I wondered why he chose me to meet her. He knew the guards at Kentucky's stretch and most of them were handsome and athletic. Apparently he had a higher regard for me then I'd been aware of.

I said I'd see him later on, not anticipating I would. I was meeting and dating good looking girls all the time. One more was no big deal. Another reason I didn't really think he'd be back was because he could sell more ice cream uptown. I soon forgot about our conversation.

About 3:00 P.M. as the day was winding down the majority of bathers began their afternoon exodus. It was mostly the hard-core that stayed until the closing bell. I happened to glance up beach and saw Don coming my way. Next to him was the most stunning girl I'd ever seen. Even observing her from a distance caused my heart to do flip-flops. Though I had never visualized the girl of my dreams, I knew right away she was it.

As she drew closer I was unable to take my eyes off her. Up until that day I had never believed in love at first sight. I came down off the stand as they approached. Don introduced me to Mickey and told me she was an aspiring dancer and model.

This lovely vision was about 5'7" long dark hair, smiling Irish brown eyes, straight nose, and perfect teeth. Her smile displayed a happy impishness. She wore a red one piece bathing suit with white piping down either side. The color of her suit was in stark contrast to her smooth white skin and complimented her dark hair and eyes. She had a lovely figure, with the long shapely legs of a dancer. When she moved, it was with a lightness of step revealed in her sensual gait.

I didn't expect she'd stay, well, maybe just long enough to make a gracious exit. Instead, she appeared right at home and engaged me in conversation about my job. She said the first day she came to the beach with her girlfriend they witnessed a few rescues. They thought it was an uncommon occurrence but said they'd seen more in the week since.

I explained that rescues were a common occurrence on Atlantic City's beaches. I told her to expect a lot more if she was staying for the summer.

Then I asked about her. After high school, she'd decided to pursue a career as a dancer and model. She was nineteen and had been dancing in night clubs for a couple of years. A lack of tourism in N. Y. during the summer left little work in the entertainment business. She and her girlfriend heard Atlantic City employed a lot of workers during the summer. They tried finding work as dancers in one of the night clubs, but, having arrived too late found all those jobs filled. Undaunted, still wanting to mix work with pleasure, they found employment as cocktail waitresses at a western themed night club on the boardwalk called the Dude Ranch. This allowed them to spend their days at the beach.

We fell into easy conversation. I had never felt so comfortable talking to a girl. She had a vivacious personality and was completely free of guile. As beautiful as she was, she didn't talk much about herself unless you asked her a pointed question. Mickey, to my delight stayed for a couple of hours. During this time I was completely mesmerized by her and hoped she was feeling some attraction toward me.

The hours sped by so quickly that Dick had to remind me it was time to close the station. As we bid goodbye, I said I hoped I'd see her the following day. She promised to return and as she was leaving, turned back and asked me if I knew of a good place to go at night. I told her there was a place called the Senator Hotel, on South Carolina Avenue, that had a bar, where everybody hung out. She nodded and left. I watched as she walked away, again taken by her sensual gait, borne of a dancers movement.

I was hooked! Dick carried on a one-way conversation as we transported the boat and stand to their nightly resting place. I think he was extolling the virtues of her beauty and personality. I was in my own world, having experienced the true meaning of the expression, "love at first sight."

When I got to the tent, some of the guys asked me who the stunner was, and "had I known her before?" When I told them I hadn't, they said I should get an award for snagging the prettiest girl of the day.

On the way home I couldn't get her off my mind.

I was living in a basement apartment on Iowa Avenue with my brother Mick and Jack, another ice cream vendor and buddy of Mick's he'd met in the Army. I discussed Mickey with my brother while we sat around puffin' on a few beers. I didn't carry on too long for fear of seeing Mick's eyes glaze over. He didn't have much to say but I could tell from his demeanor he knew I was smitten.

The three of us ordered subs from the Whitehouse Sub Shop, a recurring theme when it came to our epicurean desires. We certainly weren't following the healthiest diet but no doubt, it was the tastiest.

Atlantic City's bars were open twenty four hours a day seven days a week. No one went out before 9:00 or10:00 P.M., but if they did, they'd pretty much find themselves a party of one.

We arrived at the Senator around 10:00 P.M. As usual we ran into friends, who, like ourselves were regulars. We lingered for a few minutes, saying our hellos, before heading to the end of the bar whose location held a special attraction. There was a raised two-level platform composed of tables and chairs. This is where most of the girls sat since it was considered more lady-like.

HEAD OVER HEELS

As I approached the bar immediately adjacent to the tables, I was aware of a form hurtling toward me. I turned just in time to catch Mickey, literally, who in an effort to greet me had lost her footing and stumbled off the platform. I was euphoric, realizing she had come to surprise me. When she had inquired at the beach where there was a good place to go at night, it never occurred to me she would be there. My main thought was of seeing her at the beach the next day.

She took my hand and guided me to the seat next to hers. It had only been several hours since we'd met but I knew right away she was the one. Now she was letting me know she felt the same. I was beyond cloud nine. She introduced me to her girlfriend Anne. Anne was also a dancer and very attractive. Mickey and I had no trouble engaging in conversation and did our best to include Anne.

The bar was starting to fill up. The two guards who worked Michigan, Geza and Mike had just arrived and came over to say hello. Geza was handsome, of medium height with an athletic build. He had been a star fullback on our high school football team. Mike was tall, rangy, athletic, and at that time, the best swimmer on the beach patrol.

Mike had boyish looks, charm and an infectious laugh that made him very attractive to women. He locked on to Anne right away and turned on the charm. She in turn had not taken her eyes off him from the moment he appeared. Geza, to Mike's delight left to join another group.

Mike joined us at the table and he and Anne hit it off right away. This was the break I was waiting for. Now I had more time to concentrate on Mickey. We talked for a while, but as the bar got busier the noise-level grew louder. It became more difficult to hear each other and Mickey suggested we go for a stroll on the boardwalk.

We said our goodbyes to Mike and Anne who barely acknowledged our departure. They were caught up in their own moment. I was thrilled to be alone with Mickey.

We walked south on the boardwalk in the direction of Million Dollar Pier. Stopping along the way, we gazed in the shop windows. Mickey enjoyed admiring the clothes, jewelry, leather items, etc. on display in these pricey stores. She was like a little girl, excited by her surroundings. Her displays of joy had a contagious affect on me as I observed this beautiful girl from another perspective. I had walked that boardwalk a million times and was only now really seeing it for the first time.

The boardwalk was lit up and dressed in its finest splendor, with a display of colorful lights that sent beams reaching far into the ebony night. The hotels stood like stately sentinels, lining the wooden way from one end to the other. The famous Fountain of Light in front of the Claridge Hotel shot huge geysers of colorful water into the sky, changing hues at regular intervals.

The most unique light show emanated from atop Million Dollar Pier. This was the immense Seagram's sign, featuring a replica of a race track constructed from steel. It used electric lights to simulate eight colored horses. At different intervals, the horses would break and race around the track. Most of the time a different colored horse would win but occasionally the same one would win twice.

People lined the railing of the boardwalk to watch and bet on the races. Most viewers would make friendly nickel or dime wagers. But there were also the ever present horse degenerates who were ready to bet the hacienda if someone covered the bet. We watched the races for a while and each time Mickey's color won she would clap her hands with glee.

It was well past midnight when she asked me to walk her home. She and Anne were renting a room on a street called Mount Vernon Avenue. It was a boarding house located above an Irish bar called McMenamins.

We held hands until we reached her residence. I walked her up a flight of steps that opened on to an expansive veranda. She invited me to sit for a few minutes. I sat there awkwardly, vying for time, trying to work up the courage to kiss her.

She solved that problem by giving me that impish smile, teasingly, asking me if I was going to kiss her goodnight. I kissed her, softly at first but then with more intensity as I held her tight. She returned my passion with abandon. I had never been with a girl who affected me the way she did.

We embraced for a while, savoring the moment, knowing we had found something special. I kissed her a final time and said I'd better go. As I got to the bottom of the stairs she called down to say she'd had a wonderful evening. I echoed her thought and asked if I'd see her later in the day. She assured me I would.

It was about twelve blocks to my apartment, but that distance held no relevance. I was walking on air. I had met this gorgeous girl less than twenty four hours earlier, and that quick was hopelessly in love.

The lateness of the hour didn't matter. I knew sleep wouldn't come but I didn't care. Thinking of her was all that mattered.

LOVE WALKS RIGHT IN

I arrived to work early and sleepwalked through the morning. Dick asked me if I'd gone out the night before. I relayed the entire evening's events.

When I finished he said, "This sounds serious," and thought she was certainly someone worth pursuing. I couldn't have agreed more.

All morning I kept looking up beach, waiting to catch a glimpse of her. Finally, just after noon I recognized that familiar walk, but she wasn't alone. Anne was with her. As they approached Michigan, Anne dropped off to visit with Mike.

I couldn't take my eyes off Mickey as she covered the short distance between stands. She was well aware of my gawking behavior and smiled knowingly. When she reached the stand, our greeting was, at first, slightly awkward. Maybe it was because we were still so surprised by the suddenness of this romantic encounter.

She handed me a bag that contained lunch for Dick and I. Any awkwardness disappeared. Not only was she beautiful, charming and fun to be with, she was also thoughtful.

Mickey stayed all afternoon. Her joy and verve were so contagious I had a desire to forget about what I was doing and join her as she frolicked in the ocean.

Murph, who was watching from the tent, was not unaware of my growing infatuation. Unfortunately, he did not share my newfound distraction, or lack of responsibility for the job. We ventured out in the water together, as far as the tops of our knees, a serious breach of Murph's-Law.

The shrillness of his whistle got my attention. I looked up to see him giving me the baseball sign informing me I had just struck out. I told Mickey I was going to have to cool it since the captain did not share my enthusiasm for behaving like a tourist.

Later that afternoon Murph made his rounds as he did every day, visiting each of the four stands on our stretch. We were always his first stop. Murph, in his uniform was a picture of sartorial splendor. He was an imposing figure in his white tank suit, blue trunks and white navy-style captain's hat.

By the time he arrived I was in a total mode of military comportment. Mickey sat demurely on her beach towel a safe distance away.

As was his usual M.O., Murph would stand on the beach conversing until one of us insisted he take one of our seats on the stand. On this day I was quick to be the insistent one. He accepted with a knowing smirk and some good natured ball busting, "Have you decided to take the day off, he asked, because I don't think the bathers have." I told him it wouldn't happen again—an obvious lie.

Mickey, whose impish nature got the better of her, came over under the pretense that she was in need of her suntan lotion. I introduced her to Murph, to whom she responded with a dazzling smile. It didn't take long before he was won over by the full charm of her personality.

I knew she was just trying to take the pressure off me although I think, we, including Murph were all in on the fun. By the time Murph left to visit Michigan, I sensed he was aware of why I was so captivated by her. It didn't take long for him to recognize how special she was and to cut me some slack for my minor indiscretions.

As the summer progressed my love for Mickey grew deeper. We spent every moment together, except when we were working. She made excellent tips at the Dude Ranch which is not surprising since guys were falling all over themselves to impress her. I was bothered by this. These guys weren't innocent country boy types. Many were lowlifes and con artists.

Much of my free time was taken up driving a cab three or four nights a week. Mickey was coming to the beach every day but this wasn't the same as having time alone. I was pleasantly surprised one day by her statement that she and Anne were looking for an apartment. Their weekly rent at the rooming house was getting expensive. During her previous visit to our place she had noticed an apartment for rent next door and found the rent to be much cheaper than what they were paying. Once they moved in I saw Mickey more often. Mike and Anne were also pleased with this arrangement.

There was one thing I learned about myself that presented a growing problem in our relationship. I had a serious jealousy streak. I was shocked to discover this. I had never thought of jealousy as a character flaw in my personality On the other hand I had never experienced love that took me to the depths of a relationship for which I had no control.

JEALOUSY REARS ITS UGLY HEAD

One night Mickey and I went to a bar called Eddie's Shamrock. It was located just off the boardwalk on Kentucky Avenue. The place was popular with the guards, since both of the owner's sons were members of the beach patrol. Mickey and I took seats away from a group of guards. None of them were with girls, opting instead for a stag night. I knew the crude stories and language would be flying back and forth. And though Mickey was far from a prude, there was no reason to expose her to that environment.

Mickey and I were enjoying each other, unaware of those around us. At one point, I excused myself to go to the men's room. When I returned, some guy I'd noticed staring at her earlier was in my seat trying to make conversation. My blood pressure was already rising as I approached and asked him if he'd been invited over. He hadn't. I asked if he knew Mickey. He didn't. Then I asked what the hell he wanted? He snidely replied he wanted to meet her.

Some of the guards came over as they saw me getting in this guys face. I challenged him again to tell me why he thought it was alright to move in on her. He said if I didn't want anyone talking to her I shouldn't leave her alone. That did it. As I went after the guy a couple of guards restrained me. I was furious and yelling for him to step outside so I could kick his ass.

Mickey was visibly upset, trying to calm me down. I was having none of it. Eventually the owner came over and told me to leave and not come back. That was very embarrassing since I was friendly with both of her sons.

As we stepped outside Mickey turned to me and for the first time displayed her own Irish temper. She told me in no uncertain terms how stupid it was to make a spectacle of myself. She said she hadn't done anything to encourage him and I should have just calmly asked him to leave.

She was right of course but I was so incensed by his nerve in taking uncalled for liberties I became irrational. Unfortunately, it was not the last time this would happen. I would get upset anytime I thought a guy talked to her too long.

One night I dropped off a fare close to The Dude Ranch and stopped to see Mickey before she got off. She said she and Anne and some other girls were going to a party after work. It was being thrown by one of their steady customers. The guy had a big house with a swimming pool in Ocean City (a seaside resort about fourteen miles southwest of Atlantic City).

I balked at the idea knowing there would be a lot of guys at the party. She asked me if she'd ever given me reason to distrust her. I had to admit she hadn't. Still I didn't think it right she should go without me. I wouldn't have gone without her if the situation were reversed. She just gave me that good-natured smile and told me not to worry.

Back in the cab, I sulked through my entire shift and got home around 2:00 A.M. I spent the night tossing and turning, still unable to shake the thought of her going to a party without me, or for that matter going at all.

Next morning she came over to our place in her usual pleasant mood to make breakfast. She asked if I was still mad. I sulked out of the apartment and went to work. She came down about noon and approached me with a serious look on her face. She informed me if we couldn't have a relationship based on trust then maybe things weren't going to work out.

Hearing those words jolted me from my state of immaturity. I understood in the most realistic terms and would do anything to keep her. I quit sulking immediately, feeling embarrassed by my stupidity. Here was this wonderful girl of 19, acting much more mature than the twenty four year old dolt she was involved with.

Mickey became her good-natured self again and started teasing me for the way I'd acted. She went into a dramatic enactment of my childish behavior. Throwing her forearm over her brow, as in a silent movie, she exaggerated my immature reactions. Laughing out of control I tried to get away from her but she followed, having great fun at my expense. It was impossible to be upset with her.

Unfortunately, that infantile behavior would surface again in the future, eventually impacting the fairy tale nature of our relationship.

PERIL AT THE POOL

The Lifeguard's Ball was held each summer in August. One of the features of this affair was a beauty contest to select Miss Atlantic City Beach Patrol.

Guards from all stations were encouraged to submit an entry. I of course entered Mickey

The ball was a culmination of the season's events and we all considered it a big deal. Awards were presented to those guards who had finished 1st 2nd and 3rd in both the boat and swim races. Guest dignitaries such as the chief, mayor or state senator would attend to present the trophies.

Most of the guys brought dates, and tourists were encouraged to attend, many of whom we solicited to buy tickets. Having the tourists kept the event a fairly dignified affair. Years earlier, the ball had been more of a boy's night out gathering. Some guys would get roaring drunk and fights would break out. This could be the result of a guard bird dogging another's girl. Or it might be between two guys who'd had problems with each other on the beach. They'd wait for the ball to settle accounts. Embarrassingly, for awhile, it had become known as the "Lifeguards Brawl."

The gala was held at various locations each year. One year it was held at the 500 Club, which was a move up in prestige since the '500' was nationally known. In 1957, the year of which I'm speaking, it was held at the Brighton Punch Bowl on the site of the Brighton Hotel.

The Brighton was a small elegant hotel with not many guest floors. The Punch Bowl was a large outdoor area with a big spacious bar and grand swimming pool. The hotel served a drink they'd made famous called a Brighton Punch. The secret to this recipe was more closely guarded than the gold in Fort Knox. A few of the known ingredients were rye, rum and brown sugar. The drink was so potent that women were limited to two.

The first order of business was the trophy awards. The usual congratulations were extended by the chief as each awardee accepted his prize. It made me proud to have a horse in this race. My partner Dick, who rowed shell in college, and his partner Jack, took first place in the doubles competition.

The next event was the Miss Atlantic City Beach Patrol beauty contest. There were about twenty five girls vying for the title. The contest was based on looks, poise, and personality. The girls were required to circle the pool, while the judges narrowed the field, until they were down to five semi-finalists.

When the girls had completed their final lap the judges were ready to decide the winner. This year featured an unusual array of pretty girls, but, in my opinion, Mickey was the prettiest. Apparently many others thought so too because when she was announced second-runner-up the crowd responded with an audible groan.

After the winner was selected, I went over to Mickey and embraced her. I told her how proud she made me. I kissed her and said she was the winner in my heart, not only of a beauty pageant but in every way. With her usual graciousness and good humor she said how much fun she'd had. She commented on how nice all the girls had been and she meant it. I couldn't have loved her more.

As mentioned previously, we had sold tickets to tourists who were not that familiar with the A.C.B.P. We were not comfortable just offering a beauty contest to our new guests. Because the Brighton had a fabulous pool one of the guys had suggested a water show. Some guards got together and came up with a skit to offer our visitors, who were at the ball for the first time.

As it was every year the liquor was free-flowing. A number of younger guards were taking advantage of the free rein they were given. Some were scheduled to be in the poolside water show and drank to calm their jitters. Another guard in the show, Jackie, was a friend who worked out of States.

Jackie was fearless, and a little nuts. Working States was the perfect spot for him. He was easily bored and, if not kept busy, would find a way to attract trouble. For example, one overcast day while on duty, he went to the boardwalk to have lunch with his girlfriend. He told his partner to cover for him. By the time he got back the sun was out and the beach was crowded. He was suspended for five days without pay. He didn't give a shit.

But there was not a better guard on the beach than Jackie. The guy would follow you into hell. As far as Jackie was concerned the scarier the ocean, and the more dangerous the rescue, the better. One other thing he loved was a good fight. If you were in his company and he got drunk you'd better have an exit strategy. Otherwise, chances were good you'd wind up in a brawl.

Jackie, who usually didn't drink consumed his share on this night. His girlfriend had lately been giving him fits because of real or imagined slights. He never seemed content unless he was involved in some emotional upheaval in his life.

The show featured a circus act with some of the ideas being lifted from the water circus on Steel Pier. The finale included a stunt with Jackie diving under a barrel. As with lifeboats, when turned over, you can dive under a barrel and come up into an air pocket and breathe oxygen. The oxygen under the barrel was sustainable for a few minutes.

All the guys were dressed as clowns. On cue they started chasing Jackie around the pool, Keystone Cops style. As they got close he dove in the pool and under the barrel, the pack following him. Surfacing, they found no Jackie. They feigned carrying on and searching for him. His role was to re-emerge from a farther vantage point and thumb his nose at them as the chase continued.

Suddenly, our instincts alerted us that Jackie had been under the barrel too long. The pool had been darkened where the barrel was located so no one saw him slip from underneath. Because he'd been drinking, his oxygen was used up faster.

Bert, a good friend and one of the guards who worked States with Jackie dove in fully clothed—suit, shirt, tie, everything. He was followed in the same manner by a few other guards. They found him at the bottom of the pool, pulled him out and laid him on the tile.

Some spectators were yelling and screaming. Girls who knew Jackie were sobbing and holding onto their dates (so much for a fun filled night).

Bert and another guard began administering C.P.R. Jackie's complexion was ghostly. A chill ran up my spine at the thought he might be dead. The guys took turns working on him for what seemed interminably long. The first hopeful sign was when he began to spit up water. Suddenly, his body thrashed about violently as he emitted blood-curdling screams and frightening obscenities.

The hospital was only two blocks away. An ambulance arrived just as Jackie was coming around. They placed him on a stretcher and took him to the Medical Center.

Whether spectators got their money's worth or not I couldn't say but one thing I was confident about, they sure as hell weren't bored.

Everyone was too concerned to do anything other than go home. Mickey who knew and liked Jackie was shaken and a little horrified by this incident. She had become accustomed to seeing rescues and was always nervous when I was involved but this was a new experience for her.

The next morning when I arrived at the tent, Murph was on the phone to the hospital. I listened to his responses, trying to read his facial expressions. Looking serious his few comments were, "Yes" and "I see." When he hung up I looked at him anxiously. He said Jackie was in critical condition but expected to live.

Five days later when he was out of danger I visited him. As soon as I entered his room his first words were, "Bobby, I should be fuckin' dead. "That's what the doctors told me Bobby, "I should be fuckin' dead." Then he broke out in his maniacal laugh.

When he was sure no one was listening he motioned for me to come closer. In a whisper he said, "Bobby, there was a guy next to me in that bed last night and when I woke up he was gone. I asked the Doc when he came in the room where he was and he mumbled they had to take him for tests. I asked him why he's been gone all day and the guy ignored me and left. Bobby, that son of a bitch is dead, I know he's dead."

I came to the hospital filled with trepidation for Jackie's well being and he sends me away in stitches (no pun intended).

A couple of weeks later Jackie returned to his beloved States Avenue. He was back in the environment he craved, happy to face danger at a moment's notice. His brush with death did nothing to deter him. He was a true fatalist. Later he would be transferred to our stretch. Then the fun would really begin.

Because of events that transpired both uplifting and near-tragic Mickey and I were now inseparable. My biggest concern was the rapidly approaching end of summer. We had discussed marriage on a number of occasions but thought it best I finish a few years of college. We were not yet prepared to take on that kind of financial burden. Besides, she had her own career goals to consider.

Mickey studied ballet as a young girl and hoped to eventually score a part in a Broadway Show. She was finding gigs in some of the better Manhattan night clubs but her dream was Broadway. She was also making the rounds of modeling agencies and had shown me pictures she carried in her portfolio. They were stunning. It was hard to believe she wouldn't catch on somewhere.

THERE SHE IS…

Mickey's plan was to go back to Manhattan right after Labor Day. She had no obligations in New York but wanted to get back and seek out auditions. The theatre season didn't start cranking up until October so she had time. I talked her in to staying for the Miss America Pageant. She had only seen it on television and was excited at the thought of seeing it live.

The first phase of the pageant was the boardwalk parade. It was a colorful spectacle composed of elaborate floats, bands (including the Mummers) and organizations such as the police, firemen, military, etc. The contestants waved to the crowds from their own personal floats, each one featuring the name of their home state. In later years contestant's floats would be replaced by chauffeured driven convertibles. The pageant was held the second week following Labor Day, in order to extend the summer, giving hotels, rooming houses and merchants an extra two weeks of business. Winters in Atlantic City were long and the added infusion of tourists benefited the local economy.

On parade day, besides left over vacationers and locals, people from Philadelphia and other nearby towns and hamlets swarmed into the city. Spectators jockeying for boardwalk seats began early in the morning. The parade route was approximately three miles long but hours before the event started the boardwalk was jammed with people.

Spectators viewed the parade from any vantage point available. Rolling chairs were rented by the more affluent. They were placed against the railing on the ocean side of the boardwalk. The other side of the walk had bleachers in some areas. Where there weren't any bleachers people brought their own seating. Others watched from hotel rooms, roofs of stores, raised areas of the piers and any other locations featuring elevated views.

We had our own unique method of watching the parade. At the end of the day, instead of taking our stand to its usual resting place, just beyond the high water mark, we carried it to the boardwalk. The stand was about ten feet high so Mickey and I sat on the roof where we had a fine view of the proceedings. Dick stayed below where he had no trouble seeing because of his substantial height.

Dad and mom in front of our Pitney Village house

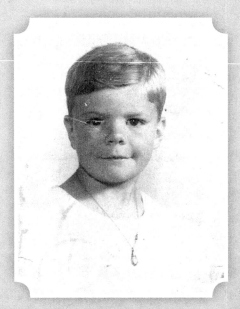

Could this angelic face belong to the same person that gave Les the hotfoot?

BROTHER JIM DURING HIS GRAMMAR SCHOOL YEARS, CIRCA 1940's

BROTHER MICK , SOWING HIS WILD OATS DAYS IN SITGES SPAIN

WITH BUDDY JACKIE, HONING OUR SHARPSHOOTING SKILLS
AT A BOARDWALK SHOOTING GALLERY

ROOKIE PARTNERS BOB AND BOB SERVING OUT OUR SENTENCE IN THE INLET

MACHO POSE, TRYING TO IMPRESS GIRLS.

BELOVED CAPTAIN MURPH AND HIS LOVELY WIFE JEANNE

BROTHER MICK, AFTER A HARD BUT SATISFYING WORK DAY ON THE BEACH

MODELING FOR ONE OF MY MIAMI HURRICANE STUDENT NEWSPAPER ADVERTISERS

Our new tent, compliments of Murph. That's Tommy leaning on the railing

Jackie looks like he's enjoying what may have been a misjudgement by Tommy

MICKEY AND ME IN THE EARLY STAGES OF OUR ROMANCE

MICKEY, WITH GEZA ON THE LEFT AND MIKE

A COMPOSITE OF MICKEY'S MODELING PICTURES

As the parade rolled down the boardwalk Mickey reveled in the excitement of the huge crowd. She was in awe of the contestants and impressed when those we'd met at our station recognized us. They rewarded us with big waves and smiles.

Dick had invited a friend (not a guard) to join us. Because the front of the stand was butted up against the boardwalk the guy started climbing up from behind. Due to the way lifeguard stands are constructed they're very top heavy. When Dick's friend grabbed the stand and put his feet on the cross braces to pull himself up, it was with too much force. The stand came over backwards. My first thought was of Mickey being hurt. As soon as we hit the sand I looked around for her. She was stunned and somewhat shaken, but fine otherwise.

When I knew she was all right I turned to Dick's friend. I knew he'd meant no harm but I was angry knowing Mickey could have been seriously injured. I verbally assaulted him delivering a good ass-chewing. Mickey came over assuring me she was fine. I was greatly relieved that she hadn't been hurt. I apologized to Dick's friend for my outburst. We watched the rest of the parade from the regular seat below.

During the week of the pageant, contestants stayed at one of the major hotels with each getting its quota of girls. Since the Shelburne and Dennis were directly behind us, contestants would gather at our beaches for publicity shots. Even though the girls were accompanied by chaperones we always managed to get acquainted. Most of the publicity shots were taken alongside the boat, giving us easy access to them. The majority of the girls were friendly, no different from pretty girls we'd meet every day, except for their status as beauty queens.

Bert Parks stayed at the Dennis Hotel every year. He would come down each afternoon and leave his things with us while he took a stroll along the beach. His walks were very long and I believe he was somewhat of an exercise buff. He always talked with us for a few minutes before his jaunt. One year he brought his two sons, who, on this day preceded him to the beach. Both were handsome kids in their teens. After depositing their values on the stand with us they raced for the water, cleared the break and continued swimming. They were very strong swimmers, and the day was mild, so we had no concern. When Bert came down he saw how far out they were and instructed us to "kick them in the ass if they give you any trouble." It was evident how proud he was of them.

During one of their publicity romps five of the Miss America contestants frolicked and posed by the water in front of our stand. They were all trying to act natural in their unnatural poses. One girl picked up a donut from the boat and started tossing it in the air, as if someone would really do that. Mickey and I were talking and watching the action. She enjoyed witnessing this exhibition firsthand. A woman, who had been observing, came over to Mickey and said, "You're the winner dear." Mickey's jaw dropped as she said, "Thank you, but I'm not a contestant." The woman looking somewhat surprised, and before turning to leave said, "You should be."

END OF A DREAM

Sadly, the dreaded day arrived for Mickey to return to Manhattan. I drove her to the bus station where we embraced and kissed until the last moment. We promised to write often kidding ourselves that Christmas was not far away. I watched the bus drive out of sight. With an empty feeling in the pit of my stomach I returned to my apartment.

I didn't have much time to dwell on my loneliness without Mickey. I was leaving for Miami in a few days, and had to pack and make arrangements for the trip. Ronnie, a beach patrol brother, had also enrolled at the university and we were driving down together.

The trip was inauspicious but long. Upon arriving I wasn't prepared for the beauty of the University. The grounds were expansive and charming with palm trees looming majestically from all corners of the campus. The grass, an emerald green, was in lovely stark contrast to the azure sky highlighted by billowy white clouds. Other species of trees lining the campus were of a rich forest green dotted with orange flowers (Miami's school colors are orange and green).

It didn't take long to fall into the routine of university life. Unfortunately for me, there were a lot of pleasurable distractions at Miami. I began falling back into my early high school Harry days. Having to discipline myself to study more complex college subjects didn't come easy. And constantly thinking of Mickey didn't make things easier. Lucky or un–I met some ex-G.I. screw-ups like myself. Having been in the military, we found these rah rah college types to be immature kids.

For example, freshman with the exception of G.I.'s had to wear beanies. Upper classman were allowed to question beanie infractions and report the offender. Most couldn't care less whether you wore it or not. Walking across campus one day I was approached by some little weasel who alertly spotted my freshman books. In a rather authoritarian manner he asked me why I wasn't wearing a beanie. I told him to beat it. He challenged me a second time. Speaking to him in an aggressive manner I said, Listen, you little shit, if you know what's good for you you'll skedaddle. That did it. He high tailed his ass across campus. Even though I still looked young at twenty four, I didn't look like an eighteen year old freshman.

Mickey and I wrote regularly and spoke by phone a few times a month. Staying in touch hastened the oncoming Christmas holiday. In spite of the longing, time went quickly and it wasn't long until I bundled myself into a car with four other guys to make the long trip home.

I was spending the holiday at my parent's house. They lived on the mainland, about nine miles from Atlantic City. Just prior to my discharge from the Navy they had bought their little dream house. Both had toiled for years to turn their dream into reality. My mother had hoped her three boys, back from the service would settle with them for awhile. This was not to be. We all had plans of our own. We were however, all going to be together for Christmas.

When I was settled, the first thing I did was call Mickey. It was exciting to know we were only 120 miles apart. She was dancing in the chorus of a club where Ted Lewis was the headliner. The club was going to be dark for a few days over Christmas. I was thrilled when she told me she was taking a bus to Atlantic City the next day to spend Christmas with us.

The following day I drove to Atlantic City's bus terminal and anxiously awaited her arrival. It was hard to believe I would actually see her after all these months. I had fleeting thoughts that something had happened and she wouldn't be on the bus. My fears were unfounded.

When she emerged from the bus I realized she hadn't changed at all. If anything, she was even more beautiful. The tan she had cultivated over the summer was long gone. The whiteness of her skin accentuated her lovely dark hair, eyes, and full red lips. During the summer I had only seen her in casual dress, uniform or bathing suit. The outfit she wore now revealed the chic New York model she hoped to become. We embraced for a long moment before heading for my parents.

My parents were crazy about Mickey. She and my dad had a special relationship due to their similar personalities. They loved to kid each other and she was on to his Irish blarney. Mickey gave as good as she got. My dad was capable of making people laugh in almost any situation. Even after a family funeral, when everyone was feeling morose, it took no time until he'd lighten up the room with his charm. Mickey was one of the few people who had this same ability and could get him laughing harder than anyone I'd ever seen.

My mother loved Mickey like the daughter she'd never had. The first thing Mickey would do when visiting would be to ask my mom what she could do to help. My mother was always taken by her thoughtfulness.

We had a delightfully happy Christmas. Everyone was in a jovial holiday mood bolstered by carols playing in the background, enlivening the spirit of the season. My mother and Mickey had spent hours preparing Christmas dinner only to have it savaged by four brutes. This was without a doubt the best Christmas I'd ever had.

Those few days Mickey visited passed much too quickly. However, we'd made plans to spend New Year's Eve together.

A New Year's Eve party was planned by a wealthy Miami classmate who lived on Long Island. A significant number of students from the University were from New York, New Jersey and Pennsylvania. Most of us knew each other and many had marked the event on their calendar.

Even though Mickey would not know many of the attendees she was nonetheless excited to attend. My friend Jack drove up from New Jersey with a date. He was picking up Mickey and I and we were driving out to the Island together.

When we arrived we were surprised to see how many people were there. In addition to those of us from the University, friends of the host's family were also in attendance. The house was a mansion with one large room being set aside as a dance floor. There was a variety of food being passed around.

Booze was flowing like Niagara Falls and I wasted no time staking a claim to my share.

A lot of guys were paying attention to Mickey. This made her feel comfortable, less like a stranger. I of course, was not thrilled by these circumstances. As soon as the music began guys asked her to dance to which she gladly obliged. Except for one guy, those dancing with her all looked like rank amateurs.

Larry was a very popular guy to those of us who knew him. He had impish Irish good looks, a terrific sense of humor and a charismatic personality. He carried himself with an unaffected air of mature sophistication. He was also a very polished dancer. My skills in the dancing department might qualify as one step above those of *Lurch*.

Mickey and Larry quickly shed the intrusions of the clumsy ones. He was now her sole partner and they were enjoying themselves immensely, too immensely for my liking. Every so often she'd come over to see how I was doing. I was trying to act nonchalant, talking to the boys like I was enjoying myself. Beneath this facade I was seething and drinking too much.

I was determined to keep my temper under control and not make a scene. The evening had turned miserable over the thought that Larry was making headway with my girl. My fear of losing her was palpable. Finally, and with much relief, the evening ended.

On the way back to Manhattan, Jack, who was driving, somehow wound up getting lost in Brooklyn (not a difficult thing to do). Mickey, who was originally from Maspeth in Queen's, knew the territory better than any of us. We felt she was our best hope of getting out of this morass. As we drove around blindly she became as confused as the rest of us. I was well into my cups, getting frustrated, because she'd laugh each time she chose the wrong route. I made some snide remark about her not knowing any more than the rest of us.

That remark pissed her off. She knew I was being a jerk over Fred Astair (Larry) and said so. I pleaded guilty to the charge and expressed surprise she hadn't let Larry take her home. That did it. She turned toward me and with lightening speed delivered a slap to my face that set my ear ringing. I was shocked and subdued. Everyone became silent.

Eventually we made our way to Manhattan and Mickey's girlfriend's apartment, where we were staying. We discussed the earlier events, each holding the other to blame for the evening's dust-up. She hadn't felt she was doing anything wrong in dancing with Larry. I felt I was being made a laughing stock because Larry was moving in on my girl. She expressed concern about why I cared so much about what others thought. We continued trying to resolve things until I had to admit I had a serious jealousy streak.

The next morning we went to breakfast and I apologized for my behavior. She apologized for slapping me. In a stab at levity I suggested if she didn't make it as a dancer/model she might try boxing. Things got close to normal but when it was time for me to leave we still had unresolved problems. I said I'd be home for Easter and would come to see her. She smiled but it was not the same smile.

Our parting did not have the same desperate sense of separation as before. As I boarded the bus it was with an empty feeling.

Returning to Miami I tried to settled down and concentrate on my studies. Instead, I found myself constantly thinking of Mickey. She wrote less often and her letters were not filled with the same loving quality as before. I wrote back with the same lack of emotion, feeling hurt and rejected. I sensed she was seeing another guy. The few months until Easter dragged on, but eventually the day arrived and I found myself making the long drive home.

My first day home I purposely didn't call her due to a fear of rejection. The next day I was afraid not to call and worked up the courage to hear the news, good or bad. She was friendly but not enthusiastic. I asked if she wanted me to come and see her. She agreed, saying we had things to discuss. I didn't like the tone of her voice.

The following day we met at Port Authority and went to her roommate's apartment where I had stayed during Christmas. We didn't have long to chat. She had to get to a rehearsal to learn a new routine for the next evening's performance. Ironically, she was opening again for Ted Lewis, the headliner.

There was a diner next to the night club where Mickey said I could wait. It was a cold, dreary day, a perfect setting for my worst fears. I ordered coffee and struck up a conversation with the counter guy who asked me about myself. I told him I was a freshman attending the University of Miami on the G.I. bill. I was surprised by his response. He said, "Oh, I tried that at

N.Y.U. It's too hard getting by on what Uncle Sam gives you, you'll never make it." To this day I still credit that guy for part of the reason I graduated. I'd had my own doubts but when he made that statement with such authority it really annoyed me. My thoughts were: just because he lacked the perseverance to succeed didn't mean others couldn't. That guy turned out to be my inspiration.

Mickey finished around 5:30 P.M. and suggested we take in a movie. To this day I remember the picture, *Run Silent, Run Deep* with Clark Gable and Burt Lancaster. Neither of us paid much attention to the movie, nor were there any little signs of affection. I was relieved when the picture ended but apprehensive for what was to come.

Regardless of what transpired, I assumed I'd be staying the night. Mickey's roommate's apartment was on the second floor. As we entered the building's downstairs hallway she suggested we sit on the stairs and talk. I was now fully aware of what was coming and my heart raced anxiously.

In a barely audible voice she made clear she didn't feel our relationship could work anymore. She felt because we were so far away, with so much school time in between, it wasn't realistic to think we could sustain a relationship. She said she wanted to pursue her own career and was not ready for a long term commitment. I sat stunned. Even though I had prepared myself, I wasn't quite ready for such finality. So this was it, this was how it would end—just like that. A few well-chosen words and suddenly you're plunged into the dark depths of despair.

By now, the emotional stress of the evening had reduced her to tears. She sat sobbing as I embraced her, hoping my effort at bringing consolation would help. It was a strange moment for an irreverent thought but I thought to myself, hell, why am I consoling her, I'm the one who should be crying.

Now I couldn't wait to get out of there. I needed air. I quickly mumbled I hoped all would go well for her and scurried out the door, leaving her somewhat surprised. In a parting thought I realized she had been able to convey her thoughts in a few sentences. For Mickey, the romance was over. For me, it was the beginning of a lifetime without her.

As I walked the cold, rainy streets of Manhattan in a daze, I thought, how ironic, that what had begun in such a beautiful setting, ended so appropriately on this cold dismal night.

I was in need of a pack of cigarettes and ducked into a corner store. It was after 9:00 P.M. and I wasn't keen on going back to New Jersey. I wanted to be alone. The store clerk pointed me in the direction of a Y.M.C.A. a few blocks away. The Y had plenty of vacancies and I was given a room on the eighth floor.

The room contained a small bed with a dreary spread cover, a drab chair and night table. Even if I'd taken a room at the Four Seasons, it would still have seemed as colorless on this night. There was a Bible in the drawer and if ever there was reason to seek comfort from the Good Book this was it. Regrettably, at that moment, at that low point, there was no comfort.

It was slightly past 10:00 P.M. and though I never went to bed before midnight, I was anxious to get this night over and get out of Manhattan. How naive of me to think I'd sleep. I tossed and turned thinking of Mickey. The reasons she gave for the breakup didn't ring true. I knew my jealousy factor had contributed significantly to her decision but I sensed there was more. Was it another guy? I didn't want to believe it but what else could it be? I eventually convinced myself it was true.

The next day with my mood matching the gloomy morning I made my way to Port Authority Terminal. I boarded a bus and rode those depressing 125 miles back to Atlantic City.

My mother was home when I arrived. She knew there was a problem since I wasn't due back until the next day. I told her what happened. She simply sat in a chair and cried. When my dad returned from work, my mother broke the news. My dad was not prone to expressing emotion, but I'll never forget the way his face looked. Everything about his demeanor changed. His eyes took on a look of incredible sadness and his features sagged. Despite my own pain, my heart went out to both of them. In their anguish they had lost a daughter.

I found out a couple of years later, from one of my brothers, that when my parents went to Manhattan to see a Broadway Show, and spend a couple of days, they spent considerable time trying to locate her. I don't know what kind of a search they would have conducted since they had virtually no information on her.

When I returned to the University I tried to put thoughts of her behind—to no avail. During class I would fantasize she would be waiting outside at dismissal. Imagine, actually thinking she would travel fifteen hundred miles to surprise me. I was definitely living in la la land. Going to bed at night merely involved the act of laying my body in a prone position. There was no sleep, no relief.

Finally, I put aside my pride and wrote, hoping it would result in a cathartic experience. I apologized for all my acts of immaturity and any pain I'd caused her. I also noted that it was difficult to believe things could have ended so suddenly. My feeling was that people who are truly in love don't end a relationship that easily, and closed by saying I was convinced she'd found someone else.

I looked for a letter everyday but none came. Anything would have been acceptable, whether it was to tell me to drop dead or go to hell, but hearing nothing was excruciating.

After a couple of months I succumbed to the realization that the fairy tale was over.

I never saw her again.

CHAPTER 6

FROM ONE RESORT TO THE OTHER

My first year of school ended not long after the breakup with Mickey. I had squeaked by maintaining a C average. Grade wise, I was assured of returning for my sophomore year. I looked forward to the summer, and my return to the beach, though I knew it would be with a feeling of emptiness.

Because it was necessary to live on the cheap brother Mick and I acquired a large house on Morris Avenue. We had no trouble finding roommates to help defray the rent. Jocko attended college with Mick at Glassboro State in New Jersey. Geza, who I previously mentioned, plus Al and Tiger went to Miami with me. The house had two floors with three bedrooms upstairs and plenty of room downstairs for extra sleeping accommodations.

Mick and Jocko sold ice cream on the beach, Geza and I were lifeguards, Al was a waiter and Tiger kept the girls happy. Al worked steadily, because like the rest of us, he had to save for college. Tiger worked when the mood struck him. His family was well off and he didn't suffer financial concerns. His decision to come to Atlantic City was so he wouldn't have to spend the summer in Detroit working in his father's meat business.

Tiger, whose real name was Bob met a girl named Arlene at the Senator bar that summer. Arlene was a very pretty girl who hailed from Atco, New Jersey, a small town some thirty miles west of Atlantic City. They married several years later.

Going out at night was kept to a minimum in order to save money. Instead, we'd chip in, snag a case of beer from the liquor store with whom we shared a common wall and sit around playing cards and bullshitting. Our place was like the boy's clubhouse and there were always friends dropping over. It was a base of operations, as in, "What's on the agenda tonight?"

Usually when we'd go out it would be to the Senator bar, still the local hot spot. Many a summer romance, and beyond, began at the Senator.

For instance, one night I introduced a girl named Aggie to a brother guard named Jay. I don't think he talked to her fifteen minutes when they disappeared. I rarely saw him the rest of the summer, but if I did, it was with her. They were married a short time later.

I returned to the beach just prior to Memorial Day. What a thrill to walk across the boardwalk and be greeted by a newly designed shiny blue and white lifeguard tent.

As I walked through the door there stood Murph with a big smile on his handsome face. We took a short tour through the building. This new layout was not unlike that of the older tents. The only difference was this version was bigger, afforded more inside room and boasted a modern design. No more changing for us in the bowels of the Dennis Hotel; no more headquarters for Murph to be shared with cabana boys. Having our own tent gave us a renewed sense of pride. Now when we walked through the doors of that structure it was under the distinguished lettering: **ATLANTIC CITY BEACH PATROL.**

My station once again would be Arkansas to which I was totally agreeable. Murph informed me that besides having a new tent I was to have a new partner. It pleased me to find out it was a high school buddy named Joe. We'd played on the football team and had become fairly close friends. Something that always impressed me about Joe, was that on my first day back from the Navy he stopped by to welcome me home. It was something I never forgot.

Joe, who I'll call Joe M. was a real character of sorts and transferred to our stretch to avoid negative influences that could have landed him in trouble. He and another beach character, we'll call Joe R, had worked as partners at Connecticut Avenue and may have stepped on some toes. Working Connecticut was like working an outpost. The guard's in the States stretch who were located to the right of the Joe's station weren't very accessible. To their left was a pier that isolated them from their own stretch. A large rock jetty extending into the ocean alongside the guards station caused hazardous offsets, dangerous conditions and not much help from backup crews. It was not a station that offered a feeling of security.

The two Joe's were good lifeguards and took part in their share of risky rescues.

They were also master pranksters and diabolical in their quest for the perfect caper. Most tent crews were peaceful and didn't let pranks get out of hand, but because of Rhode Island's alcoholic captain and interfering wife, the same rules did not apply. Usually two rascals of the Joe's nature were enough for any tent. However, Rhode Island boasted two more experts that were, in every way, the Joe's equals. The competition to see who could be the most creative, became perilous. Things were close to getting out of hand and Joe M decided it was time for a change. A few years later Joe R would follow, for much the same reason.

Eventually, this was in effect a tribute to their humorous antics. Guys transferred for various reasons. Maybe partners were incompatible, or, two guys were rowing together in the boat race and training would be more practical if they worked the same station. In some cases guards might prefer easy beaches and others tough ones. The two Joe's transferred because the contest to see who could come up with the biggest prank was becoming dangerous to their futures as members of the A.C.B.P. In a word, they were having too much fun.

Being transferred to Arkansas didn't mean Joe M. had reformed in any way. It was just that from here on, he was performing as a solo act. He knew I didn't want to take part in, or be affected by his antics. He also knew if I was, there'd be some trouble in paradise.

KENNY, OUR THIRTY-SOMETHING MASCOT

One uneventful day, early into the summer, Joe and I were watching the bathers conversing about nothing in particular. Something to the left caught my attention as I observed an odd looking character approaching the stand. Drawing closer he appeared to be spouting gibberish at no one in particular, and at the same time, slobbering all over himself.

I had recently become aware of how these beach characters could pass up ten stands until they got to ours. This oddity was no exception. Still babbling away in French we identified him as being from Canada. Moving into our space he leaned on the stand, chin cupped in hand, and smiled up at us displaying a fine mouthful of brown stumps that in an earlier incarnation may have passed for teeth. This was too much for Joe. He pointed his finger in the guys face and broke out laughing. Incredulously, this strange creature laughed just as hard back at Joe, as if they were sharing a secret joke.

Suddenly he started speaking in rapid fire English punctuating the end of each stuttering sentence with "y-y-ya know eh?" As he jabbered away we realized he was relating his exploits of the previous night. Obviously he was still drunk and hadn't left the bar that long before he stumbled upon us.

It was difficult to determine his age but I judged him to be somewhere between 31and 35. Physically, Kenny was of medium height and wore a crew cut. His skin had a peculiar yellowish pallor and his eyes were red rimmed, like those usually associated with Down Syndrome but he exhibited none of the other features.

His physique was worse than that of the guy in the Charles Atlas *before* advertisement. He had shoulders like a sparrow, arms like a kewpie doll and a protruding gut with no waist. The calves of his legs were shaped like those of a woman's and he had a gay duck like walk. He wore skimpy black bikini bathing trunks, exacerbating his schmoo like body. Bikini's on women were not readily accepted at that time. A Bikini on a guy could get you your ass kicked.

For whatever reason, he planted himself next to our stand for the rest of the day. He alternated his time between sleeping and taking a dip. During one of his waking periods we asked if he'd get us some coffee. To our surprise, he readily agreed and we included him in on the buy. We found out his name was Kenny and he was from Montreal. We gave him an A.C.B.P. sweat shirt to wear since going shirtless on the boardwalk was not allowed. Additionally, his wearing the shirt would assure us a discount.

Apparently he loved uniforms. As soon as he pulled on the shirt his whole demeanor changed. He took on a look of pride and stuck out what little chest he had. When he brought back the coffee he asked if he could keep the shirt on. We didn't see any harm, since mascots wore the uniform every day. He strutted around like a peacock when he wasn't posing by the boat. If people observed him when they passed he'd assume a look of self importance. Eventually he sobered up, but sobriety didn't make him any less goofy. The guy could talk your ear off about nothing.

When it was quitting time we told him we had to go and needed the shirt. Reluctantly, he gave it to us and said he'd be back the next day. We sloughed that off with a wave goodbye, thinking, don't do us any favors.

Sure enough at 10:00 A.M. the next morning Kenny showed up ready to go to work. Happy to have someone go for coffee we gave him the shirt and off he went. We didn't know it at the time but Kenny was to become both a blessing and a curse.

Murph, who never missed a trick, had been observing this grown man wearing a lifeguard sweat shirt. We'd just finished our coffee when he appeared to confront us. Why, he wanted to know, was this adult non-lifeguard wearing an A.C.B.P. sweat shirt? We said we thought Kenny would make a good mascot and would do anything as long as he could wear part of the uniform. Murph asked if we thought it prudent that Kenny be considered representative of the Atlantic City Beach Patrol. We had to admit he had a point.

There was only one flaw in Murph's argument. He wasn't prepared for Kenny's persistence. Kenny was there every morning like clockwork. He would do anything or go anywhere we asked. Murph eventually acquiesced and Kenny became a permanent part of our stretch. We heard he was from a well to do family and his parents paid him to stay away, which wasn't hard to believe. We'll hear more from Kenny later.

JOE MEETS HIS MATCH

Joe M did not have the looks of a Tyrone Power but he may have had something better, a very persuasive gift of gab. If he saw an attractive girl he'd call her over. Often her initial reaction would be a shake of the head. But Joe had this pleading look of sincerity and using a soft voice, feigning guilelessness, he'd succeed in luring girls to the stand.

Climbing down from his perch he'd approach a girl like he had the most important information imaginable to relate. Affecting an obsequious manner he'd act like he was unworthy to talk to her. I don't know what the hell he'd say but within minutes he had the girl smiling and warming up to him. Soon he'd be luring her toward the pier, and hopefully, from his perspective, underneath, in an effort to do God knows what in broad shadow light. At times he would emerge from beneath the pier with lipstick on his face and the victim... err, girl, staring at him adoringly. It was a good thing Murph never caught him because Joe would have been consigned to the excrement house. Not a place you wanted to be.

It wasn't long before Joe's little game with the ladies backfired. My best high school buddy Moe, was a tall handsome Irishman with dark hair and warm smile. He was a good athlete and a person of high integrity and steeped in core values. He had met some girls from a Pennsylvania college who were down for the summer. Among them was a co-ed named Mary Jane. Mary Jane would be described by most guys as a knockout. She had sparkling blue Irish eyes, dark naturally curly hair, full lips and beautiful wide smile displaying perfect teeth. She laughed easily and had an infectious personality. Moe was immediately smitten.

Moe was also friendly with Joe, from high school, where they played football and basketball together. Moe started going to the beach at Pennsylvania Avenue, where Mary Jane and her girlfriends gathered with other like-minded co-eds. One day he suggested they take a walk to see his lifeguard buddy, Joe, at Connecticut Avenue. As soon as Moe introduced them Joe went into his act. Birddog that he was, and unbeknownst to Moe, Joe somehow got Mary Jane to promise she'd come see him again.

Moe continued pursuing Mary Jane and made a date to meet her one evening when she got off work. Many of the college crowd hung out at a bar called Mort's. There are certain bars that have a comfortable feel to them, and that's how Mort's was. I don't know if was the tasteful subdued lighting, or the mellow atmosphere but it was a huge hit with the college crowd. The defining feature of Mort's, though, was its juke box. All the biggest hits of the day received continuous play. They mostly included romantic ballads by The Ames Brothers, The Four Aces, Joni James, June Valli, Nat "King" Cole, Guy Mitchell, etc. It was a great place to take a girl, especially, if you were involved in a budding romance.

Moe waited for Mary Jane, while sipping beers for several hours, until he realized she wasn't coming. It was a hurtful slap in the face finding out later she'd met Joe that evening.

It was shortly thereafter that I inherited Joe, and with him, Mary Jane. By now, they were a romantic item. When girls who attended Catholic colleges found a mate, they pursued him with deadly seriousness. There was to be no more fooling around with other women. The most important priority for them was setting a wedding date.

Mary Jane and I had become good friends and I loved her bubbly personality. Regrettably, I had a sense of what she was getting into and hoped she would be able to deal with coming events. Though Joe loved her, he was not quite ready to avert his roving eye.

Trouble started brewing immediately. Mary Jane came down every day. At times she'd bring us sandwiches from the hotel where she worked. We made it through the first few visits without incident. Inevitably she showed up on a day, when earlier, Joe had lured two girls to the stand. She glared at them with such an intimidating look they quickly said their goodbyes and continued on up the beach.

The third degree was quickly forthcoming. Joe tried to stutter and stammer his way out of his predicament. Finally, he told her they were *my* friends. Now it was my turn to glare, the seriousness of which was not lost on him. I guessed he'd rather face my wrath then hers.

He took her for a walk down by the waters-edge. She angrily gestured pointing her finger in his face and chewing his ass out. He listened, trying to squirm his way out of this helpless predicament.

When she left to go to work I laid into him for trying to involve me in his peccadilloes. I told him if it happened again, not only would I rat him out, I would become her confidant letting her know every time he cheated. He got the message.

Joe couldn't help himself though, and continued his womanizing ways. I adopted the strategy of talking to girls down by the boat. That way, if M.J appeared, and Joe was talking to a girl, there could be no question.

He got so cagey he worked out a network with guards up beach. Using hand signals from one stand to another Joe was warned ahead of time when M.J. was heading our way. She however hadn't been born under a rock and knew he was up to no good. M.J. had a few tricks of her own. Instead of walking down the beach to our station, at times, she came via the boardwalk.

Now Joe had no idea when she'd arrive and his illicit rendezvous took on new risk.

His luck was bound to run out, and of course did. She appeared one drizzly day when he thought she was working. I was on the stand watching a few hearty bathers brave the surf. Joe had performed his disappearing act with a cutey beneath the pier. M.J. had come by way of the boardwalk with a bag lunch in hand. She asked me where Joe was. I lied and said maybe he was up in the tent. Just at that moment Joe came from under the pier with his arm around the girl and lipstick covering his face.

Mary Jane, by nature, was a sweet loving girl, so it was surprising to see how quickly she turned into a raving shrew. As M.J. charged the hapless Joe, the girl took off running in the opposite direction. I was in awe as M.J. mounted her attack, swinging the bag lunch like Mickey Mantle and connecting with every blow. Wax paper, bread, lettuce, tomato, meat, cheese were flying in all directions. Joe had put his hands up to thwart her blows but she was on a roll. She beat him with her fists and delivered expletives that were impressive considering they were coming from a good Catholic girl.

Joe got unlucky in another way. Murph witnessed the entire event. He wasted no time closing the distance to our stand. He asked what was going on (as if he didn't know). Joe tried to make light of it but Murph wasn't buying. He told Joe his nonsense was at an end and if it happened again he would find himself being shipped to the leper colony. The leper colony was an unflattering term used to mean a transfer to the down beach area which consisted of sprawling beaches, sparse local bathers and little or no action. In a word, BORING!

Joe had no choice but to toe the line. My summer became peaceful and Mary Jane was exorcised of having to tolerate a steady diet of bimbo's on parade. It turned out to be Joe's only summer with us. He and Mary Jane married, and shortly thereafter he left the beach to pursue a career.

RESCUES AND RESTAURANTS

The summer was not in any way memorable but for two (three including the foregoing) events. The first was the numerous rescues we had by the pier mostly involving children. We learned how to identify dangerous ocean conditions which resulted in better rescue techniques. It made our task easier to recognize a potential rescue before it happened.

For instance, a bather at low tide would wade out through a waist deep gully to a shin deep sandbar. Once on the sandbar he might venture out to chest deep water. Usually there was no danger in that part of the ocean. The bather at this point would test his swimming skills. Adopting the prone position, he'd cup his hands and bend his arms slowly alternating the stroke. While swinging his arms and head wildly from left to right, he still managed somehow not to move an inch. The feet, that should have been used like fins in a fluttering motion were lifted out of the water and plunked back in, creating small geysers, but little movement. This method of swimming won't get you from one side of a pool to the other let alone through a dangerous offset. After taking about ten strokes and suffering near exhaustion, the bather would have to stand up. This swimming technique we referred to as the "come get me stroke."

So as the tide rose the water would pour into the gully causing a swirling offset. As the previously described swimmer was trying to make his way to the sandbar, we had already launched our boat knowing he'd never make it through the gully. We guessed right almost 100% of the time.

An important technique, involving swimming rescues, was the proper use of a can buoy (flotation device). When approaching a drowning person you had to be careful not to get too close. First you'd remove the rope harness from your shoulder and push the can buoy towards the bather. Naturally they'd grab on for dear life. Diving under water you'd resurface behind the person, lock your arms around him, and wait for the boat to pick you both up. The boat crew would row the mortified victim to shore and watch him disappear into the crowd.

The second memorable event was a girl I met. Most of the girls I encountered that summer only appealed to me peripherally. I was not looking for, or expecting to meet another Mickey. But a girl started appearing at our beach every day laying her towel close to our stand. She was showgirl statuesque, very pretty, with a fine figure. I realized early on she was a bookworm, usually immersing herself in the latest popular work of the day. I thought it interesting a woman with showgirl looks, maybe the reason for my attraction, spent so much time reading.

It was too tempting not to approach her blanket which was not usually my M.O. but I was curious to meet her. My opening line was to ask her what she was reading. Not unfriendly, but not very open, she replied, *"The Catcher in the Rye."* I think my response was, The Catcher in the—What? She said it was written by J.D. Salinger and very popular among college students. When I asked her what it was about she warmed somewhat. Maybe up until that moment she had thought all lifeguards cretins.

As she related the story I became fascinated by its contents (the books). She said I could borrow it when she finished. Things became more relaxed. I found out her name was Connie, a college student down for the summer. Not surprisingly, she was a waitress along with her girlfriend Eleanor (Ellie). Ellie was not nearly as attractive as Connie. They had just quit their jobs because the hotel where they worked was not giving them enough hours. I was surprised when she said they had gotten jobs at a seafood restaurant called the *Ship Ahoy*. It just so happened, my uncle tended bar there. Never wanting to linger at a female's blanket, fearing the wrath of Murph, I returned to the stand.

Connie however made a couple of visits throughout the day. I realized quickly she did not have a killer personality. She was serious about everything. Even though *The Catcher in the Rye* was written as an American tragedy there *were* some humorous passages, "He put my goddamn paper down then and looked at me like he'd just beaten hell out of me in ping pong or something."

She didn't find any humor. Her major was something difficult, like physics. Every time I'd make an attempt at levity she'd give me an odd look. I wasn't sure if she didn't get it, had no sense of humor or simply thought I was weird.

By the end of the day I had made plans to visit her at work. Normally, this is not considered kosher. In this case it was okay since my uncle was the bartender. I could chat him up without distracting her.

My uncle (my mother's brother) wasn't surprised by my visit, since he and I were close and I went there on a regular basis. My uncle George was a very good looking man with a great personality. He had always been popular with the ladies. Age did not concern him. If he saw something he liked he was a dog.

As soon as I got there he started telling me about the new blond who'd been hired. Right away I knew his horns were up. When Connie came out of the kitchen she spotted me, came over, and said hello. She went to wait a table while George gave me the first degree. I told him she was camping on my beach.

I knew that wouldn't deter him. Even though I would see her most days on the beach, he would see her at nights. Actually it didn't bother me. I knew I wouldn't become that interested. Her personality was too weird. If he wanted to make a play for her, fine.

As it turned out she was more interested in me than I thought and I began to see more of her. It wasn't like an every night thing which was okay with both of us. On her night off we would go to a movie or if some of the guys from the clubhouse had dates for dinner we'd join them. The relationship was casual and we liked it that way. Neither of us was interested in a romance. I would still visit George, who apparently wasn't having any luck. Any night I'd go there to meet Connie he'd tell me how lucky I was and what a knockout she was. He wasn't crazy about Ellie though and referred to her as that "dumb broad."

One night the restaurant was busy, both the bar and tables, and George was the only bartender. I would never describe George as the most patient person I'd ever known. If someone was making his job difficult he could get very testy. At one point I saw Ellie come to the bar and ask for something. George got a perplexed look on his face and sent her back to her customers table. She came back to the bar and repeated the order. Again he looked puzzled. He came over to me and asked if I'd ever heard of a drink called a "crabtee cocktail." I admitted I hadn't.

He told her to ask again. She was afraid to go back a third time. Pissed off that he had to go to the table, George gave her a look that would melt metal. When the man at the table spoke to George he nodded and with pursed lips went back to the bar. Looking thoroughly aggravated he said something to Ellie that sent her scurrying to the kitchen.

He came over to me and said, "Can you believe that simple shit?" the guy asked for a "crabmeat cocktail."

I don't recall how long I continued seeing Connie but I know it wasn't until the end of summer. There was nothing like a breakup, we just went our separate ways.

The rest of the summer was not memorable. In a way I was sorry to see the season end. On the other hand, I was looking forward to school and activities that would occupy my mind. I was even determined to buckle down and make better grades, although would soon be reminded of the quote "The best laid plans of mice and men etc."

FRAT BOYS

My first year at Miami had been spent at two different frat houses. The first semester was at the Kappa Alpha house which I was asked to pledge. However, I had nothing in common with this Southern themed fraternity. At certain times, these guys would dress in Civil War uniforms and parade around campus on horses. But even my love of horses couldn't persuade me to join. It wasn't that I felt there was anything wrong with them. It was just that my upbringing and environment were so different.

The second semester was spent at the Sigma Nu house. A few of my friends from Atlantic City, including Jack and Al were already Sigma Nu's. Al and I became roommates and hung out together. He hailed from Connecticut where his father was a golfing professional. Al was quite a golfer himself and he and other Sigma Nu's would take full advantage of the great Florida courses.

Offers to pledge Sigma Nu started as soon as I moved in. At first I thought, why not? I knew a lot of these guys and the living arrangements were comfortable. But soon after settling in some of the more unsavory features of fraternity life became obvious. In some ways it was akin to the same kind of political infighting that was Atlantic City.

Many of the frat boys had their own agenda, and egos abounded. Additionally, many were rah rah, types which was definitely not my style. You had to be careful regarding your actions for fear of offending someone. I went along with this childishness for most of the semester.

Each year during Greek Week, Sigma Nu played Sigma Chi in an annual football game. This was more than a two hand touch scrimmage. Both teams practiced for weeks and used the varsity's game day uniforms. The game was played on the University's practice field and raised money for charity. There was a large contingent of fans on both sides.

On game day I was issued a uniform with the number 44. When I first became a lifeguard, we were issued numbered uniforms and mine was 44. After we'd suited up for the game, a guy named Bruce approached and asked if we could switch jerseys because he wore #44 in high school. I explained to him that it had also been my number. Besides, getting that jersey on over my pads was like getting a size small on over a large and the game was getting ready to start.

Well, you'd think I'd taken away his puppy. He started whining like a child. Ooooh, I want that jersey, that was my number in high school. I ignored him, joined the team, and went out on the field. We'd been friendly up until then.

When it came time for me to be voted into the fraternity I was called before a group of judges, of which Bruce was one. I forget what questions they asked but from what I recall they were just silly. The next day I found out I had been blackballed by the entire group. I had been under the impression that most of those guys liked me.

Later that day I ran into Jack. He told me Bruce lobbied the other guys against me regarding the jersey incident and got them to vote his way. I was later told by someone that over a period of time my name would be brought up again for a second vote. I don't recall who gave me the message but I do remember telling him they could kiss my ass. When the semester ended I bade them a fond farewell.

G I'S R US

At the beginning of my second year I was determined to find some veterans, like myself, to live with and share expenses. I visited the Student Union and found a promising candidate listed on the bulletin board. "Veteran looking for roommate: Call John at xxxxxx." I dialed the number and a male with a well modulated voice answered. We exchanged information and agreed to meet at the Union. John was from Teaneck, N.J. and we hit it off immediately. He was a Navy vet like me, pursuing a degree in Engineering.

We spent the next few days searching for a place to live, finally locating a house on Douglas Road. It was nothing fancy but did include three bedrooms, a kitchen and living room. The rent was a little steep for two but quite manageable for three.

A few days after John and I settled in I ran into a friend on campus named Arnie. Arnie was a guy I knew from Ventnor, N.J. (a city down beach of Atlantic City). I told him I was looking for another roommate, hopefully a vet. It wasn't long before I received a call. The voice on the other end introduced himself as Norman, a friend of Arnie's from whom he'd gotten the message. Ironically Norm was also a Navy vet. He came over within the hour. We talked for awhile and though he seemed to scrutinize us as much as we did him, he seemed like a solid guy.

The three of us settled into a routine of going to classes, while sorting out our separate social agendas. For the most part I hung out with guys from Atlantic City, or my ex-roommate Al. Norm had a friend, Dave, who like Norm was from Rhode Island. Having gone to high school together they both opted for Miami. John tended to hang with guys, who like him, were majoring in Engineering.

There was a beer and wine place just off campus called the Campus Canteen, affectionately known as the Can. The nickname couldn't have been more appropriate, since drafts were served in beer cans with the tops cut off. The Can was frequented by both sexes and a great place to meet girls. I would see John there often. He may have been a serious engineering student but he was still Irish. I never saw Norm there since he wasn't a drinker.

Weekend football games at the Orange Bowl were a big deal. Home games, generally played on Friday nights, were electric with excitement. *The Band of the Hour,* Miami's world famous marching band performed before kickoff and during halftime. One of the unique things about the band was, in addition to their official band uniforms they would, at times, appear in white shirts, black Bermudas, black berets, and knee high socks. The crowd went wild. I had seen a few college games before attending Miami. However it's an entirely different experience when you're wedded to a university. As a fan, the team becomes an integral part of your entire experience. It stays with you for life.

Norm and I were cordial toward each other but far from close. Little did we know at the time we would form a bond that endures to this day. At first, maybe being older, having been through a four year growth period and not into rah, rah crap we were a little leery of each other. All that changed one night.

Norman loved women. If he saw a girl he liked he had zero qualms about pursuing her. I was at home by myself the night he brought Michelle to the house. She had short black hair and a distinctive Nordic look with high freckled cheek bones. Michelle was very attractive and an aspiring model. Norm introduced us and watched with amusement as I reacted with surprise to her greeting, in a thick Swedish accent.

We sat and talked awhile with Michelle's use of English being barely comprehensible. Norm was getting a kick out of her accent, laughing when she wasn't looking. Watching him made it difficult to stifle my own amusement. Finally, in a discreet manner he asked if I could disappear for awhile. She said something like *"It vass veery pleasing to meet viss you."*

I went to the Can (not that one, the bar), ran into Jack, and had a few beers. When I got back to the house Michelle was gone. Luckily, John hadn't gotten home before me to interrupt Norm's romantic interlude.

Norm related his exploits not leaving much out. When he was finished I remained silent for a few moments. Always possessed of a certain talent for mimicry I responded, *"vass she ass goot ass you zought?"* I was unprepared for his response. He literally exploded with laughter that was so contagious it set me off too. That was all the encouragement I needed. Every time I recalled something she said I would imitate her accent sending him back into hysterics.

I'm not sure how long we laughed but it was more than enough to launch a lifelong friendship. After that night we were basically inseparable.

I was working two part time jobs as a bartender and serving as Advertising Manager for *The Miami Hurricane*, our student newspaper. Getting this position was a result of Al having being selected Business Manager and recommending me for Advertising Manager. Al had a lot of experience in that end of the newspaper business, having worked for his local Connecticut newspaper prior to attending Miami. He taught me a lot over the next couple of years. My income from these jobs, in addition to my G.I. bill, afforded me a comfortable financial cushion.

DOWN TO THE SEA IN CARS

Some of the customers frequenting one of the bars I worked in Coconut Grove, might be generously described as lushes. They often spent the entire day guzzling glasses of beer from large pitchers. Buying a pitcher made the per glass price cheaper. They basically did anything they could to support their habit.

It was no surprise then when a customer came in one day offering a ski boat for sale. The package included a 35 hp motor, skis, rope tow, detachable hitch and trailer. The exact price he was asking escapes me but as I recall it was about a third of its value. When he got no bar stool takers he approached me. I feigned disinterest. He dropped the price further. The deal became impossible to resist. I may have bought the whole package for as little as seventy five dollars.

Making the deal was contingent on my seeing the craft. He brought it to the bar within the hour. When I examined the boat, other than needing a paint job, it looked sound. The trailer had some rust but that could be fixed. Still I was not buying it without testing the motor. The next day I got out of class early and met him at Matheson Hammock County Beach. When we launched the boat, I started the engine and listened to it roar into action. The boat slid smoothly across the water. My heart soared. Wow, my own ski boat.

I towed the boat home and proudly displayed it to Norm and John. All three of us finished classes the same time each day, shortly after noon. The next day we went to the beach and spent the afternoon skiing. Norm and John had never skied before. Watching them trying to get up on skis was hilarious. I almost lost control of the boat. They would just about get up and then keel over in slow motion letting go of the tow. The rope handle followed the boat, skipping jauntily over the water, as if bidding good riddance to the bumbling amateurs.

Time that should have been spent studying was often spent with the boat. Norm and John learned how to ski and were welcome to use it whenever I couldn't.

Norm and I had our last class of the day together. One day it was cancelled and we were finished at 11:00 A.M. It was a great day to take the boat out but we had a problem. My car was out of commission. John, who had to study for a test and couldn't go with us offered his car, an old beat up Dodge. We took the hitch off my car transferring it to his.

Two more friends, Tom and Nick were joining us at the beach. Before we left John warned us that the parking brake didn't work and the regular brakes were a little shaky. We assured him we'd be careful.

Tom and Nick were already there when we arrived. I proceeded to back the trailer down the boat ramp. When the trailer was in position Norm suggested it might be a good idea if he sat in the car with his foot on the brake. The rest of us would push the boat off the trailer. I found a piece of wood to use as a chock and wedged it under one of the trailers back wheels.

It was difficult pushing the boat off the trailer because of rust in the track. Our first efforts were unsuccessful. I urged the guys to really put their shoulders into it. With a Herculean push we felt the boat start to move toward the water, unfortunately so did the trailer. Apparently, Norm having his foot on the brake that long caused it to slip. The trailer rolled easily over the chock. I watched in horror as trailer, boat, car and Norm, like a good sea captain, held fast to the brake as his ship slowly slipped into its watery grave.

Luckily, the car didn't go all the way under. Water was up to the steering wheel and at chest level for Norm. Prankster that he was Norm climbed out through the driver's side window and scurried up onto the roof. He cupped his hands and scooped up water spilling it on the roof saying, "I baptize thee in the name of the Father…"

The other two clowns started making remarks, like, "Should we try the engine?" or, "Do you think we'll get charged for parking?" Meanwhile the boat, which was unattached, set sail on a course of her own, heading for sea. I had to strip to the waist and go rescue her.

My first thought was how in hell are we going to raise the car? My second thought was how in hell am I going to tell John?

We found a park official who said deep-sixing a car was not uncommon. The park had a portable winch for such occasions, which included a fee of course. We knew the car was unsalvageable since cars don't respond well to salt water. Luckily, we were able to attach the hitch to Tom and Nick's car and tow the boat back to the house.

Tom and Nick weren't content to drop us off and leave. They had to be in on the fireworks. John knew immediately from the looks on our faces something was wrong. They stood behind me as I fumbled for the right words. John listened patiently with a serious expression. I relayed the information about the brakes and the chock, trying hard to convince him it wasn't my fault.

When I described the trailer rolling over the chock, and Norm riding the vehicle to Davy Jones Locker, his reaction was totally unexpected. He chuckled at first which quickly turned into a belly laugh. All of a sudden he was out of control holding his gut and shaking like Santa Claus. The relief was overwhelming as we all bent over in hysterics, reliving the day's events.

I had liked John from the first time we'd met, but my admiration for him soared following his incredible reaction to this incident. I promised him when I went home that summer I would get him a car, and I did. Jack's father Hector sold used cars as a sideline. He found a 1950, Electric Company cast off, puke green colored Ford, in good condition and made me a nice deal. As I recall it cost about a $100.00–well worth it.

NORM'S NEW ROOMMATE

One thing I disliked about Miami was the incredible number of flying bugs, insects, etc. that came in all different shapes, sizes and colors.

We'd pig out at a place called the Royal Castle, ordering two or three 15 cent "barfburgers" and a birch beer. While stuffing our faces we'd suddenly hear a loud thump at the window. A red, green or other colored flying creature, the size of a small B-29 had just committed unintentional hari-kari by crashing into the brightly lit plate glass window. Outside they'd be swarming by the thousands, as if on a convention. I hated encountering those air borne aliens, especially when pigging out on a barfburger.

Imagine our chagrin when Norm, John and I returned at night to a dark house. As soon as we entered and turned on the lights we'd be greeted by a small army of palmetto bugs running helter-skelter throughout the house in all directions. These things were totally disgusting. What they were, were giant cockroaches. Norm was especially repulsed. Our weapon of choice for combating these horrid creations was the common household broom.

We'd chase them around the house, military style, yelling "general quarters, general quarters, all hands man your battle stations." The disgusting critters were quick though and would race to hiding places in crevices and behind counters. On a good night we would manage to get a few.

One night just John and I were home and he happened to kill an especially large brute. I think the force of the blow itself killed the creature because the body was totally intact. We decided to have some fun and scotch taped one of its legs to Norm's headboard, so when he came home and saw it he'd think it was alive.

When Norm arrived he stayed in the living room for awhile. Our anticipation was palpable. Finally, he went to his room. The next sound we heard was a shriek followed by footsteps moving toward the kitchen and then back to the bedroom. The reverberations from the broom slamming the headboard, with such force, seemed somewhat excessive. In stitches by now, we ran to his bedroom and told him the roach had already been conquered. I knew Norm was a clever guy but the creativeness of the expletives directed our way were truly impressive.

NOT QUITE BULLDOGGING FRED

I worked my three part time jobs during the day. That left my nights free to study, not something I looked forward to. When a friend told me he could get me another part time job at Flagler Dog Track I accepted. I had never been to a dog track and didn't even know greyhounds were the breed of racing dog used. What I did know from others who worked there was that the pay was good.

We were required to wear these silly military drugstore jackets and chincy looking captain's hats. Before the races started it was part of our job to parade the dogs before the spectators. Many bettors placed money on a dog solely on its looks. We'd march the dogs back and forth in front of the stands in order for the oglers to get a better look.

With the amount of time the dogs had to relieve themselves before the race, you'd think their potty habits would be a bit more disciplined. But no, the dogs always waited until they were on the track to take their ill timed dumps. If it wasn't embarrassing enough standing there while hundreds watched, you also served as their designated pooper scooper.

When my friends found out I was working there they said they were going to come out one night. None of them had any idea what my job entailed since they'd never been to a dog track either. I didn't try to discourage them, since doing so might have aroused their curiosity. I just prayed they'd forget. No such luck.

Predictably, the dreaded night arrived. I was going through my usual routine, parading the dogs. Without warning, I heard my named being called. I turned to look, already fearing the worst. It was Tom, Nick and another buddy, Gene. These guys were master ball busters.

They waved and hollered drawing the attention of others toward me. I was mortified. As luck would have it and as if on cue the dog I was walking decided to drop a load. When I glimpsed them from the corner of my eye they were draped over each other in hysterics. Furthermore, I couldn't begin to describe their glee when they saw me wielding the pooper scooper.

Mercifully it was time for the race to begin. We led the dogs to the starting gate away from the crowd and my tormentors.

Just before the race was to begin the chief dog handler approached me. He told me one of the guys had called out sick and I would be handling his dog. This was no ordinary dog and definitely not good news. The guy he was referring to boasted a talent comparable to that of a steer wrestler. The dog he was referring to was the steer.

Over the course of many years, the name of the dog escapes me and the only one I can think of is "Fast Fred." Whether that was his name or not, it applies. The dog won almost every race in which he was entered. Unfortunately, he had a colossal negative.

At the end of the race there were no little jockeys atop the dogs to rein them in. In order to stop them, all the handlers stood on the track waving their arms. If the dogs went by the handlers a canvas curtain was drawn across the track. For 99.9 percent of the dogs, the handlers and barrier were enough, not so Fast Fred. Whether he had vision problems or psychological problems I couldn't say, but that dog was not right.

If there wasn't someone to stop him, Fred was destined to make contact with that barrier. Enter the previously mentioned steer wrestler. He would get himself in position as Fred raced headlong toward his destruction. When the dog sought to go by, the handler would leap on his back and wrestle him to the dirt track, putting an end to the animal's suicidal attempt.

I would bet the chief handler asked everyone to handle Fred before approaching me and they all said, "Give it to the new guy." Unlike them, I was *told* not asked. Furthermore, because the dog was a winner he was worth a lot of money. The owner didn't want anything happening to him and this was made abundantly clear. I thought, screw you, I'm not killing myself over a dog. Additionally, I had the three ball busters to worry about.

As the dogs were put in position we assumed our places at the finish line. Whenever I glanced toward my three tormentors their eyes were locked on like lasers, waiting for another hysterical moment.

The gun went off and the dogs broke from the gate. As usual Fred forged into the lead. As I watched the dogs rounding the final turn my heart started pounding. I didn't know what I was going to do but whatever it was, it wasn't going to be my rodeo debut.

As the dogs approached the finish, the guys started waving their arms. This was supposed to give me just enough time to corral Fred. As Fred came at me I made a fake lunge that would make a linebacker proud and may have launched my future amateur acting career.

Fred, who'd continued on, hell bent for *canvas*, slammed into that barrier at mach speed. Hitting the wall, he looked like something out of a Tom and Jerry cartoon. When Fred's body collided with canvas, it lingered for a moment before crumpling to the dirt. I thought the dog was dead. As everyone raced toward him he slowly rose. Like a punch drunk fighter who's just had his bell rung, Fred staggered around the track trying to collect his senses. I wondered what Fred would do in his next race that was, if he had a next race.

The handler came to me and chewed my ass out. I feigned innocence saying I did my best. Apparently I convinced him since I wasn't fired.

Safe to say, I was never asked to tend Fred again.

My "friends" had come to the finish line after having witnessed the entire event. I waved, signaling I would see them later, and headed for the handlers room.

When the semester ended John informed us he was departing our living arrangements. He said he'd enjoyed living with us but was moving in with some guys who were majoring in Engineering. We certainly didn't blame him. He was a serious student and wasn't interested in living with two clowns who were a source of constant distraction.

NEW DIGS

Norm and I didn't like the cockroach infested house anyway. Besides, it was too far from campus. Shortly thereafter I ran into my friend and brother lifeguard Geza. He too was looking for a place to live. A couple of days later we found a house in South Miami, within walking distance of the university.

This house, like the other, had three bedrooms, kitchen and living room. The previous house was furnished but this one wasn't. To say it was sparsely furnished would be an understatement. Other than a cheap sofa, table and lamp in the living room, I don't recall much of anything else. I believe the flooring was called terrazzo, made from marble or stone. The great thing about our new digs, was, after a party we'd just bring a hose in, move our paltry furniture to one side, and wash it down—very informal.

Jack visited often, especially around dinner. He would drive over in his late model Cadillac, compliments of his father, wearing a Palm Beach suit, sans shirt, with loafers and no socks. His timing was impeccable. We served as his home away from home.

On one of Jack's visits he brought a friend with the name Michael Leland Fairchild Kerry Jr. (not his real last name). Mike was from a well to do family but was always talking about living in "tap city," as in tapped out. Mike later became known simply, as "Dingle-Berry Kerry" or just "Dingle." Upon first impression Mike seemed the quiet sort. That supposition would prove not quite accurate.

Mike was good looking with a distinctly leprechaun, impishness about him. He had a ready smile and as we'd discover loved to have fun, as long as it was at somebody else's expense. He was sturdy and broad shouldered and had the look of a wrestler, which he'd been in high school.

We learned Mike was an ex Marine. Like us he was looking to live with guys his own age. Our group would now include three sailors and a marine, a full compliment from the Naval Service (marines are a branch of the navy). We welcomed him aboard.

One thing we all shared was our distaste for academics. Norm was especially outspoken on this subject. Even when inspired to study, which was seldom, he performed this task with mental anguish. He'd sit with a textbook squirming like a kid who was forced to be on a long car ride. "Are we there yet?" I'd constantly hear him mumbling to himself, "What a bunch of shit this is."

Norm had acquired ice cream trucks in his adoptive home town of Newport, R.I. This is how he supplemented his G.I. bill. He did well enough financially to comfortably carry himself through the school year. In the summer he scoured neighborhoods ringing his bell to attract "the little bastards" (his customers) and collect their "grubby dimes." Some kids would come to the truck looking longingly for an ice cream only to be turned away for lack of funds. After a few incidents like this, as soon as a kid appeared for ice cream, Norm would inquire of him, "Ya got cash?"

Norm's idea of a good time was going to the movies, probably to get lost in a fantasy world that took his mind off school. The problem was, he went every day and there were only so many movies before demand outstripped supply. On his way home, he'd stop at Stevens, a supermarket, and pick up a huge horrid looking chuck steak and onion. His whole meal topped out at about 59 cents. He'd sit at the table of our non-air conditioned apartment in his shorts, sweating, devouring the steak and eating the onion like an apple. For him, this was a gourmet's feast.

Naturally because of our academic avoidance we'd search for the easiest classes. We all scoured the college bulletins for snap courses. I found a good one that Norm and I signed up for. It was Music Appreciation 101. We asked around and found out the professor was an easy grader. We were reassured of this on our first day of class. There must have been close to a 100 students in attendance.

Actually, I was glad I'd taken the course; it dealt with classical composers. Having always been a music lover I was anxious to learn more about the classics. Not so Norm, he hated it. Each week fewer and fewer students, including Norm, would come to class. Just before midterms the class was down to about 20 students. On exam day, voila,' all hundred students were back in their seats. The professor was a laid back type with a droll sense of humor. When everyone was seated, he said, with a glint in his eye and all the sarcasm he could muster, "Good morning class, welcome to Music Appreciation 101."

I was conscientious about that course and put some serious time into studying. Norm's text gathered cobwebs. On the day of the final exam he sat next to me and copied my answers verbatim. He received a B and I was awarded a C. Go figure. To this day he loves to remind me of that academic injustice.

My car had died but thanks again to one of the bar lushes where I worked I was able to get a great deal on a Vespa motor scooter. The guy who sold it to me needed money and I was in the right place at the right time. Except for going on a date, or some other minor problem the scooter was perfect. I could get up late, throw on a T-shirt, Bermudas and sandals, jump on the scooter and be on campus in a couple of minutes. Wherever my class was being held I could drive right to that location without ever having to worry about a parking space.

Geza didn't have transportation so whenever I wasn't using the scooter, he was welcome to it. He had gotten a job at a place called Super Subs that sold East Coast style submarine sandwiches. The people who operated the shop were from previously mentioned Ventnor, N.J. where they had opened their original business. They had decided to take a flier and open a second store in Coral Gables, just off Miami's campus.

Geza worked a deal with them, where the owners would make up various types of subs for him to deliver and between them receive fifty percent of everything he sold. He suggested this would bring them business they didn't ordinarily have. They loved the idea. He would visit the frat houses and hawk the subs to students. This business proved very lucrative because the frat boys were always hungry toward late evening. Geza's little entrepreneurial endeavor proved quite successful.

Every so often, a frat weasel would try to get over on Geza. While one would distract him, asking about the different kinds of subs, another would try to grab a sandwich from the box. He was on to this ploy quickly. Geza was not a guy to fool with and a few rah, rahs were quick to find that out.

Depending on business there were times when he returned to the shop for more sandwiches. One night he came home late and we were all sound asleep. Suddenly, we heard this roaring sound coming from the living room. Scrambling out of bed we rushed to the source of the disturbance. Geza had driven the scooter into the living room, continuing to rev it up until we told him to turn the damn thing off.

I asked what the hell he was doing. He had been to the Campus Canteen having a few beers and had locked the scooter outside. When he left, and took off the lock and chain, he didn't realize until he got home that he must have left them behind. The lock and chain had come with the bike and we were not interested in buying a new set. As a result, the living room became home to the scooter and part of the furniture. At least the wheel lock still worked.

PIED PIPER OF CATNIP

Mike, we discovered, had a Jekyll and Hyde personality. At times he would be in the living room plotting his next fiendish caper. Other times he'd stay in his room for days on end. During these latter periods he was moody and wanted to be left alone.

Geza was not a big drinker. He kept a busy schedule and had little time for socializing.

One afternoon Geza ran into Jack after class. Jack, who was a big party guy, talked Geza into a few beers at the Can.

By the time Geza got home he was really drunk. He went into his room took off all his clothes and fell into bed. When Mike got home he looked in

Geza's room and saw him lying on his bed, bare assed naked. Geza was snoring loudly, dead to the world.

That was all Mike needed. He started moving about like a gleeful child. He was trying to figure out what he could due to Geza in his vulnerable situation.

There were these cats that hung around the neighborhood. They were always in the garbage cans looking for food. Mike's brain quickly shifted into high gear as he swung into action. We knew he had come up with one of his diabolical schemes and waited to see how it played out.

Mike went into the refrigerator and started rummaging around for leftovers. The first thing he spotted was a can of whipped cream. He ran to the bedroom and proceeded squirting the gooey mess all over Geza's genitals. Norm, Jack and I looked at each other perplexed. Our expressions changed in a hurry when he opened the kitchen door and invited the cats in. These neighborhood toughies were not bashful and let Mike lead them through the house like the Pied Piper.

We quickly got the picture and joined Mike in the bedroom. The felines, at Mike's urging jumped on the bed. In no time they were licking the whipped cream and with it Geza's genitals. Now you'd think this was enough but with Mike nothing was ever enough. He ran back to the kitchen, grabbed the ketchup and shook that onto Geza's affected area.

From there the recipe grew with anything Mike could find. Some of the items I recall were: mustard, mayonnaise, raw eggs, bread, Maraschino cherries, tuna fish and God knows what else.

The more items he added, the more diabolical he became, looking like one of those mad scientists from a Boris Karloff movie. The cats feasted contentedly and just licked around anything they didn't find appealing. In all this frenzy I was hoping Geza's genitals weren't mistaken for catnip. Geza slept peacefully through the entire episode. Norm, Jack and I had to leave the room. We could hardly stand up. The worst thing you could do was laugh at Mike's antics. That just encouraged him.

I don't think we ever said anything to Geza but Mike might have. If he did, I'm sure he blamed it on us.

That was the best semester in my four years at Miami. I was almost sad to see it end. On the other hand, how sorry could I be when I was going back to a job I loved and one that offered so much excitement? As in the previous year, grade wise, I just squeaked through, but the worst was over. I had confidence I would make it through my four years.

The trip home was long as usual but more interesting this time. Jack's brother Tom (also a student at Miami) wanted to avoid the long drive home. He decided to fly and asked me to bring his car, a late model Corvette. Every time I stopped for gas, those big ol' southern boys would look at me as though I'd just landed in a space ship. With every red light I stopped at through Georgia, and the two Carolina's, somebody wanted to drag race. I obliged most and left them at the gate.

That was a fun trip.

CHAPTER 7

THE GOOD THE BAD AND THE BEAUTIFUL

SHAKEUP AT MICHIGAN

Michigan's stretch was about to undergo some personnel changes. It would not happen right away since the moves would be dictated by circumstances. Ultimately, the changes would bring together a crew that would be transformed into a team working as a single unit. This team would perform as one, not only under lifesaving conditions but in all beach-related activities.

Camaraderie among crews was paramount otherwise a stretch could be dominated by political cliques, all vying for their piece of the turf. This kind of turmoil, at times, could be instigated by the captain in charge. If he was the type who enjoyed gossip, and some did, it was not unusual to see it filter down among the troops. What ensued were little power groups acting out that stretch's equivalent of, *As the Beach Patrol Turns*. Much of the infighting had to do with who was worthy of promotion. There were other less significant jealousies, but they all contributed to a pettiness that affected efficiency and socialization among the crews.

We were proud to have Murph as our captain, a leader in every sense of the word. He was above talking about his charges to any outsider in a negative way. If there was a serious rescue, or scramble, he was part of the action. He encouraged social events such as the crew going to dinner every payday. We were required to practice rescues and CPR in order to stay sharp. Crews were encouraged to compete in the annual boat and swim races. He urged us to find pretty girls to enter in the Miss Beach Patrol Contest so our stretch might boast the winner. *And,* he had an unstated philosophy but one that we all understood—he was firm—but fair.

Returning to the beach each year and this kind of brotherhood does not make leaving an easy choice. It would be difficult to carve out a better life if given the opportunity, and so it was why I returned each summer. This was *my* kind of fraternity.

I do not wish to imply a utopian environment. Guy's had differences but it wasn't over some squishy insignificance and it was rare. During a rescue, if three boats were involved, we competed like hell to be first to the victim. This was a healthy competition, the victim being the beneficiary. Ball busting abounded, the more creative the better, and all lived by the creed: "I don't get mad, I get even."

My return to Arkansas found me with yet another new partner named Tommy.

Tommy and my brother Mick had become friends during their senior year in high school.

After graduating they both enlisted in the Army. Upon being discharged they enrolled in Glassboro State College (now Rowan University). Tommy had also passed the test for the beach patrol. His early years were spent at the Chelsea Avenue stretch where there wasn't much action. Chelsea was not far from the previously mentioned dreaded leper colony and so, not the most exciting place to be. He had put in for and was granted a transfer to Michigan and assigned to Murph.

Tommy was handsome and exuded in his persona an instant likeability. In addition to a charismatic and disarming smile all who met him would immediately seek his friendship. He was of medium height with a well proportioned square shouldered build. Displaying a laid-back subtle sense of humor you had to be on your toes to pick up on his witticisms. An impeccable dresser, whether he was wearing a tuxedo or his lifeguard uniform, he could have posed for the cover of GQ. He was generally on the quiet side unless you were able to engage him in a subject such as history (his major), which he articulated with passion.

Tommy was a terrific lifeguard. He was very conscientious and kept his eyes on the bathers at all times. In all the rescues we were involved in over the years I always felt a complete sense of security knowing he was my partner and stern man. And though he never appeared aggressive, when engaging the gentler sex, there were always plenty of girls dropping by the stand to see him.

I never knew what Tommy was up to. There were things he'd do that would catch me by surprise. For example, people were forever picking things up along the beach and bringing them over to have us determine their derivation. One day a sea-matter-bearing creature came to us with her motley find. It was one of those ugly green colored pieces of seaweed that have those little snapping air bubbles.

The woman held out her hands, offering up the slimy mass, like she'd just made the discovery of the century. Pointing to the gross substance and looking horrified, Tommy, in a contrived effort to get away, scooted up to the back railing of the stand pointing and shouting, "Oooooh!! **serbungy!**" or "**magongoo!**" The woman rapidly shook the item free as if ridding herself of a warm turd.

It was difficult stifling laughter but the fear of her reporting us to Murph if we did, helped. Another reason to stifle was it gave the bather a sense of discovery and bravery for bringing it to our attention. Later we'd see that same woman pointing out the mess to others, seemingly, discussing its history. What the hell she was telling her audience was beyond us. Tommy had said nothing more than what was just described.

JACKIE AND GEZA

Michigan underwent its own change. Mike, Geza's partner, decided to end his carefree lifeguard days in order to explore new vistas. Geza welcomed his longtime buddy Jackie, as his new partner, who had requested a transfer out of States to join us.

Jackie, he of the near death, pool fiasco, was not someone you would look at and say, "That guy looks like a lifeguard." Not very tall or muscular he didn't have an athletic build, yet was athletic. His upper body was roundish and unintimidating but to take him lightly would be to underestimate him. His Irish good looks were accompanied by the requisite gift of gab. He was aggressive with women and would have had no problem asking Miss America for a date.

Perhaps a little background on Jackie is in order to help the reader more clearly identify with him and understand why he operated on the edge.

Jack's father, Merit owned what was arguably the most popular restaurant in Atlantic City, Bishops Savoy. Formerly a bank, the restaurant opened sometime around the late 1930's to early 40's. It drew all the well known local celebrities of the day. This included the previously mentioned Enoch "Nucky" Johnson, the Boss who ran Atlantic City and who the television series *Boardwalk Empire* was based on.

Atlantic City drew many of the largest conventions in the country. The conventions are what kept the city viable during the long winter months. During times they were in town, conventioneers spent hundreds of thousands of dollars. They were especially enamored of the restaurants and bars. Bishop's Savoy and another restaurant called Jack Guischard's, less than half block away, probably relieved conventioneers of more of their money than any place in town other than the gambling joints.

Jackie and his brothers, Richard and Danny who my brothers and I went to grammar school with, were products of the "too much, too soon" class. All of them were a little wild and found their share of trouble. Nothing serious— just the usual kids pranks—but on a more consistent basis.

They were the only family I knew as a kid who actually had a maid. Her name was—I'm not kidding—Mary Christmas. Mary was more like a part of the family than a maid. She may have had as much to do with raising the kids as either Merit or Josephine, their mother. Mary loved the boys and did what she could but they were spoiled and somewhat out of control. Jackie was the wildest and paid little attention to parental controls.

As Jackie got older, he was rewarded with the usual privileges of the well-to-do. He attended a military school for a time but was not comfortable in that environment. He lived the life of late-model cars, girls, trips to places of interest, parties, etc. He led a life his peers envied, but he took it all in stride.

Much later, his father would relocate the restaurant to the Warwick Hotel in downtown Atlantic City. One summer, Jackie tended bar for his father and because business was good brought me in as a backup. The clientele were sophisticated and we were required to wear madras sports jackets (madras being all the rage then) and ties behind the bar. Jackie never paid attention to Merit who liked to drink with his buddy, movie actor James Barton and seldom drew a sober breath. Jackie sauntered around like he owned the place and in a sense, did.

Once he took the test for the beach patrol it gave him a sense of identity and became his home. The beach patrol took on the role of a mistress and he loved her with all his heart. Unfortunately, he never had the discipline required to stay out of trouble.

Jackie, like Tommy, was a great lifeguard. Ostensibly he never seemed to be watching bathers. He was like a whirling dervish whose motion never stopped. Anyone observing might think him derelict in his duty. To judge him thus, would be a mistake. He was like a hawk and would take it as a personal affront if anyone beat him to a rescue.

Geza, on the other hand, was not intense. He was quick on rescues but it was usually Jackie who spotted them. Jackie could be talking to a girl but he always kept one eye on the bathers. If they were involved in a rescue directly off their beach we would act as their backup. During one of these events we'd be coming from a block away and wouldn't even get close before they had the bather(s) in the boat. They never failed to needle us as they headed to shore. Of course the opposite was true when the rescue was off our beach.

At times, a rescue would take place directly between both stands. This made it a fair race to see who could get to the bather first. Invariably, these wound up in a dead heat. If there was more than one victim we'd divide them between us. If there was only one person, the guard with the more accurate donut throw was the one whose boat the bather was put in.

One relatively quiet day, with not many bathers, we sat enjoying the solitude. There was a nasty offset brewing between Arkansas and Michigan. Neither station was concerned, since bathers were staying grouped in front of both stands away from the danger. But as was often the case a kid who swam out past the break was now making his way back to shore. The gentle current carried him over toward the path of danger. Not realizing he was swimming at an angle he headed right for the churning set.

Tommy and I stood ready to break for the boat. I looked toward Michigan, and, incredulously, Jackie, who was talking to a girl, did not see the impending trouble. As the kid got closer to the set Tommy and I sprang into action. Normally, we would blow run whistles, in short shill bursts, to warn bathers to get out of the way of the boat and oars. On this occasion we waited until we were launched and rowing, so as not to give Jackie a heads-up.

At the sound of our whistles Jackie's head snap around with a look of disbelief. He and Geza ran for the boat but our start was insurmountable. He knew he'd been had. Before they cleared the break we'd snagged the kid and had him securely in the boat. We really rubbed it in, as Jackie would have, had we been on the losing end. "What's the matter with you guys, don't you ever watch the water," was our good natured response.

Jackie did not react in a sportsmanlike manner. He started calling Geza every name he could muster. When they reached shore and were pulling the boat up on the rollers he was still swearing. At one point he put his finger in Geza's face. Geza's body stiffened. That was the signal for Jackie to back off. You didn't want to push Geza too far.

Later he approached our stand to tell us how lucky we were to catch him off-guard. He told us to enjoy our victory, because it wouldn't happen again and we'd better be on our toes. That was one competitive little bastard.

Jackie and I were good friends and he would do anything for those he liked. However, he had a hair-trigger temper and a reputation as a sucker puncher that spared no one. We were having a friendly argument one day about something silly concerning rescues. As things became heated I saw his body tense. My own instincts warned me to be ready to parry an impending blow. Finally, I just said, Jack, if you sucker punch me you'd better make it count, because if you don't I'll come after you with everything I've got. Apparently he thought better of it. I had a good three inches and thirty pounds on him and was no stranger to street fighting. Our friendship grew stronger from that day on.

Much of the time the ocean floor was flat at Michigan, but not so Arkansas. Because of Arkansas's close proximity to the pier the ever-present holes in the ocean's floor made for dangerous conditions. The danger could be compounded by a dry nor'easter, a condition of weather we disliked. As previously discussed, winds would come out of the north with great velocity.

Nor'easters usually bring heavy rains that keep people off the beach. Dry nor'easters are windy, but sunny, and usually suitable beach days. Still, they could be dangerous even for those not in the water. A beachgoers most popular piece of paraphernalia was probably an umbrella, which was not allowed to be raised on extremely windy days. Some of the umbrellas had sharp metal points just above the crown. The wind would send them hurtling down beach at a high rate of speed, capable of inflicting injury to others. We had to take a lot of grief from those who *owned* or *rented* them when we asked for them to be taken down.

It was on such a day, thanks to Jackie, we came to know the "bitches." The force of the wind was causing swift currents to run toward the pier. We were keeping all bathers out of the water at Arkansas, and had joined Jackie and Geza at Michigan. Our main task was to keep everyone far up-wind of the pier, away from the offsets, and in front of the Michigan station. We also did not allow bathers out very far for fear the current would carry them toward the pier.

Everyone was complying with our safety measures, since the danger was obvious. The only problem was these four older heavyset women. They were frolicking in the surf just above their waists, holding hands, playing Ring around the Rosie. Each time they got to the part, "out goes y-o-u," they would dip down raising their feet off the oceans floor. This repeated action quickly carried them, in short spurts, toward the pier before they would regain their footing. An accumulation of these moves could land them in trouble.

They were becoming a constant source of annoyance for Jackie, who decided to make them his responsibility. Whenever they'd dip, he'd blow his whistle motioning for them to stay on their feet. Apparently, they had no idea what his signals meant and just waved and smiled at him. They were having too much fun to give him any serious consideration.

In frustration, he waded out to his knees blowing his whistle and hollering for them to, "Move the hell up." The force of the wind muffled his words. Again, they'd wave and smile as if it was all a big joke. However, without any prompting, they would return to the safety and security of the bathing crowd. Then the process would repeat itself.

When again they started running the rapids he was back in the water. Now he was getting pissed. His whistle-blowing continued but was now punctuated by a new command. He started yelling, "Move up you old bitches." From our vantage point, Tommy and I could hear him and started cringing. Still the women waved and smiled.

Jackie's next move took us totally by surprise. He stopped blowing his whistle and waded out a little further. He reached under water for some ammunition—mud—and started flinging it at them, still cursing them out. We couldn't believe our eyes and dissolved into laughter. When he turned and saw our reaction it spurred him on. Every time he threw mud at them he'd look back at us, laughing gleefully. Their reaction was predictable, they waved and smiled. His whole demeanor changed. Now, with an audience, he was having fun.

When he came out of the water, still laughing, he said, "Hey! Bobby, Tommy did you see those old bitches?" He loved using shock value to break us up.

Eventually the "bitches" came out of the water and headed for their blanket. When they spotted Jackie, what was their reaction? They waved and smiled. It was amazing seeing him constantly get away with such antics. If any of the rest of us attempted this behavior we'd have been brought up on charges. However, as we shall see, his luck eventually ended when he ran afoul of Murph.

Many of the same tourists returned year after year. It was only natural we would develop a relationship with some. Beachgoers would use our stand as a safety deposit box. Before taking a dip, they'd roll their valuables in a towel and drop them at the stand for safekeeping. We were glad to provide this service and most bathers were polite and thoughtful. Our only caveat was that we couldn't be held responsible for their valuables, since rescues occurred at anytime, in which case the stand was left unattended.

Once in a while, we'd get some snob who would deposit his belongings on the stand without as much as a "Do you mind?" He would act like it was our duty to protect his stuff and plop it on the stand without even making eye contact. One of us would promptly kick it to the sand. Indignant, he would question our action. We'd tell him our duty was to the bathers not his valuables. If he wanted to leave his things, fine, but have the courtesy to ask. Surprisingly, with some of these initial offenders, we developed solid friendships.

THE CHANGING WINDS

Lest I give you the impression that all beach days were a conglomerate of nasty weather, a rough ocean and danger, let me assure you they were not. Most days were sunny and warm with a cool ocean breeze. The prevailing winds in Atlantic City come from the south and are referred to as southerlies.

Usually, southerlies started out in the morning as a gentle breeze. Somewhere between noon and 1:00 P.M. wind conditions picked up. By late afternoon these same winds came blowing off the ocean with significant force. This may or may not cause dangerous conditions. They do however, cause a choppy, sloppy ocean that can impede efficiency when performing rescues.

Because the choppy seas came in on a south to north angle it was necessary to keep the bow of the boat pointed into the wind. Still, the boat was rocked by the continuous lapping of seas against the port bow. Rowing was difficult since the constant rocking motion affected the placement of the oars. If the boat was listing to one side, one oar would be deep in the water on the low side, whereas, you'd be pulling air with the oar on the high side. With experience you learned to deal with these conditions.

In the way we were affected by the wind regarding rescue conditions, so were we affected sitting high in the stand. After a couple of hours of having a strong southerly wind blow on you it begins to get chilly. The first item of clothing to go on would be our sweatshirts. As the afternoon progressed sweatpants would be added and finally jackets. We also took turns standing down in the sand where it was sunny and warmer.

Southerly winds made little difference to bathers. If I were to describe what's written above to a beachgoer about one of these days he would think me daft. The way the wind affected us did not in any way affect the beachgoer. For them, the southerly was just a nice cool ocean breeze to be enjoyed as they took a stroll along the beach, or relaxed on blankets in the soft sand. The air temperature was just warm enough to require an occasional dip. The water temperature–a refreshing 70 to 74 degrees–was ideal.

Often, when friends or others stopped to chat, they'd ask, "Why are you wearing all those clothes." We'd tell them they'd know soon enough if we were to exchange places for a couple of hours.

There were three other relevant wind conditions. nor'easters, of which you're already familiar, wet or dry, were by far the most dangerous for bathers. With them came swift currents, big waves and treacherous offsets. Fortunately, they only occurred a few times a summer.

The most hated wind by far was the westerly. It came off the land, bringing an uncomfortable windy, hot, dry heat and very cold ocean. What makes Atlantic City's ocean warm in the summer is the Gulf Stream. It is only about 100 miles off the coast. The prevailing southerly pushes the Gulf Stream's warm water toward the land, bestowing mild temperatures, perfectly compatible with land temperatures. The total opposite was true regarding westerlies.

As if this wasn't enough to put a crimp in your day, westerlies brought little biting flies. These things were faster than jet planes, making them impossible to swat. They competed with their bigger cousins, the dreaded Greenheads. There's a resort just slightly northwest of Atlantic City called Brigantine, where Greenheads call home. These things are almost twice the size of a common house fly, actually have green heads and bite like hell. The only good thing about them is they're slow and easy to swat. During a westerly, you could count on these beach-day blood suckers being blown into Atlantic City, assuring you a miserable experience. Fortunately, westerlies don't occur that often.

One of the most peculiar things about Brigantine, and its Greenheads, is they actually bragged about having them. They even sold T-shirts with Greenhead images. Why any person would be proud to display those flying Dracula's was beyond me.

God may have decided to impart the first three wind conditions upon us just to make life interesting, but he also took pity. The easterly was a wind that came straight off the ocean but should more properly be referred to as a gentle breeze. These days brought exquisite sunshine, warm water, a calm ocean, gentle waves that lapped the shore and no humidity. The entire day remained that way making it a joyful experience.

Ironically, this benign beach and ocean condition would come close to claiming the life of a favorite bather.

BILL, A NEAR DISASTER

During our first summer together Tommy and I met a man named Bill. He was very courteous and likable and appreciated us watching his valuables.

Since his two week vacation was spent alone we watched over his things every day. He soon began bringing us coffee to show his appreciation. He would stay and chat for awhile before going for his daily dip in the ocean. Bill usually smelled of alcohol though never appeared drunk.

Certain individuals are tuned into the ocean and they may or may not be good swimmers. The thing they all have in common is a lack of fear. This is not to suggest they are foolhardy–they're not. It's more like they have an understanding and respect for the ocean, with which they're in harmony. This would describe Bill.

I don't remember ever seeing him swim. He merely turned on his back and floated. That guy could float in any ocean condition, whether it was out past the break, in calm water or in the middle of a churning offset. We were seldom concerned for his safety but always kept an eye on him. He never resisted the nature of the ocean, but as one who uses another's strength against him was how Bill dealt with the sea. Whereas others we described as going for a swim; in Bill's case we'd characterize as going for a float.

His routine was consistent. He came at noon each day alternating his time between lying on his blanket, reading, and going for long ocean floats. He'd leave the beach about 4:00 P.M. and we'd not see him until the next day.

Uncharacteristically, one afternoon after leaving, he returned about 6:00 P.M. We were working the 6:30 shift and the three of us shot the breeze for awhile. As usual he smelled of alcohol. When we asked him why he decided to return he said the weather was so perfect he wanted to extend his day. He dropped his stuff on the stand and headed for the ocean.

At closing, we moved the equipment to the soft sand. The beach still held a smattering of late sun worshipers and a few die-hard ocean goers, including Bill, who floated contentedly in a peaceful sea. The other 6:30 crew was already in the tent when we arrived. We waited for them to take their showers.

Tommy had stepped out on the porch, as he often did, to take a last look around. Suddenly, in a stricken voice, he called my name. Instinctively I knew it was Bill. I grabbed my trunks struggling to pull them on as I stumbled down the porch ramp. Tommy was almost halfway to the surf.

The other guards had donned trunks and raced to help us with the boat. Together we flipped the boat, picked it up, and carried it to the water (It's amazing how fast four guys can carry a 500 pound boat when the adrenalin is flowing). We were launched and rowing in seconds. Heading toward the spot where Bill had last been seen, we looked frantically from side-to-side hoping to see some sign of him. All at once Tommy shouted, "I see him, he's off the stern." We backed the boat to the spot and spied Bill two or three feet below the surface. He was still in a floating position, eerily facing upward in peaceful repose.

Tommy dove from the boat, grabbed Bill and brought him to the surface. We got him in the boat and laid him over the stern while Tommy administered C.P.R. As soon as we reached shore one of the two guards joined us, the other having called for an ambulance. We laid him out on the hard sand and took turns working on him.

All the while we worked on him he kept throwing up sea water. Finally, after what seemed an eternity, he began gasping, moaning and thrashing about. The hospital, only a block away made the ambulance very accessible and able to get there in no time. The medics lifted Bill onto a stretcher as we all lent a hand carrying him to the ambulance. As they drove away Tommy and I looked at each other. We shared the same thought. Was this the last we'd seen of our friend?

We called the hospital the following day and were told that Bill was in critical condition. This came as no surprise. We were more surprised to hear he was still alive.

For the next few days Tommy and I kept reliving the events of that day, wondering what went wrong. The ocean was like a lake. Why had Bill just slipped beneath the surface? We discussed how thankful we were about the condition of the ocean that day. If it hadn't been so calm and crystal clear, we'd never have seen him.

Three days after the incident Murph called the hospital to get an update on Bill's condition. The report on Bill was that he was still in serious condition but expected to make a full recovery. We were relieved and felt like a weight had been removed. The memory of the incident gradually faded.

About ten days later Tommy and I were shooting the breeze, when suddenly, like an apparition, Bill appeared before us. We both jumped from the stand and pumped his hand. We expressed our feelings about his recovery and how good it was to see him. Becoming emotional Bill thanked us for getting to him on time. He said the doctors told him if we hadn't worked on him in the boat he wouldn't be talking to us now.

When things settled down he went to his towel and came back with a package and a couple of sandwiches. Inside the package was a beautifully crafted seashore design mounted on a laminated wood background. For a border he'd used a length of rope braided in various nautical patterns. Other decorations included paintings of colorful seashells and soaring seagulls. He had painted a lifeguard boat with the #5, and a lifeguard stand with our street name, "Arkansas Ave." At the bottom he had inscribed the names, "Bob and Tommy."

Bill had crafted the seascape while recuperating in the hospital. He had taken up the hobby of artistic wood-working while in the Navy. He told us he had many others at home in Philadelphia, that he either sold or gave to friends. Of all the gifts we received, that was the one we treasured most.

After exchanging small talk we got around to asking what he remembered of that day. He admitted he'd had a few too many "pops." Because the day had been so perfect he'd decided to prolong it by coming back to the beach. He said he loved being out by himself in a semi-deserted ocean. There was nothing different about taking his float that day, except, he was experiencing a profound sense of peace and euphoria. He told us a strange sensation overtook him as his body slipped beneath the surface. He knew he was drowning but could clearly see the sun as through a prism. Any fear of drowning dissipated as he awaited his final moment. He said he wanted nothing to interfere with his reverie. The next thing he remembered was awakening in the hospital with tubes running down his throat.

The experience did not keep him out of the water. Each day he came to the beach he repeated the same mantra, "I'm living on borrowed time, thanks to you guys." He felt he'd experienced death, and now had no fear of it. We saw him for several summers after that and then he stopped coming. We never knew if he passed away, but if so, we felt sure it was without fear.

SHIFTING STANDS

There were some shakeups along our stretch that summer but not for disciplinary reasons. Murph gave us a choice of which station we preferred to work.

Geza and Jackie wanted out of Michigan, away from Murph's microscopic eye. They didn't enjoy being in front of the tent where they were easily scrutinized. Tommy and I were ready to leave Arkansas. For all its excitement there was an eeriness involved in being next to a pier. As afternoon wore on shadows from the pier crept toward our stand creating a foreboding sense of darkness.

Since I had seniority among the guys in our stretch, I requested, and was given Michigan, of which Tommy approved. Recently, rescues had increased at Michigan due to newly formed holes being carved out in the ocean's floor. This phenomenon developed during the winter owing to fierce winter storm conditions. Not only would the number of rescues increase, but we would now be responsible for backing up Arkansas and Ohio on either side.

Two young but capable guards named Roy and Chuck took over Ohio Avenue. A guy named Basil and another guard whose name escapes me, opted for Arkansas.

Geza and Jackie, to my surprise, chose Indiana, the farthest stand from the tent. The reason for my surprise was that Indiana Avenue was largely inhabited by a homosexual crowd and had been that way as long as I could remember. *And,* of the four beaches composing our stretch, Indiana had far-fewer rescues than the others. Therefore, I was perplexed as to their reason(s) for choosing it. Later we came to realize it was some sort of a rebellious move. What they were rebelling against I never did find out.

Indiana Avenue, at this time, was referred to as "Queer Beach." The term "gay," as we think of it today, was still more than a decade removed from its present usage. Gay, as we knew it then was still thought of in its literal sense, happy or excited. For our purposes here, and to not offend, we'll use the current term "gay," or sometimes, "the boys."

We were friendly with some of the gays from Indiana who loved to take strolls along the beach. They would stop at our stand and flirt with us. At first we were uncomfortable since we didn't know how to react to their overtures. Once we realized they were only trying to get a rise out of us (no pun intended), we relaxed and parried them as we would an unwanted female. After a while the flirting ended and conversation became more natural.

From our perspective it seemed to Tommy and I that Geza and Jackie were making a big mistake. Jackie, as we've seen, had an unstable volatile personality. Additionally, Indiana had very few rescues and Jackie without rescues was like a boat without an ocean. It didn't take much to set him off.

In no time, the two guards became friendly with many of their gay beachgoers. Jokingly, Geza even took on their mannerisms. It got to the point when girls from our high school stopped by his stand, he would fool around and talk with a lisp. After a while the word went out that Geza had turned gay. Keep in mind this guy was a standout fullback, who would run through a wall, and, had garnered many athletic awards. He didn't care what others said. He was having fun while the gossipers were turning apoplectic.

Geza and Jackie brought their friendliness with the gays to new heights. They required them to check in at the stand, write their names, and state how long they'd be in the ocean, silly stuff. The boys loved it. They would gather around the stand carrying on with the two guards and causing a distraction. Guard's who'd worked the station previously had been respectful of the boy's, but had kept their distance. Geza and Jackie encouraged the continuous gay fun and frivolity.

The first signs of trouble surfaced when the boys would pretend they were drowning. They wanted to continue their little antics while frolicking in the ocean to get the guards attention. Geza and Jackie knew they were faking but bathers around them didn't. Some of the bathers thought the guards were ignoring the boy's pleas for help.

These shenanigans did not take long to reach Murph. He had a talk with them and issued a stern warning to cut it out. Things pretty much calmed down and returned to normal after that–or so we thought.

There was a luncheonette under the boardwalk at Indiana Avenue, called Bessie's.

It was located directly behind Jack and Geza's stand, a distance of about sixty yards. Bessie sold sodas, hot dogs, hamburgers, chips, etc. The place had some tables and chairs for those who preferred to eat there and was a popular hangout, especially among the boys.

Bessie was an attractive, friendly, energetic lady, short of stature and big of heart. She loved the boys and they loved her. Consequently, it was not unusual to find a crowd there at any given time of the day. The store was also convenient for lifeguards stationed nearby. They could run for coffee or send their mascots. Bessie's little under-the- boardwalk eatery did a brisk business.

Bessie and Jackie were very friendly since Bessie operated the coat check concession at Jackie's father's restaurant, Bishop's Savoy, during the winter months. He would often patronize Bessie's place and she always made a big fuss over him. He and the boys would kid around, and some would out-wardly flirt in an aggressive manner. Jackie wasn't fond of them getting too familiar but tolerated it for Bessie's sake.

Jackie had fallen head over heels for a girl named Gerry that summer. Generally, he never got very involved but Gerry was different. She was inde-pendent and had stated goals for herself that didn't necessarily include Jackie. Another surprising thing about Gerry, she was a local girl. Though we dated local girls in the winter, shamefully, we acted as though they didn't exist come the first signs of summer. There were just too many new girls to choose from. And for the most part no involvement was required.

Whereas other local girls, feeling shunned, did a slow burn, Gerry couldn't have cared less. She was very attractive and had a certain sophistica-tion that made her interesting to men. Jackie liked this kind of women.

Once, after a heated argument fueled by his jealousy, Gerry wouldn't speak to him. Jackie felt I had a pretty good way with the written word so he asked me to write a poem he could give to her. In a Cyrano de Bergerac moment I jokingly wrote a really sappy love poem. I wasn't surprised that he loved it since he was not hard to please. Sadistically, I wanted to see her reac-tion, believing she'd think it corny and laugh at him. Incredulously, when he gave it to her she was just as impressed. Gerry got all warm and fuzzy, thinking she was seeing a new side of Jackie.

Jackie would ask Gerry for a date and she'd agree to go out. Then some-times, she'd call at the last minute and break the date. Or she'd tell him she was coming to see him at the beach and not show. These occurrences would send him into a rage and beware if you were in close proximity.

One day he came to work and right away we all knew there had been some kind of blowup. He was angry as hell and in a very foul mood. I asked him what happened. He said he'd found out Gerry was dating another guy (who, incidentally, was the guy she eventually married). My first thought was, Uh oh, I hope nothing sets him off. That was wishful thinking on my part.

Sometime during the course of the morning Jackie went to Bessie's for coffee. Some of the boys were there and started in with their usual flirtatious chatter. Jackie told them he was in "no mood to listen to their "shit." One of the boys who did not read his mood persisted. He went over to Jackie and said, "Oooh Jackie, what's the matter precious are we not feeling well today?" Jackie flushed, his body coiled, as he turned to the boy and said, "Get away from me faggot!" Still not tuned in and misreading the situation, the boy reached out his hand to soothe Jack. In an instant Jackie unleashed a punch knocking the hapless boy ass-over-tin-cups, where he sprawled on the floor.

Bessie came unglued. She verbally attacked Jackie denouncing him for hitting a defenseless customer in her store. She said, "Wait until I see your father, you're going to regret this." Unfortunately, that was an idle threat since Jackie never paid any attention to his father.

Murph was a different matter. When he heard about the incident he made a few calls, then went immediately to Indiana and told Jackie to pack his gear at day's end. Murph had him exiled back to States. I was sorry to see Jackie go, notwithstanding the foregoing incident. He always kept things exciting. He and Murph remained best of friends over the years, but he would never again work with us.

WATCHING ALL THE GIRLS GO BY

Earlier I spoke about beachgoers who would pass ten stations until they got to ours and then stop. At the very least they could be described as characters, but a stronger case could be made for these personalities.

To illustrate, one morning Tommy and I were having coffee. Usually we had the luxury of spotting characters from a distance; not so on this occasion. Like an apparition out of the mist a woman suddenly appeared from behind our stand. From her appearance she looked like she came from money. She was about 35, quite attractive, nice figure and sporting an expensive looking bathing suit. Oh, and she wore sunglasses—with only one lens.

We didn't know what to expect. We both got a little uncomfortable when she just stood there staring at us with one exposed eye. We tried to ignore her hoping she'd go away. No such luck. Then we asked if there was something we could do for her. She didn't respond and just kept staring. She gave us no choice so we just continued to ignore her.

A few minutes later a couple of good-looking girls passed by. Following the tradition of all lifeguards we gave them the once-over. Just as they got by our stand the one-lens-eyeglass-lady started marching in front of us, singing, "Standing on the Corner Watching All the Girls Go By." She didn't do it just once but kept up a constant drumbeat, parading back and forth in front of us. Strollers taking in the scene looked first at her, then at us, with strange expressions.

This continued, even though, when girls passed we'd ignore them lest she break into song again. Our strategy didn't work. Whenever she saw girls coming our way she'd join them before they got to the stand. Some of the girls tried to avoid her but she wasn't discouraged. When she got alongside the girls she'd link arms with them and once again start singing, "Standing on the Corner...," The girls giggled and hurried on.

When no girls were forthcoming she'd walk about twenty yards away, turn, face us, put her right hand behind her head and left hand on her hip like a Vegas Showgirl. With all the sexy gyrations she could muster, swaying from side-to-side, one eye exposed, she'd come vamping toward us. We were trying not to laugh to show the poor woman respect but this was too comical and we lost it. Seeing our reaction just encouraged her and she continued.

By now she was attracting people on the beach. I figured we'd better get Murph, and sent a mascot to fetch him. He came down, approached the woman, and asked where she was staying. At first she just stared, as she'd done with us. Finally, he was able to determine that she was staying at the Shelburne Hotel, which lay directly behind us and fronted the boardwalk. He told us to keep an eye on her and went back to the tent.

A short time later two official looking gentlemen came down from the Shelburne. They spoke gently and were able to escort the lady to the hotel. Tommy and I breathed a sigh of relief.

Sometime around 2:00 P.M., I was standing down by the boat watching the bathers when I felt a tap on the shoulder. I turned to see that our songstress had returned, minus the glasses. I quickly got back up on the stand. Tommy said with a groan, "Oh no." At least she didn't start singing this time and mercifully just walked to the water's edge.

All at once she sauntered over to the boat picked up two oars crossed them in front of her and posed, like she was modeling for some nautical magazine. Now there are certain no no's one can get away with on the beach, but fooling with the boat equipment is not one of them. We never knew when a rescue might be imminent so it was imperative our gear be in its proper place at all times.

I went over and told her she couldn't play with the oars. Surprisingly, she didn't resist when I took them. However, she wasn't easily dissuaded. No sooner had I returned to the stand when Tommy said, "Check this out." I turned to see her with the donut (life preserver), trying to pull it over her head. When she realized the donut hole was too small to accomplish this feat she imagined herself looking through a porthole. Changing facial expressions she posed as if modeling for a glamour magazine. We had to admire her ingenuity.

Once again curious onlookers started gathering, as others, strolling the beach, paused in their sojourn to observe this curiosity. We didn't need this kind of attention and contacted Murph, who contacted the hotel. The same two men came once more and escorted her back to the Shelburne.

Murph only received scant information on the woman. There was talk of problems with her husband in New York and she had come to Atlantic City to get away from him. Apparently, somewhere along the way she'd had a breakdown. The word was that on her second return to the hotel she tried to commit suicide by jumping out of a window. None of this was ever confirmed and we heard nothing further.

THE DROWNING

I have wrestled with myself, trying to decide whether to include this section as part of the book. If I've ever talked to anyone about it other than Tommy (with whom it was experienced), I have no recollection. It is a subject I have held inside for close to 50 years. Since my brother Mick is very familiar with just about all the stories recorded here, I decided to test his memory on the one I'm about to relate. From the quizzical look on his face as I relived these events I knew it was unfamiliar to him. This reinforces my belief that, except for Tommy, or others involved, I have never spoken to anyone else about the following.

During my lifeguard years covering the 50's and 60's, Atlantic City's beaches drew hundreds of thousands of tourists every summer. Captains from each of the nine beach patrol stations called headquarters at South Carolina every day to report estimated crowds, number of rescues, lost children recovered and deaths by drowning if any.

Of the vast number of people who enjoyed the ocean each summer the number of deaths by drowning were almost non-existent, almost—but not quite. The Atlantic City Beach Patrol recorded about five-thousand rescues each summer, and averaged one drowning a year. Even though our record has been lauded as a noble achievement, one drowning, to myself and my proud beach patrol brothers, was one too many. This was especially true for those of us who experienced this painful misfortune.

Throughout the course of this book I have spoken of gullies (holes in the ocean's floor) and their potential for danger. When conditions are right the ebb and flow of tides can have a profound affect as to the degree of this danger. For example, conditions sometimes create perilous offsets in gullies, making these areas extremely dangerous to all bathers, but especially children.

Where these circumstances existed we were on high alert. We tried to keep bathers away from those danger areas without interfering with their overall pleasure. Sometimes due to circumstances beyond our control, bathers would find themselves swept into an offset. Because we were able to anticipate these circumstances, we would have launched the boat and been on our way. At times we were asked by either the victim or an onlooker how we knew they were in trouble. Because of the complexity involved in explaining how we could do this, we'd just say it was because of our training, which was true.

At other times gullies could be completely benign. There were days when things were so calm gullies presented no danger, or at least no anticipated danger. In an earlier chapter I spoke of how, at low tide, a gullies depth might be around waist-high for kids of a certain age. Beyond the gully was the sandbar. After fording what the kids perceived as a real test of bravery they'd reach the bar and climb to a level that was barely above their ankles. It was fun to watch them turn, and in a moment of triumph, wave to someone on the beach.

One of the reasons sandbars were appealing to kids, was because there were waves out on the bar. Waves don't continue once they reach a gully. The reason for this is that waves require a flat ocean floor to sustain movement. As soon as a wave moves from a flat ocean floor to a gully, it dissipates due to water displacement. This is where a smaller volume of water pours into a larger volume of water which just absorbs it.

Naturally, as soon as the first kid reached the bar every little *Magellan* on the beach had to follow suit. It was not long before the sandbar, filled with rollicking happy kids, saw the tide turn and start rising.

I am of the opinion, from observation, that all humans have built in body barometers. As the tide started making, the sandbar would get deeper. The kid's human barometers would instinctively alert them that since the sandbar was getting deeper the gully must be getting deeper. Seldom was it necessary to whistle kids, or adults, off the sandbar. Consequently, with the rising tide, you'd see an exodus of bodies heading for the beach.

As I've already stated the gullies were calm but deep by now, in some cases over a kids head. However even a nominal swimmer or wader usually had no problem making it to shore.

Tommy and I had been watching the kids as they journeyed to the bar. After observing for a few hours, we were familiar with all of them and aware of their swimming skills. This is not to say we knew all of them thoroughly, but we did have a good working knowledge of their positions and where to look for them.

There was a threesome we had observed, a girl of about 14 who had taken two smaller kids, a boy and girl, ages five or six, out to the sandbar.

The older girl was a good swimmer and had held the kids' hands on the way out.

Upon their return the water would be well over the smaller kid's heads and slightly over hers.

At some point, I had occasion to make a visit to the tent for a pit stop. I was there less than five minutes when I headed back to my station. The bar was still packed with bathers but others were making their way in. Just as I got to the stand I reached for the upper railing, put my foot on the brace and swung up in a motion similar to mounting a horse. In the instant of making that turn my eyes scanned the ocean. I saw the girl step off the bar into the gully. As soon as I was facing the ocean I looked for three kids but only saw the two girls. My heart skipped a beat. I waited a second for some reaction but none came. She appeared calm as she helped the little girl in. At that moment I doubted my eyes and thought maybe I'd had an illusion. I quickly asked Tommy if he saw the kids. He knew the kids I meant but had been watching another set of bathers cross the gully.

Our faces said it all as we dashed for the boat and launched. We searched the spot the girl had stepped off–nothing. In a near panic we raced back to the beach. By this time other crews were alerted. Not seeing the normal type of rescue activity, or knowing what to look for, they were confused

We approached the fourteen year old, who still had the little girl with her and asked if she hadn't also had a boy. At this point she started sobbing uncontrollable. That was enough. We raced for the boat again and went back to the spot where Tommy dove out and started feeling his way along the bottom. Soon other guards joined us. We hunted for the boy for what seemed an eternity with no success.

By the time we got back to shore the kids' mother was there. She was wailing in an unearthly manner, "My baby, my baby," a plea that almost ripped our hearts out. Murph ran to the tent to call the Coast Guard. As soon as I was able I asked the girl, who we found out was the baby sitter, why she hadn't made some response. It turned out the poor kid was so scared she just blanked out and lapsed into a state of denial.

All of this occurred about 1:30 P.M. Three hours later the boys' body washed up on the other side of Million Dollar Pier.

Tommy and I sat in stunned silence the rest of the day.

In the following days I tried to act somewhat normal, while Tommy, outwardly, was having trouble coming to grips with this tragedy. I know we both experienced some sleepless nights. All the guys in the tent were extremely supportive. It took both of us time to erase the events of that day, especially our memory of the mother's anguish.

LAYOUT

Layout, discussed briefly in an earlier chapter was not a part of the job most guards enjoyed. Layout by guards was mandatory each day between the hours of 2:00 to 4:00 P.M. These were considered peak bathing hours (which they really weren't). In order for layout to be cancelled, headquarters would have needed proof of an impending tsunami. Not really–that's an exaggeration but the ocean would have to be very rough.

At least, we only had to layout one of the two hours. Stations alternated times. Half of the stretch went on layout from 2:00-3:00 P.M., the other half from 3:00-4:00 P.M. I had a running debate with Murph, saying headquarters should leave the decision up to each captain whether layout was necessary. After all, who knew their stretch better than the captain's who commanded them. Those words fell on deaf ears.

I found layout on most days to be boring, and thus, a pain in the ass. There were days when it was enjoyable but not often. Usually, by this time of day the wind was kicking up at a good pace and you had to keep the boat under control in the slop and chop.

On days the ocean was calm, and with big waves, we loved to use the boat as a springboard for catching waves. The bow man would handle the boat and wait for the right wave to come along. When that happened, the stern man, with one foot on the stern-sheet, waited for the wave to lift the bow. As the wave moved toward the stern it would propel the diver with tremendous lift. With just the right timing, the diver would land on top of the unbroken wave, take a few strokes, and ride that baby all the way to shore. Tommy and I would alternate this fun activity on those special days.

Salt water taffy is an Atlantic City staple. When you have no gift to give, give the gift of cavities–salt water taffy. That could have been our slogan. Not that it was unappreciated, but over the years Tommy and I received so many boxes of salt water taffy as gifts we just gave it away, or found some other creative use for it.

Our favorite thing to do with the taffy was to take it on layout and throw it to our bathers–one piece at a time. Tommy would stand up in the boat and holler to a bather, "Here catch." In no time, a crowd of bathers would gather behind the boat all waiting for Tommy to throw the next piece. He would hesitate letting the anticipation build.

Each time he'd throw a piece the crowd would jump all over each other practically killing themselves to get at it. You'd think we were throwing gold coin. I was always reminded of the ships that pull into Hawaii, where the natives swim out and wait for the tourists to throw money.

One beautiful balmy day we were on layout and the ocean was unusually crowded. Everyone was having a good time frolicking about while Tommy and I were dying of boredom. We had been out for half an hour, when, without a word, Tommy stood up, grabbed an oar, and started jabbing frantically at something, or so I thought. The bathers around us were in chest-deep water. Many others were out further swimming in the calm ocean.

One quizzical bather, watching Tommy jab his oar asked what he was doing. Tommy in a noncommittal manner replied: "Nothing." The guy was having none of it and asked, "Its shahks ain't it?" (Time Magazine had just put out a feature article warning of an increase in shark attacks). Again Tommy said "No" and kept jabbing away.

Suddenly, the guy cupped his hands over his mouth and in a booming voice, hollered to his son who was farther out, "Hey Billy, ged outta da wahta, dere's shahks. Well, talk about the Red Sea opening, followed by a mass exodus, I never saw people get out of an ocean so quickly. Normally, ordinary swimmers, who weren't very fast, could have competed in the Olympics that day. Others were half swimming, half chugging, not knowing which to settle on. It seemed only seconds and our entire stretch of ocean was completely empty.

The formerly happy bathers all stood on the beach waiting for us to come ashore. Finally, with layout over, we rowed in, secured the boat on the rollers and strolled casually to our stand, like the crowd wasn't there. We sat on the stand talking, as if nothing had happened, purposely ignoring them. Strangely no one in the crowd said anything or asked any questions. I guess they were waiting for us to say something or give them the all clear sign. We didn't.

Eventually, the originator of this group panic attack decided we'd been screwing around. He announced to the crowd, "Dere ain't no shahks." Slowly walking away, muttering to themselves, they drifted back into the ocean. Tommy turned to me and said, "What did I say?" My answer: nothing!

JIMMY THE THIRD

Murph announced one morning that we were getting a third man. Our first thought was, we hoped he'd be compatible. Our second thought was, now we only had to go on layout a half-hour each day.

Third men are selected from rookies who have passed the test. Stations already have their full complement of two-to-a-stand so these guards are extras and become third men. They're usually placed in a stretch that experiences a high volume of rescues. As mentioned earlier, Michigan had undergone dramatic changes to its ocean floor over the winter. Since we had a significant increase in rescues, and Arkansas always had the potential for danger, we were given a third man.

The purpose of a third man, or can man, is to back up boat crews on rescues. They follow the boat swimming with a can buoy in tow. If a boat gets swamped before reaching its victim(s) the can man is expected to stabilize the situation until more help arrives. This can subject a swimmer to perilous situations. We learned about this in an earlier chapter concerning Murph's tragic outcome with a bather.

However, like Ivory Soap, about ninety-nine and forty-four one-hundredths percent of the time the boat would reach the bather much before the swimmer. Serving in this capacity was an excellent training-ground for the third man. He learned to recognize danger areas and witness what happened to a swimmer when he got caught in a treacherous offset.

Ironically our third man turned out to be my friend Jack's kid brother. His name was Hector James after his father. Jimmy was about 17 when he joined us. He was of medium height and maybe 135 pounds soaking wet. He looked younger than his 17 years, had a baby face with freckles, an infectious smile and bright blue eyes. We liked him immediately.

Though Jimmy was not naïve, being new, he was somewhat shocked by some of our shenanigans. For example, sometimes when the ocean was in a foul mood and rescues heavy, instead of going to the tent to relieve ourselves, we'd pee in a bottle. We executed this feat by putting our jacket over our lap and firing away. I guess because of its grossness, Jimmy's face would turn red and he'd laugh like a little kid. He'd walk away from the stand, shaking his head, asking himself how he'd gotten stationed with these two cretins.

Sometimes while we were in the act of relieving ourselves someone would come to the stand. They never realized what we were doing. If they thought at all about why we had a jacket over our lap they probably surmised we were protecting sunburned legs. We'd put the bottle with its contents on the floor of the stand. Invariably when girls came by they'd ask what was in the bottle. We'd tell them it was pineapple juice, and ask if they'd care for some. They were always suspicious enough not to accept. This was too much for Jimmy and he'd scurry for cover.

Another antic that took Jimmy by surprise: Million Dollar Pier had a huge Coppertone sign high above the pier. You know the one, with the dog pulling down the little girl's bathing suit. Attached to the sign was a huge clock directly in line with a tourist's vision as they strolled down the beach toward us. Still, they'd walked ten blocks in the direction of the clock then stop and ask us what time it was. As soon as they asked, we would slowly rise from our seat to the edge of the stand. In painfully exaggerated gestures we'd turn our heads upward and look ever-so-slowly toward the clock. The stroller would just as slowly mirror our movement until his eyes became one with the clock, and the absurdity of the moment struck him. Then, even more ridiculously, he'd say, "OH!!!! I DIDN'T SEE THAT!" The first time we went into our act Jimmy broke up right in front of the person while unwittingly embarrassing himself.

It didn't take long until Jimmy was as jaded as we were and came up with his own creative pranks.

Though Jimmy seldom went on boat rescues, he got plenty of experience rowing. Each of us spent half-hour a day with him on layout. We would row parallel to the beach for a block up and back. We taught him to row in rhythm, how to feather his oars (bending the wrists upward placing the blades in a horizontal position so they skipped over the water). He was a quick study and in short time became a good oarsman.

For as slight as he was Jimmy was fearless and had a quick temper. Woe to the bully who tested his manhood. He wasn't afraid to go up against somebody twice his size.

We later found out how tough he was when he won the University of Miami welterweight boxing championship. Like his brothers, Jack and Tommy before him, he also graduated from Miami.

Jimmy was a guy who found his life's partner at an early age. Her name was Pia, short for Olympia. She was diminutive and quite attractive with dark hair and eyes and the olive skin of a Mediterranean. She was every bit his equal in temperament and could give as-good-as she got. Those two were meant for marriage and it didn't take long for that to happen. So except for his preference for married life, as opposed to us, who embraced bachelorhood, we welcomed him as a brother.

CHAPTER 8

THE BROTHERHOOD

The next two semesters at the University went by quickly. Norm and I found a decent house a few miles from campus and his friend, Dave joined us. During the year we would take in roommates to share the expense. Most of these guys were interesting characters and fit right in with our life-style. One guy was so broke he would go to a stream nearby and fish for his supper. He'd catch sunfish so small that by the time he prepared them there was practically nothing left to eat.

I resumed my position as Advertising Manager of The Miami Hurricane newspaper. Since my major was Marketing and Advertising I was gaining valuable experience in the field. I laid out the paper, created and sold advertising, wrote copy and worked with the printer. I even modeled for some of the retail clothing stores who advertised with us.

As soon as the school year ended I made the long trip home and was back on the beach in a matter of days. Tommy had also finished school and we resumed our duties at Michigan Avenue.

HIS "FODDERS" SON

Murph's son Steve was older now and came to the beach every day with his "fodder." In the ensuing years Steve would grow into a good-looking, well-built 6'1" specimen and follow in Murph's footsteps, carving out his own lifeguard career. For much of his early adolescence he was just a thorn in everyone's side.

Even though Murph and Jeanne spoiled Steve, somewhat, they were both disciplinarians and didn't allow him get away with too much. No matter how you tried to win him over he was always resistant to acts of kindness.

One of his more annoying habits was whining and he'd cry at the drop of a hat. Witnessing this on a daily basis earned him the nickname, "Meyer the Cryer."

Toys were always a big part of his arsenal. He brought an assortment of cars, trucks, soldiers, rubber animals, etc. to the beach every day. Mercifully the toys kept him occupied much of the time, so we didn't have to deal with him on a regular basis.

During times when he did come to our stand, it was usually to bring a message from his father "My fodder says you have to work until 6:30." This meant an hour of over time because the beach was so crowded. He could never leave without some annoying pronouncement, for example, "My fodders taking me to Steel Pier tonight and you can't come." We'd respond saying, "That's great Meyer have fun." "I'm going to tell my fodder you called me Meyer," he'd say." Our rejoinder would be, "Go ahead and have a good cry while you're at it." Back to the tent he'd go–screaming his ass off.

It wouldn't take long for Murph to appear. He'd chew our asses out, telling us to knock it off, with a reminder that we were supposed to be the adults. Steve would hide behind him with a smug look thinking he'd scored a coup. But Murph would turn to him and say, "If you come crying to me again, I'll really give you something to cry about."

Million Dollar pier was still a popular attraction for kids. However, it had changed dramatically from what I had experienced during my adolescent years. The new version was more honky-tonk. The movie theatre was gone, as were all the great rides. In their place were booths with the same tired games you'd see at any carnival event. Still, it was a fun place for an impressionable kid to spend his time.

Consequently, Steve, much to our satisfaction, spent considerable time at the pier.

JOE R, NEVER A DULL MOMENT

As with the previous summer changes occurred in our stretch and we were greeted by new faces. Jimmy was still there but now had been given his own station at Arkansas. Two new guys, Bill and Teddy, manned Indiana, where

Jackie and Geza had been. Roy, whose partner had left, was still at Ohio. He was joined by a seasoned veteran and well known character, one Joe R., who I mentioned earlier.

Joe R earlier worked Connecticut Avenue with Joe M who you'll recall had transferred to our stretch. Their station was next to a dangerous rock jetty where rescues were common and could be extremely dangerous. The two Joes were working out of the New Hampshire tent at the time. The captain in charge, along with his wife, might generously be described as boozers. She came to work with him every day and constantly stuck her nose in beach patrol business. She was also a gross individual and not at all liked by the crew. As indelicate as some of my stories may be in this book, they would pale in comparison to ones I could tell you about the captain and his wife. Suffice it to say, as difficult as it was for us to be shocked by anything; in their case, they succeeded smashingly. Consequently, the crew was always looking for ways to make life miserable for them. Additionally, some of the guards were real hellions and having the captain and his wife to feed off managed to produce, at least, an antic du jour. Some of these little capers were of the no-nonsense variety and as culpable as Joe R was, he smartly decided that staying around could land him in serious trouble. He was also overdue for a change.

As in my case, Joe knew of Murph but had never met him even though they had not worked far from each other when Murph was stationed at States. Though I didn't know Joe at the time I would come to recognize him as one of the most unique lifeguards of my time. He would also become a lifelong friend.

Joe was slightly older than me. He was of average height, good looking, had a powerful stocky build and had played football in both high school and college. You'd be hard pressed to meet someone more laid back than Joe. He taught school in Delaware during the winter. For an educated guy he was the worst speller I've ever known, though a very competent writer. Being a teacher you'd think having a spelling problem would be cause for embarrassment and serve as a handicap. Not so in Joe's case. If he didn't know how to spell a word, which was often, with no embarrassment he would ask his students. Because of his candor and likeability they thought nothing of it.

Joe at first seemed like a model of decorum. He was particularly friendly and courteous and didn't usually instigate pranks, unless forced or cajoled into it. But when he did they were beauties. Steve, because of his annoying habits, would manage to come to Joe's attention.

When Steve brought his collection of toys he often made us the subject of his irritation. Playing with a monster toy he'd stick it in your face and affect a low growl. He didn't just put it near you, but rather about an inch from your face waving it back and forth. He aggravated Joe a few times too many and inadvertently put himself at the top of Joe's shit list.

One day he brought his collection of rubber Arachnids, including scorpions, spiders, mites and ticks–such a lovely child–and proceeded waving them in our faces. The scorpion was his favorite as Joe was becoming painfully aware. He kept putting it to Joe's face and growling (Do scorpion's growl?).

Steve, at some point, one day, must have gotten on Murph's nerves. Murph was only too glad to grant Steve's request to let him go to the pier. He gave Steve strict orders to be back before 5:30 P.M. Murph was a guy who followed a set schedule everyday because it had to be coordinated with Jeanne's. So as he was always early to work in the morning, he was always prompt in leaving the tent each evening at 5:30. Unfortunately Steve hadn't seen fit to cooperate this day and was nowhere to be seen at 5:30.

To make matters worse, Murph and Jeanne were meeting friends for dinner. As the hour grew late Steve came up M.I.A. By now, Murph's patience had grown thinner and he paced the tent while we looked on nervously.

He asked one of the rookie guards to go and fetch Steve. Apparently, on the way back to the tent, the guard told Steve he was in deep shit and his father was really pissed off.

Afraid of what awaited him, Steve was wailing like a banshee when he arrived at the tent. Murph was trying to control himself. He told Steve to gather his toys and be damned quick about it. As soon as they were ready Murph hurriedly shooed Steve, who was still crying, out the back door.

Meanwhile there were four of us working the 6:30 P.M. shift including Tommy, Roy, Joe and myself. We had just closed our stations and were sitting on the porch shooting the breeze. We had observed Murph becoming more agitated and were glad when he retrieved Steve and left. But things weren't over yet.

Joe discovered Steve's beloved scorpion had been inadvertently left behind. Joe, who just couldn't help himself, saw his opportunity to have some fun—and extract a little revenge.

He went to his locker where he kept an impressive array of tools and returned with hammer and nails. He picked up the scorpion like it was his mortal enemy and nailed it to one of the railings that ran parallel to the ramp leading to the beach.

Joe was not content to drive one nail into the dreaded scorpion's rubber midsection. Like a crazed man, he drove several nails, burying them deep into the scorpion's body. At that moment we heard Steve's familiar piercing howl coming closer. He had discovered his missing treasure. We braced ourselves.

As the door swung open we heard Murph telling Steve he'd better make it fast if he knew what was good for him.

When Steve got to the porch, he looked around for his scorpion. We sat with angelic expressions—pictures of innocence. Quickly, and with a look of triumphant relief, he spotted his trophy on the railing and rushed to retrieve it. He was in such a hurry, that as he grabbed for it he was already turning to rejoin Murph. His hand came away empty as a look of shock crossed his face. He made a few more futile stabs before he realized the scorpion and railing were now wedded. Though we thought we had heard the best (or worst) of his laments, we were unprepared for the volume of decibels he now emitted.

Murph, who again, had started toward the boardwalk, thinking Steve was right behind, came scurrying back. By the time he reached the tent he was fully enraged. He knew we were responsible for whatever sent Steve into orbit, as Steve pointed out the scorpion's embedded corpse.

We hurried for the locker room to take a shower and get the hell out of there. Instead we got a different kind of shower—the one Murph rained down on us as he delivered a stream of expletives. Hurtfully, one of his curses alluded to our association with our mothers, while another suggested illegitimacy. But the word that hurt most was the one with the regressive K's, questioning our sexual preferences.

Murph told Steve to "Forget the scorpion, we'll get it tomorrow." He let us know we now resided in his major shit house and we'd better be careful from here on. He gave me an especially malevolent stare. Up until now I had been the instigator of several pranks, so it was automatically assumed that I was the culprit.

LADY FINDS A TREASURE

Joe's partner, Roy, didn't know what to make of Joe. Roy's father Gene had been a lifeguard and retired as captain. Gene had a reputation as a serious guy and I seldom knew him to smile or laugh. I came on at the tail-end of Gene's career and only knew him slightly.

Roy was short in stature and had a sturdy compact build. He, like Jimmy, had piercing bright blue eyes. He always wore his hair in a crew cut style. Roy reminded me of a small, cuddly, teddy bear. Like his father he was usually serious, but, unlike his father he had a lighter side and liked to laugh. Joe would provide many.

Roy was shy around girls whereas Joe was just the opposite. Joe was extremely candid and had no compunctions about discussing any subject. If he had something on his mind he just came out with it. For example, when girls stopped by the stand he would immediately win them over with his soft-spoken manner. He always made them feel he was a trusted ally they could depend on. If they told him they'd recently broken up with a boyfriend, he would, in the most genteel manner ask how they were being sexually gratified. He had won them over so completely they would actually tell him.

This was way too much for Roy. Embarrassed, he would grab his sweat-shirt and pull it over his head trying to stifle laughter. Roy had an infec-tious out-of-control laugh that affected everyone around him. The poor kid had been serious for so long, that now, being around Joe more than made up for it. Joe became Roy's mirth-mentor and looked for ways to keep him entertained.

One of Joe's fondest pleasures was coming to the beach early. He enjoyed taking a morning swim, at the end of which, he would relieve himself by depositing his daily constitution in the ocean.

Tommy and I decided to enter our beach patrol boat race held every year in July.

Lifeguard boat racing was/is a big deal along the Jersey Shore each summer. All area beach patrols held their own events. At the end of the summer this culminated into the winner-take-all South Jersey Championship. Whoever won this race, took home the title of South Jersey Champs and a year's worth of bragging rights. Consequently, like Joe, we came early every morning to train for the race.

The beaches were mostly deserted at that time. One of those mornings, after our workout, we observed a lone woman flitting happily about. We quickly identified her as one of the curious types, who enjoyed examining different species of sea matter. The lady was having a field day discovering all the ocean oddities that washed up on shore. She picked up seaweed, clamshells and starfish and poked at dead king crabs, jellyfish and sand sharks with a stick. We thought she might be a marine biologist.

After tiring of exploring as a landlubber, she ventured into the water to see what new discoveries awaited. She scrutinized anything of interest.

As she scanned the ocean for valuable sea matter, one of Joe's little treasures came floating by. Incredulously, the woman reached out and picked it up. She placed the bauble in the palm of her hand and began mashing it with her forefinger. Not being able to determine its derivation, she slowly brought her hand to her nose and sniffed. Instantly, her arm shot out like she'd been hit with a cattle prod. She violently shook off her trophy and dipped her hands in the ocean rubbing them furiously.

She looked to see if anyone had been watching and caught Tommy and I staring, totally mesmerized. As if in a movie, our eyes locked for a few seconds before we could break the spell. We knew right away what had happened.

Exiting the ocean, red faced and muttering to herself, she quickly disappeared up the beach. We had been so shocked witnessing this scene that the humor of it didn't strike us immediately. When it did, we draped ourselves over each other and almost collapsed to the beach. That story grew legs over the years making it a Michigan stretch classic. Joe achieved celebrity status and forevermore became known to one and all as: "The Phantom Shitter."

TITTIES IN A TEMPEST

Roy loved his working relationship with Joe, which he described as, "never a dull moment." The two were having a lot of rescues due to holes that had formed in the oceans floor over the winter. Historically, Ohio hadn't been a dangerous beach and still wasn't for the most part. But under certain ocean conditions, they found it necessary to keep bathers away from the holes located to their down-beach side. Roy was now gaining valuable first-hand experience working with Joe, who was a seasoned veteran.

It was an unusually overcast warm and windy day that Joe and Roy had a troublesome offset brewing. There were many bathers because the ocean temperature was ideal. The two guards were kept busy whistling people up-beach, away from danger.

The guys were having success, except for a clueless couple who paid little attention to their warnings. The twosome, he especially, was more intent on pursuing a sexual agenda. He kept reaching for areas of his partner's body that she coyly parried—unconvincingly. They were so distracted, by their lustful quest that they kept getting closer to the offset. Just in time, they'd heed the whistles shrill blast and unwittingly move away from the danger.

After recovering from each whistle warning they became more carried away by desire. Finally, during one passionate exchange, they threw caution to the wind, groping each other, while heading swiftly toward the offset. This time the whistles had no affect as they were hurled into a deep swirling vortex.

When they realized their plight they tried heading for shore. He was a good swimmer but she was a student of the come-get-me-stroke, school of aquatics. It was seldom our experience not to see a guy choose the heroic role and try to save his damsel in distress—not so Chick. As he headed for the beach she screamed, "Chick Chick," but Chick was having none of it. Chick had turned tail and was stroking like a champ, as if a shark was on his ass. She continued yelling, "Chick, Chick" but Chick was more interested in saving his own sorry butt, leaving his amorous partner to fend for herself.

As Joe and Roy ran for the boat, Roy was having trouble containing himself. While the Chick and chick show had unfolded Joe was carrying on a running narrative of the event. Roy, by now, was addicted to Joe's humor and was finding it hard to control himself. He told us later, "Here I was going on a rescue and could hardly launch the boat because Joe had me in stitches."

They reached the woman who was flailing about, still calling for Chick. Roy tossed a perfect donut strike and reeled the woman to the boat. The woman was very heavy and Roy was having trouble getting her aboard. He tried to get her to lift a leg to the gunnel, so he could use her weight to roll her in. Finally, Joe had to leave his oars to help Roy pull her aboard. When they got her in the boat they realized her top was down–compliments of Chick. With each heave of her chest, her mammoth breasts flopped from side to side.

Roy was beside himself. While the poor woman gasped for air Joe casually asked if she could please put her boobies back in her bathing suit. Not being quite lucid the woman said, "What, what?" Joe added, "You know, your boobies he said pointing… just as she looked down horrified… back in your bathing suit." Poor Roy was bent over his oars, out of control, as the woman pulled her top up.

As soon as the boat touched shore the woman scrambled from the craft and hurried up the beach. She spotted Chick, who, incredibly, was waiting dutifully by the stand. "You dirty son of a bitch, bastard," she yelled, along with some other more inspired profanities. The woman pummeled Chick about his face and body. She called him a no good coward as the rubbernecking crowd, who had witnessed the entire event, looked on with bemused interest.

Joe was back on the stand, but Roy who was still trying to regain his composure went back down by the water to whistle bathers away from trouble.

An hour later when all had settled down Joe and Roy were discussing the bizarre incident. Suddenly, the heavy lady was back in front of the stand to extend her thanks.

Upon seeing her, Roy's sweatshirt went back over his head as his body convulsed.

Turning to leave, with a look of concern, the lady said, "Please don't let this get in the newspapers. My brother is Captain of the Ocean City Beach Patrol" (a sister patrol about fourteen miles south of Atlantic City). That did it for Roy. He leaped from the stand and walked up the beach holding his sides. The woman must have thought he was nuts.

BOOMER PUTS TO SEA

It would be neglectful of me to write a book about the Atlantic City Beach Patrol without mention of Boomer. Boomer was, and is, an Atlantic City lifeguard legend. He and Murph had been partners at States for a number of years, winning two doubles rowing championships together. Boomer would later become a captain and retire as Assistant Chief. His life, other than the beach, was as a carpenter. He was always armed with the tools of his trade.

Boomer was a giant of a man who stood well over 6 ft. and probably weighed in at about 300 pounds. Not only had he rowed in doubles races but in the singles events as well. Rowing in the singles requires the agility of a cat. You had to push the boat out by yourself, jump in over the stern, straddle a seat and be rowing in a matter of seconds.

Usually, a person of Boomer's size wouldn't have the skills to perform this feat at such a high level. But Boomer had the gracefulness of a ballet dancer and strength of a Goliath. Once he started rowing, the oars looked like toothpicks in his huge hands. He was so powerful, that with every stroke, the bow would dip violently into the water, seemingly, impeding the boats motion. However that was not the case. He would quickly gain the lead on his competitors and from there it was no contest.

Over the years Boomer won six doubles races with various partners and eight singles races. The most singles races won, before or since, by any guard were three.

Boomer, when he was sober, was reasonable and likable. When he was drunk, which was often, watch out. One of his more enjoyable pastimes was coming to work still loaded, picking up the nearest lifeguard and throwing him over the porch railing onto the beach.

Arriving to work one morning, still inebriated, he was greeted by a furious ocean, the waves frighteningly massive. They were breaking in rapid succession—huge whitecaps—as far as the eye could see. It was one of those days you'd rather not be there. Bathers weren't allowed out beyond their knees.

Allow me to digress for a moment. The beaches along the stretch from Million Dollar Pier to Steel Pier contain rock jetties, groins, and smaller piers. One doesn't realize the full expansiveness of the ocean due to the enclosure these structures create. It almost gives one the impression of being in a privately closed off section of the ocean, while offering greater security.

Once you get to the north side of Steel Pier there are only a couple of jetties, which are not obstructionist. A new vista opens up revealing the awesome expanse of ocean before you. I always found, that looking out to what seemed infinity, a more majestic ocean, at that end of the island. One other point: Brigantine is a resort that lies just north of Atlantic City. The distance to Brigantine from States Avenue, where the following event took place, is roughly two to three miles.

Back to Boomer and that awesome day. Someone proposed a bet, the basis of which was that Boomer couldn't get a boat out and back without wiping out. He of course accepted.

As I heard it from the guys at States, they stood at the water's edge watching him head out getting smacked by one huge breaker after another. They expected at any second, to see him get slammed by one of those monsters, catapulting him to shore, and dumping him unceremoniously on the beach.

Incredibly, he was moving steadily. The guys couldn't believe their eyes. Soon he had gotten out so far he disappeared behind walls of white water. They waited expectantly, hoping they'd see the bow of the boat appear. To their consternation there was no sign of him.

A couple of hours later the word came back that the Coast Guard had found Boomer not far off the shores of Brigantine. The boat had turned over with Boomer clinging to it probably content to ride it to its chosen destination.

I have sometimes wondered, as I'm sure others have, what must have been going through his mind as he battled that awful fury. I don't think any of us would have tried it in the first place. If so, I'm sure we'd have left an unintentional trail of Joe R. treasures along the way.

It was well known among us that Boomer was not fond of rookies. They were not a species of lifeguard he held in high regard. For the most part, unless rookies were special, they were basically useless for the first two years—and sometimes beyond. Few were good oarsman and didn't know how to read the ocean or spot a rescue. However, most were good kids, who kept their noses clean, their mouths shut and were willing to learn—but not all.

States had acquired a rookie one year named Jerry who came to the stretch with an extremely cocky attitude. Maybe he thought, because his father was an Atlantic City big shot, he was entitled to special treatment. Ultimately, he would be, but not in the way he envisioned.

A clash between Boomer and Jerry was inevitable. It wasn't long coming.

Jerry was in the habit of strutting like a peacock and at times being disrespectful to his fellow guards. He was not highly thought of, especially by Boomer. One day when Jerry came to work he brought a change of clothes with him. He had a date for dinner and wanted to be dressed and ready to leave from the tent. He was being particularly obnoxious that day, which did not go unnoticed.

At 5:30 P.M. he hurried to the tent to get ready. As soon as he finished his shower he jumped into his shirt and pants and reached for his shoes. They didn't budge. Upon closer examination he discovered three or four nails had been pounded into each. He had been scorpioned! Poor Jerry wasn't going anywhere, at least for awhile. He knew Boomer was responsible, but what do you say to a 6'7" 300 pound giant—in a foul mood?

You'd think this would have been sufficient warning but Jerry was not easily dissuaded. The next time he overstepped his bounds the treatment became a little more, shall we say, harsh. Boomer and some of the other guards threw him into one of the boats, took the donut line and tied him to a seat. They pushed him out into deep water where the boat floundered, while Jerry, *struggling to be free*, awaited his fate. States being States, it didn't take long.

The first and only wave that hit him was a big hollow-back that made up quickly and crashed over the boat. He must have been horrified to see that thing come down on him knowing there was nothing he could do. He, along with the boat, was dashed to the beach in what may have been world record time.

Fortunately, except for his feelings, he escaped unscathed. The guys untied him and walked away. Jerry became a model of decorum and ultimately one of Boomer's best friends.

THE PHANTOM STRIKES AGAIN

States was not the only station that experienced rookie rebellion. The problem reared its ugly head in, of all places, our peaceful little stretch or more specifically, to Tommy and me.

Now that Geza and Jackie were gone Indiana was in need of a new crew. Two rookies named Bill and Teddy joined our stretch. Both were incredibly cocky.

Bill was of medium height with a stocky build. He was anxious to pass himself off as a leader right away. However, since we already had a captain, Bill would have to wait his turn. He did organize some functions, including at times, our bi-weekly dinner events and always took a conscientious approach toward his responsibilities. At times he would display a superior attitude flashing an annoying grin like he was privy to something the rest of us weren't. Bill and his future wife Jane would eventually introduce me to my future wife. We would become good friends and neighbors living in New York State.

Teddy, on the other hand, was about 5'10," slender but with a wiry muscular build. He was swarthy, handsome and had just graduated from high school where he'd been on the wrestling team. One day while we were goofing off on the tent porch, he and Tommy got into a friendly tussle. At one point, he got Tommy in a headlock and wouldn't let go. Tommy told him that was enough but Teddy wanted to impress the rest of us. Tommy became serious and warned Teddy what would happen if he continued the hold. Teddy got the message and let go. Tommy was laid back unless you pushed him too far, then he could get very nasty. We had to talk him down from taking a punch at Teddy.

After that incident, all of us were just waiting for a chance to teach those two a lesson. They'd oblige soon enough.

In previously discussing layout I noted the two hours were staggered. For example, in our stretch, Arkansas and Ohio would cover one hour and Michigan and Indiana the other.

There is an unwritten law when laying out that you do not leave your immediate area of responsibility, unless you're assisting in a rescue. Each station is responsible for its own bathers. At times, when partners were training for a race they'd get carried away and row too far from their coverage. It didn't take Murph long to let them know to get back to their area of patrol.

It was on one of these days that Tommy and I were on layout, watching the bathers, when the trouble began.

We turned to see Bill and Teddy's boat coming toward us. Immediately, alarm bells went off. We kept our distance reminding them they were out of their patrol area. They said they had something to tell us and gave assurances they weren't up to anything. We didn't trust them but were confident they would not have the audacity to try anything.

Before we rowed over we warned them it better not be a trick. As we drew close Bill stood up and heaved a large bag of garbage into our boat. Naturally the bag broke spewing egg shells, banana peels, apple cores, some kind of gross liquid mess and other unwelcome items of disgust. They immediately pulled away laughing and racing for their station. We dared not give chase, knowing all hell would break loose if Murph saw us.

Tommy and I were livid, not so much at what they'd done but at the nerve of those little bastards, and after we'd warned them; first would come anger–then revenge.

When layout was over we put our boat on its rollers and commenced cleaning it. Apparently the two sneaks had raided several of the trash baskets along the beach and picked the juiciest garbage they could find. Following our *good boat cleaning* chores we spent the rest of the day planning our retaliation.

At 5:30 P.M., we closed our station and headed for the tent. Bill and Teddy weren't far behind. They came strutting in with grins on their faces, proud they had put one over on the old vets. Tommy and I hung on the porch while they took showers. They dressed, and with frozen grins still in place left for the day.

Tommy and I scurried to Ohio, where Joe was working the 6:30 P.M. shift. We told Joe of the two rookies' brazenness, and how we wanted to teach them a lesson. He was as incredulous as we at such insolence. We told him of our plan, saying, we thought this was a job for the "Phantom." He happily agreed, stating this kind of disrespect could not go unpunished. When Joe's shift ended, as per our plan, he made a visit to their boat.

Segue to the next morning. Tommy and I were already in the tent when the guilty pair arrived. Joe, who was working the late shift, came early on the pretense he'd had an earlier chiropractic appointment. Incredulously, the two offenders still had grins on their faces—were still cocky as hell.

The rookies changed into their uniforms, grabbed oars and other equipment, and headed for their station. As previously discussed, boats are turned over at night a safe distance above the water line and laid on two rollers. In the morning they are righted and rolled to the water's edge.

As the pair made it to their station we each grabbed a pair of binoculars. We watched them pile their equipment on the stand and dutifully proceed in turning the boat over. As they grabbed the gunnels we braced ourselves. As soon as their hands made contact, and they started lifting the boat, they suddenly froze as if suspended in time. Ever so slowly, they lowered the boat back on its rollers. Already suspecting the worse they looked at their hands and recoiled in horror. Yes, the Phantom had struck again.

Even though they were a few blocks away we could plainly read their body language and see the rage build. Not wanting to know how Joe had applied the excrement (his artist tools), whether by paint brush, stick or—I shudder to think—a more personal touch, he'd done a masterful job.

We watched as Bill and Teddy headed up to the tent. When they arrived their skin tones had taken on a purplish hue despite being deeply tanned by their many hours in the sun. They were pissed! Neither said a word as they headed to where the cleaning materials were kept. After gathering them they hurried back to their station. We never gave the slightest hint of having had anything to do with their misfortune. We had discarded the binoculars so as not to leave any clues—as if they needed any.

They spent the next few hours cleaning. Lifeguard boats have networks of hidden crevices, especially where the ribs attach to the floor. Getting up under the bow and stern seat to clean requires the flexibility of a *Houdini*. Those obscure hiding places were all part of the affected areas. Add to that the drying effect that took place overnight and you'd need the skills of a *Hazel* to clean that craft.

The more the villains cleaned, the more they discovered. Ultimately, it was necessary to launch the boat, take it out beyond the break, turn it over, and scrub underneath to get rid of the infectious obscenity. Lifeguard boats have air pockets when turned over so the boys were able to spend considerable time cleaning underneath. I'd bet nobody knew the inside of that boat better than Bill and Teddy. It only took them a few hours. The boys had performed a Herculean chore, not one they'd wish to repeat again—ever!

Normally, guards would wander up to the tent, once or twice a day to get their lunch, relieve themselves or shoot the breeze with Murph. On this day Bill and Teddy never left their stand. They had been totally defeated in front of the entire stretch, and of course we saw to it the tale became known to one and all.

At the end of the day the two came to us with a total look of defeat. They said something to the effect that they surrendered, we had won and that was the last time they'd show disrespect. To Joe they gave the nastiest most disgusting look they could muster. He was gleeful. The boys were pretty much subdued for the rest of the summer. The virtue of humility was forever ingrained.

KENNY'S EXCELLENT ADVENTURE

Murph's son Steve had begun to shed his pain-in-the-ass-factor. His new-found likableness, I'm sure, was somewhat influenced by his cousin Bobby. Bobby was the nephew of Murph. He was a few years older than Steve, tall for his age and handsome, with a pleasant disposition. Both boys became mascots. Years later Bobby would become Chief of the A.C.B.P. For now we were sitting on a bonanza, one station with three mascots? Unheard of!

Lest you've forgotten, Kenny, our adult mascot, he was still with us and in his third summer. Animosity among Kenny and the boys began immediately. Kenny decided they would be his own little crew of gofers. If we asked him to do something for us he'd try to make one of the kids do it. They'd tell him to shut up and do it himself. They'd say he was nothing but a mascot like them. Kenny would respond that he was a junior lifeguard and senior to them. They'd just point at him and laugh.

Because Kenny was out to prove to the kids he was a lifeguard he dogged Tommy and I to let him take the boat out. We had no intention of letting that happen. If Murph had the slightest inkling we were entertaining such a thought he would have shipped us to the leper colony. But as often happens, things sometimes have a way of spiraling out of control.

We told Kenny we'd sleep on it and see if we could find a good time to let him earn his wings (oars).

A couple of times each summer, it usually occurs, during a full moon that the ocean rears its majestic head and for anywhere from three to five days tremendous waves pound the shoreline. They form a huge cavity in an area of the soft sand where bathers normally place their blankets during the day. Overnight, this cavity fills with water due to the constant influx of waves. By the next morning, a massive pool has been created and can extend for the length of a city block.

The kids and even some adults love it, the latter particularly, because of the safety factor. At the pool's highest point it is only thigh deep, but deep enough to row a boat. As we contemplated this phenomenon, flashbulbs went off. We had found the perfect opportunity to get Kenny off our backs.

We'd have to make Kenny's debut as a sailor an early morning event. Luckily the tide was high so the ocean was not far from the lip of the pool. If an extra large wave came up it would roll over the lip adding to this body of water. Our lifeguard stand was next to the pool and we could float the boat in it. This also gave us quick access to the ocean, in case of a rescue.

Kenny came to the beach at about 9:45A.M. We greeted him with the good news. He smiled at us with that goofy look of adoration, and with the satisfaction he had worn us down. We knew Murph wouldn't mind Kenny paddling up and down in a kiddy pool for awhile.

We suggested he wear his A.C.B.P. sweatshirt and red hat. When he was ready, we steadied the boat while he climbed in. He inserted the oars in the tholepins and we gave him a gentle shove.

His first few strokes were spastic, one oar going low and forward the other high and in the opposite direction. It didn't matter, because the pond was so calm the boat could have rowed it-self. As he passed the few waders tending their kids they gave him quizzical looks, wondering who the goof-ball was rowing a 17 foot lifeboat in a kiddy pool.

His look suggested one of pride and a feeling of accomplishment. For the first time he considered himself a real lifeguard. He maneuvered his way the length of the pool a few times, as more and more beachgoers watched and wondered what was going on.

We soon had to tell Kenny it was time to quit. The tide was starting to fall and we had to get the boat on the rollers and placed by the water's edge. We didn't want Murph to get nervous. The pool remained for the next few days, replenished each night by the abnormally high tide and large waves.

Kenny continued to practice rowing, the waders continued to stare and he continued to act like a peacock. After a few days, the seas diminished, the tide was down, the pool disappeared, the soft sand resumed its original state and things returned to normal.

We felt we had pulled off a real coup and Kenny would cease bugging us about the boat. Not so. If anything he got worse. He had tasted "the thrill of victory." It seems we'd created a monster. Luckily, we were able to fend him off by using Murph as an excuse and telling him it was much different rowing in the ocean.

Kenny was persistent though and he had an annoying habit of nagging. Even when we'd get pissed off and tell him to get off our backs, it didn't take long before he'd come at us through another door. If it weren't for the fact that he was such a good mascot, we would have given him a swift kick in the ass and sent him on his way.

One day after work Murph informed us he wouldn't be in until 10:30 or 11:00A.M., the following day. He was scheduled for a chiropractor's appointment. Murph was practically never late to work and probably never would have been if not for his back. He had taken part in so many hairy rescues and competed in so many boat races, the years had taken their toll.

Unfortunately, Kenny was there when Murph made the announcement.

Next morning when we arrived there was Kenny, waiting in his blue lifeguard trunks, belly hanging out, a shit eating grin and look of anticipation on his face. As soon as we began changing into our uniforms he started. "M-murph's n-not g-going t-to be here t-today, c-can I t-take t-the b-boat out?" We gave him all the reasons why we thought that wasn't a good idea but he persisted.

All the while we were putting the boat and stand down by the water's edge he kept up a steady dialogue, begging us to let him go for a row. Just to get rid of him for awhile we asked if he'd get us coffee and told him we'd think it over.

We admitted he had a point about Murph being gone and if we let him go out it might get him off our backs. Even better, the ocean was a little rough, the sea was choppy and the waves were a decent size (not a big deal for a seasoned guard but a potential problem for a novice). This might be the solution we were looking for.

When he came back we accepted our coffees and took him aside as a professor would a student. We told him with magnanimous gestures we were deferring to his wishes. He gave us his best stumpy grin, as we set about preparing him for his maiden voyage. We outfitted him with the kind of rowing trunks we wore in competition; raggedy cut off sweats with drawstrings and an old A.C.B.P. sweatshirt with cut off sleeves. To top it off we gave him a pair of rowing gloves–the ones with half the fingers cut off. Now he looked like a seasoned oarsman as he proudly climbed into the boat.

Just before he was ready to go we gave him his final instructions. We told him we'd give him a push as far out through the break as possible. It would be up to him to negotiate the rest of his course.

As he felt the boat being jostled by the choppy conditions a look of slight panic crossed his face. Tommy and I were on either side of the stern. We ask if he was ready and he answered with a nervous, "Y-yes."

We pushed as hard as we could. His oars were flailing like hell sometimes catching water other times only air. The water became a drag on our bodies as we kept pushing out past our thighs. We took a couple more strides and gave him a mighty last shove.

The boat catapulted forward thrusting him out into the break. He managed only a couple of strokes before being clobbered by a wave that turned him side-to, resulting in the loss of one of his oars. He reached over the gunnel to retrieve it, causing the boat to list, sending him head-long out of his seat toward the ocean. He caught himself and barely avoided being deep-sixed.

Luck was not with him as a second larger wave crashed into the boat, picking it up sideways, sending it bouncing comically toward shore. Tommy and I were mesmerized. Kenny was hanging on to the high side tholepin for dear life but as the keel hit the sand, he shot headfirst out the low side. The upper half of his body wound up in a couple feet of water, the lower half still in the boat. Incredulously, he was drowning—in two feet of water.

He tried to slither from the boat but was having much difficulty. Tommy and I were trying to reach him through the laughing spasms we were choking back. Finally, he was able to work his body free. He came up sputtering and coughing. He had a look of abject terror.

Though Kenny continued to come every day, it took some time before he got near the boat again. Up until that day he used to like to sit in the stern sheet, arms draped over the gunnels, with the boat sitting safely on its rollers. He had enjoyed trying to impress strollers as they went by. Now he seemed to enjoy more, the feel of sand under his feet.

It was some time before Murph had reason to come late again. When Kenny came to get us morning coffee, we told him the captain wasn't going to be in for awhile and would he like to go for a row? No need to provide his answer.

Case closed.

KENNY LEARNS ABOUT BANAPPLES

Kenny could be a blessing or a curse depending on his level of involvement. For example, because he had no qualms about approaching anyone, he was asked to sell tickets to the annual Lifeguard's Ball. The money raised, benefited the Lifeguard Organization's pension fund. It also helped defray the cost of our annual yearbook.

Kenny would go anywhere to sell tickets, the boardwalk, hotels, retail stores, along the avenue, etc. He was such a pest people would buy tickets just to get rid of him. He had a special line for beachgoers. If they didn't buy a ticket, he'd infer we (guards) might not see them if they were ever in danger. Imagine! They'd tell him to get lost.

When we found out about this outrage we were ready to strangle him. We told him in no uncertain terms, if that report ever came back to us again, we'd ride his ass out of town on a flatcar. Kenny however, was slow on the uptake.

On payday he'd go to City Hall and pick up our paychecks. Later we'd take him to breakfast. All was fine for awhile until the day he absconded with our money. He was gone most of the day but late in the afternoon he called from Philadelphia (about 60 miles away). He stuttered and stammered that he was s-sorry. I told him we had an A.P.B. out on him (we didn't). He asked me "w-what t-that w-was" and I told him an All-Points-Bulletin. He hated official sounding labels and that one scared the hell out of him. He returned in a few hours with all our money. Whatever he spent his parents probably covered.

We knew our time would come to teach him a lesson, and it did–in the way of a special order. Tommy and I were relaxing one trouble free day. It was just before noon and we started talking about ordering something different for lunch. Our conversation turned silly, and how we came up with the following I don't recall. Somehow, we started conversing about mixing various fruits. I said if someone mixed a grape and orange it could be called a *grange*. Tommy followed up with a plum and peach, a *plunch*. Our next creation was a banana and apple, what else, a *banapple*. The final suggestion was a watermelon and cantaloupe, a *waterloupe*. The thought hit us simultaneously–Kenny!

This was delicious.

At that time, there was a major upscale wholesale-retail fruit and produce market on Atlantic and North Carolina Avenues called Segal's. It was eight beach and two city blocks from our station. They carried fruit specialties for the discerning, so this would fit well with our little scheme.

When Kenny came to the stand, we told him we wanted something different for lunch. He asked what it was. We told him we were going to start eating healthier, to get in shape for the boat race, and wanted something new in the way of fruit. The problem, we told him, was that Segal's was the only place we could get it. He balked at first but we pleaded with him saying it would be a real favor and we wouldn't forget him. We also laid a little guilt on him reminding him of how he'd betrayed us. That did it.

When he was ready, I gave him the note with the list of items we wanted. Leaning down from the stand, I told him the first thing on the list was a bunch of granges. "W-what a-are g-grange's" he asked. Oh! You never heard of a grange? It's a combination of a grape and orange. He eyed me suspiciously but I went on with great sincerity. Next we'd like four plunches. "f-four w-what?" Plunches, you know a plum and a peach. After that he didn't want to seem stupid so I gave him the rest of the order. I pointed out the four banapples and two pieces of waterloupe. He still looked unsure, but took the money and note and headed up-beach.

He was gone forty five minutes and we almost forgot about him. But then, I looked up at Ohio and spotted him duck-walking furiously toward us. As he drew closer we could see the veins popping out from his neck. His face was purple and he looked downright scary. He was shaking his fist and shouting obscenities. Before he got to the stand, we jumped out laughing and quickly moved away dodging his wrath.

We continued to avoid him and after a while he disappeared.

Later in the afternoon he came to the stand. He had pretty much settled down so we asked him what happened. After his long walk to Segals, he said he went to the loading dock and found a worker. He told the guy he had an order from the lifeguards and handed the guy the note. The guy looked at the note, and then at him and said, "Are you nuts?"

Perhaps you're curious as to what happened to Kenny after the summer. Fear not.

He had another organization he ingratiated himself with during the winter months, namely the Montreal Canadians Hockey Team. Apparently he was some kind of gofer for them and enjoyed the same status with them as he did with us.

In May of the following year, one of the guards brought in a hockey magazine that showed a centerfold picture of some goofball trying to steal the coveted Stanley Cup. This characters goal (no pun intended) was to return it to the Montreal Canadians, where he thought it rightfully belonged. There was one slight problem—the Canadians had not won the NHL Championship.

Would you care to venture a guess as to who that Stanley-Cup-stealing-culprit was? If you said Kenny, award yourself a gold star.

TROUBLE IN THE SAND

Lifeguards had police authority during my years on the beach patrol. Each summer, after the Fourth of July, all guards reported to headquarters at South

Carolina Avenue for our annual group picture. There were always dignitaries including the Mayor, and during my era, Senator Frank S. "Hap" Farley, successor to none other than the boss of all Atlantic City bosses, Enoch "Nucky" Johnson.

Senator Farley always delivered a speech in his nasally voice about how important it was to honorably represent the A.C.B.P. He would tell us how we were good will ambassadors and anything that happened, good or bad, was a reflection of our interaction with visiting tourists. He always ended his speech with the same tired cliché after swearing us in. "You have now been invested with police authority, use it, but don't abuse it." He loved that quote, like it was real original.

There were times we were forced to use this authority. When drunks got out of hand we sometimes had to use physical force to restrain them. Usually, we'd take them to the tent and hold them until the police arrived. We dealt with thieves who waited for girls to go in the water before robbing their blankets of valuables. Worst of all were the mashers who preyed on females, sometimes accosting them as they walked under a pier. We caught a few of those characters and roughed them up a bit before the police arrived.

Surprisingly, one summer we were confronted with trouble from an unexpected source–the gay beach.

One day we spotted a huge blue and white striped tent that had been raised at Indiana Avenue. We didn't think anything of it, other than it looked like it could house the entire cast of the *Arabian Nights*.

Complaints started coming from the crowd that lewd shows were taking place. The word reached headquarters and they contacted Murph, and instructed him to have the tent taken down. Murph sent a mascot to the Indiana guards to relay the message from the Chief. One of the guards went back and told a hard-bitten looking woman, the one in charge, generally referred to as a "fag hag," that the tent had to come down. She started giving the guard a hard time.

The group had actors performing lewd shows that were well attended by a large gay audience. Among the crowd were four muscular tough-looking guys we came to know as the gay's protectors. As the guard and woman argued one of the protectors stepped forth. He asked what the problem was and the guard told him to mind his own business. One thing led to another and the next thing we knew all hell broke loose.

The guards in our stretch raced to enter the fray and soon guards from the Kentucky stretch joined in. Fists were flying everywhere, as the four protectors seemed to be enjoying themselves. Many of the gay boys were running up the beach screaming hysterically. If it hadn't been such a serious melee it would have been comical.

A cop whose beat was on the boardwalk radioed for police help. A swarm of reinforcements arrived and subdued the crowd. We went back to our stations, which had been left unattended, leaving bathers dangerously exposed. Incidents such as these were not tolerated during this era and soon we would be called to court as witnesses.

When our day in court arrived, about five of us acted as witnesses, together with some of the cops. Those taken into custody were the four "protectors" along with the "fag hag."

The judge listened to the testimony and at the end of the proceedings banished all five from entering the city again. He originally gave them a month's jail time but suspended that in lieu of their never returning to Atlantic City. If they were ever spotted in the city again, not only would they serve the month, he would also tack on some extra time.

Some of the gays we knew later came to tell us they had no part in that show. They explained that the participants were a rowdy group from South Philly. Their idea of fun was to push people's buttons to see how far they could go. The group talking to us said they liked maintaining a low profile, keeping to themselves, enjoying days on the beach and nights on the town. We agreed, we'd always gotten along and hoped those troublemakers hadn't impacted them in any way.

Another incident involving the gay beach came about as a result of men's bikini bathing trunks. Shamefully, there were times when the city harassed the gay beachgoers. An ordinance went out that men's bikini bathing trunks would no longer be tolerated on the beach. No one, including us, paid any attention to this ruling, since threats of this kind were common, and we never expected it would be enforced. None of the gays on Indiana paid any attention either.

One of the strollers from the Indiana beach used to wave each time he'd pass our stand. He was very distinguished and seemed to be a loner since we never saw him with anyone. His bearing was such that he gave the impression of someone who was financially well off–not uncommon among the gays. He also wore a brief bikini.

After awhile we became friendly and he'd stop and talk. We found out he was the manager of one of the famous hotels in Manhattan. At times, he would bring us great club sandwiches from the Claridge Hotel where he stayed during visits. Other than his work, he never spoke of his personal life. He was very discreet.

One day the cops pulled a surprise raid to round up all the gays on Indiana who were wearing bikinis. The city's intention was to fine them and throw them out of town. When we saw all the commotion Tommy and I went to check it out. Shockingly, we saw our friend in the roundup. We knew many of the police and spotted one we knew well, a sergeant with whom Tommy had gone to high school. We approached him and requested he let our friend go and apprised him of his background. He obliged. The gentleman was released and we returned to the stand.

The next day he came to the stand, saying he knew it was us who'd intervened on his behalf. He thanked us profusely and said if he'd been arrested he surely would have lost his position with the hotel.

KNOWING BILL

I've often been asked how I managed to get my hands on some of the black and white pictures contained herein. That's a story in itself.

I don't remember the exact year we met Bill, the photographer. What I do remember about him was his blur-like movement as he'd speed past our stand. The reason I noticed him at all, was because he was always in street clothes–never a bathing suit. I wondered how anyone could enjoy themselves at the beach without a bathing suit. The other thing I noticed was he always carried a camera–an expensive one.

ONE OF OUR LOVELY VISITORS

JIMMY THE THIRD AND ME POSING BESIDE OUR STATELY CRAFT

ALL FOUR OF OUR STATIONS ARE VISIBLE IN THIS PICTURE:
ARKANSAS, MICHIGAN, OHIO AND INDIANA

AN ACTUAL RESCUE OFF MICHIGAN OF THE ROUTINE VARIETY;
TOMMY AND ME ON THE LEFT

WITH FRIEND CAROL

L TO R BACK TOMMY BOB BOB HERBIE RALPH MURPH
BILLY GRAY JIMMY JOE ROY FRONT BOBBY KENNY STEVE

COULD MURPH HAVE LET TOMMY AND I SPEND
LAYOUT ON THE BEACH? DON'T BET ON IT

POSING WITH A BEAUTIFUL MODEL JUST ONE OF OUR CIVIC
COURTESY'S SOMEONE HAS TO DO IT

L TO R BOB MURPH GRAY LOUIE ENJOYING
A MOMENT OF CAMARADERIE ON THE TENT PORCH

JIMMY (IN THE BOW) AND ME COMING IN FROM LAYOUT

WITH NANCY SOON AFTER OUR RELATIONSHIP GOT OFF THE GROUND

FRIENDS JANE AND BILL. BILL WAS THE OTHER HALF OF THE PHANTOM'S REVENGE

SHOOTING SEAS WITH NOT MUCH WAVE ME IN THE BOW CHARLIE IN THE STERN

CHARIE AND I SHORTLY AFTER WE MET

BOB AND TOMMY WATCHING A BATHER HEADED FOR TROUBLE

Bill started appearing every weekend. Whenever he passed he would shyly look toward us and hurry by. This routine went on for several weeks until one day, as he passed Ohio, Joe called him over. As usual, Joe had no compunction about getting into Bill's case history.

Bill had recently retired from the U.S. Coast Guard as a Chief Petty Officer. He had a love of photography and decided to pursue it as a hobby upon his discharge. Bill was from Delaware, where Joe lived and taught during the winter. He and Bill became fast friends and remained so until Bill's death some years later.

One day Joe brought Bill to our stand and introduced him. We did our best to open him to conversation but he still exhibited an almost painful shyness. Once in a while if you hit upon a topic that piqued his interest, he would reverse gears and talk excitedly about the subject. Photography was one he could really get into. Trouble was neither Tommy nor I knew the first thing about cameras, except for the part where you aim and click.

Consequently, lifeguards and women became his favorite subjects and he had a plethora to choose from. Bill came to Atlantic City by bus every weekend, where he got off at South Carolina Avenue terminal. He'd head straight for the beach and walk the seven or eight blocks to our stretch.

Initially, he'd stop and snap pictures of some of the guards he'd talk to on his way down to see us. After awhile, so many guards started pestering him for pictures it began pissing him off. Subsequently he stopped taking pictures of anyone who asked. It seemed many of the guys had no consideration for his time or expense. He never charged anyone for his pictures.

Soon Bill started coming primarily to our stretch. He and Joe shared a close relationship and he spent much of his day at Joe's station. He had also taken a shine to Tommy, me and Murph. I'm sure one of the reasons he liked us was because not once did we ask him to take our picture. As a result, we became the beneficiaries of his generosity and he is the reason I'm in possession of such treasured mementos.

He also liked the class of girls who came around our stand because, in most cases, they were more mature than the college girls who frequented other beaches. He loved taking their pictures. Bill would have Tommy or I pose with them, then he'd step back and start shooting, suggesting various attitudes. He'd turn his Coast Guard cap around and snap away. As he started clicking he'd go, "Ooooh yeah, that's beautiful; Oooh yeah, lovely; oh my! Oooh oooh." With each picture he'd become more aroused, until a series of low moans escaped his lips, and we thought he was having an orgasm. I don't mean to infer any deviancy by that statement. For as long as I knew him, Bill was always a perfect gentleman.

When he went home he'd develop the pictures. Upon his return he'd hand us a pile of snapshots to choose from and then make beautiful eight by tens of those we'd select.

Over the past fifty years I have carried these pictures with me through four states and more residences than I care to remember. They have always served as an inspiration and comfort. They have frozen in time the memories of those I knew, and served with, and those I will always treasure.

I don't recall the year we found out about Bill. Joe had been calling him, as he always did during his winters in Delaware, but getting no response. Fearing the worst, Joe made a visit to his apartment, which confirmed his worst fears. He found Bill lying on the floor, dead of an apparent heart attack.

CHAPTER 9

BOAT RACING, BOOZE AND BABES

A PAIR OF LIGHTWEIGHTS

Tommy and I, as I'd mentioned earlier came in the mornings to train for the boat race. We had taken Murph's advice to represent our stretch in the annual beach patrol rowing competition. Our combined weight, soaking wet, was barely 330 pounds. This is considered small for a doubles boat crew. Most crews weighed upwards of 370, to over 400 pounds. Ironically, a few years prior to our entry, a crew who weighed in at a mere 295 pounds won the event.

So it wasn't about how much you weighed. Much of it had to do with how coordinated your rowing stroke was, level of seamanship, training regimen, size of heart and–luck. A crew could experience luck in several ways, but the two ways that made the biggest difference were either on the way out or way in. Luck on the way out was usually bad. Luck on the way in could be good or bad.

Ocean waves usually break in irregular series, not only from out to in, but from side-to-side. If ten boats line up in a heat, they stretch for a few blocks to give crews enough room in between to maneuver. At the start of the race the bow man sits in the boat oars ready. The stern man stands in shin deep water waiting for the gun to go off.

As soon as the stern man hears the crack of the gun, he pushes the boat to get a good start. Some guys push as far as practical to get the boat moving before they get in. Here you have to be careful. Push too far and your body becomes a drag on the boat as you try to jump in.

Others employ a strategy that takes advantage of the first wave, as it lifts the bow and depresses the stern. This allows the stern man to easily step in the boat and be in his seat, rowing in seconds. Which is best I couldn't say. It's a matter of personal preference. I think most veterans preferred the latter.

A crew in lane one might have the good fortune to launch in a calm sea, finding themselves swept out beyond the break before other crews have cleared their first wave. This becomes a huge advantage. Still, you have to have the rest of the package to hold on to that lead. Conversely, the crew in lane ten might run into a series of waves that slows the boats progress. Worse yet, taking water adds significant weight and usually means the kiss of death. This kind of bad fortune can strike in any lane. It depends on the luck of the draw.

Atlantic City lifeboats are made to withstand a steady, relentless pounding by waves on a daily basis. I cannot articulate on the details of their design and why they're so seaworthy, but all one has to do is observe the boat's craftsmanship to realize what sturdy vessels they are. A boat builder named Van Sant provided the boats during my era. When new, those boats weighed about 500 pounds. After several seasons of new paint and a certain amount of water-logging, they could take on an extra 100 pounds.

Normally, the oldest boats would be retired after the season and replaced with new ones. In our stretch the new boat was always assigned to the tent station which was Michigan in our case. Having a newer boat in a race does not guarantee victory; you still have to move your arms and legs. But guys who had to row a heavy boat were at a distinct disadvantage. Those boats were harder to get moving and didn't leap over seas like their newer counterparts.

Whether a boat was old or new I always saw them as proud seaworthy ladies. Viewing them poised primly against the ocean's tufted white swells, and clear horizon, the gleaming white craft is a picture of dignified beauty.

Training for a boat race requires dedication. If you're not committed to an intense program of conditioning you're wasting your time. Many of the crews are almost fanatical in their approach. They spend hours developing a rowing stroke, outfitting their boats with the right leg braces, picking out straight oars and, most important, finding soft heiny pads.

Crews are not allowed to train for a boat race during working hours, though crews get in what they can during layout. Training takes place before and after working hours. Usually, we'd get to the beach about 8:00 A.M.

This gave us time to change and get our equipment set up. We would row a mile to a mile and a half, depending on ocean conditions. If the ocean was flat, which was common in the morning, we'd row farther. A rough ocean was more difficult to navigate having to keep your bow into the wind. The choppy seas kept pushing us off course–something we had to get use to.

Training in the evening was tougher. As I stated before, the prevailing wind was southerly. After putting up with a blowing wind whipping off the sea all day, the last thing you felt like doing after working hours was rowing a mile. The ocean was sloppy and the surf splashed over the bow, spraying you with sea water. After being subjected to a chilly breeze all day, being soaked didn't make for ideal conditions. Still, if you were serious, you'd bite the bullet and carry on. Additionally, neither partner wanted to be the first to wimp out.

Initially, neither Tommy nor I had a clue about boat racing but we both considered ourselves athletic and had the desire to compete. On our first day of training, we put out our cigarettes jumped in the boat and rowed as far as we could, without throwing up. We wore our wool lifeguard trunks–brand name: Fruit of the Sandpaper, and possibly, even jock straps–big mistake.

When we got back to the beach we experienced brush burns on our butts. They were somewhat painful but tolerable–that is–until we hit the cold shower (tents did not have hot showers). It was then we found out what the effect of skin loss and cold water do *not* have in common.

Before we dressed we applied significant amounts of Vaseline to our burning bums. This was our introduction to the innocuous sounding condition known as "strawberries." They may look like strawberries, but a more fitting name would be red-hot chili peppers. When I tell you those suckers burned, they burned; worse was shedding your underwear. By the time that happened, your shorts were already securely glued to the upper part of your tush. Peeling those off was excruciating. Another interesting tidbit about strawberries was-they didn't heal until December.

It didn't take long for us to purchase some nice soft foam rubber pads and tape them to the lifeboat seats. For trunks we wore cut-off sweats which were made from softer material. The most important thing we did before each row, was grease our bums like a couple of butt boys.

In order to get more leg drive we, had braces made to extend the seats where our feet rested. This allowed for more power with our legs giving us increased leverage. All serious crews used this technique.

As a smaller crew, Tommy and I developed our own rowing stroke. Where the bigger, more leveraged crews rowed a longer, smoother, approximate 36 strokes per minute, we decided we needed something different. We hit on the idea of a shorter faster stroke—oars in the water constantly to keep the boat moving. Actually, to keep the boat moving steadily was every ones goal. The way crews accomplished this was a matter of personal choice. Since we couldn't compete with the leveraged crews on an equal basis, we rowed more strokes per minute, eventually 44 to 46.

We had no way of knowing whether this rowing stroke would work. After we had been training for awhile we decided to ask a few crews to pace us. This is where crews get together to see how you match up and how you're progressing. After competing against three crews and beating all of them, we felt pretty good. Admittedly, these crews weren't of championship caliber, but then, neither were we. However, it still gave us some standard by which to compare ourselves.

Most crews practice sprints during training and we were no exception. In our case, we threw in a lot more strokes than the average crew. As our endurance increased we found ourselves sprinting for longer periods. We developed a smooth stroke in which our oars were striking the water simultaneously. When this kind of coordination is achieved moving the boat becomes almost effortless.

In bitching about how tough it can be training in a sloppy southerly, fighting the wind and sea occurs only on the way out. Therefore, let me come clean and inform you that the opposite is true upon turning and heading in. That same wind and slop impeding you on the way out, is your ally on the way in. The conditions that cause you to swear at everything and nothing on your way out also cause you to rejoice and give thanks on the way in. It is almost as if an invisible hand is helping you along.

To illustrate what I'm talking about, I will relate an incident Tommy and I had during training one morning. This did not occur in a sloppy southerly, but on a beautiful clear windless morn over an ocean of shimmering glass. The only odd thing about the day was that the waves were huge. This combination of conditions happens infrequently, except maybe at the end of summer during hurricane season.

We were only about a week away from the race and the guys in our stretch were eager to help out. On this morning, three of the guards said they'd put a stopwatch on us to count our strokes and clock our overall time.

We had to be careful picking our way out because of the size of the waves. These were not the dangerous hollow-back variety I've described previously. They were the big, billowy, majestic beauties that roll slowly and for long distances, before reaching their apex and breaking. When they do break, it is with a gently rolling motion that begins gradually and builds into a powerful force.

On this day, these beautiful swells were breaking farther out than I'd seldom seen and rolling toward the shore in uniformed splendor.

There were a few hairy moments as we got underway. We just cleared a couple of swells before they broke. It was exhilarating to feel the boat go straight up, bow pointing skyward, then dip and slide down the other side of the wave.

What a thrill, rowing out to sea, listening to the boat glide over the ocean. The oars were slapping the water in perfect unison, keeping time to the click-click rhythm as they moved back and forth inside the thole pins.

As we turned to head back we were immediately aided by the in-going swells. As one made up off our stern we would pick up our stroke staying with it as long as possible. Each one of these swells would propel us about five boat-lengths beyond that of our normal distance. Million dollar pier, during that era, stretched the length of about three football fields, into the ocean.

As we approached the end of the pier the swells kept getting bigger. We spotted an unusually large one and I told Tommy I thought we could catch it, but I didn't think either of us was convinced. Normally, catching a wave out that far is rare. We pulled as hard as we could and moved rapidly with it. Still, I thought we would fall off as we teetered back-and-forth atop its highest point. I yelled for Tommy to pull. Suddenly, we felt the bow start to dip as the boat began its descent into the deep abyss. As that monstrous wave broke, it felt like we were being propelled down a lightning-fast, roller coaster. The thrill of that moment was indescribable.

Tommy jumped to the back, thrusting one of his oars out the stern using it as a rudder. I sprang to the bow using my body weight to help keep us straight. When that wave was fully broken we looked back to see a mountain of white water propelling us like a speedboat toward shore. We rode that wave from the end of Million Dollar Pier, right up until the moment our keel hit the beach.

The guys were waiting by the water's edge, their excitement clearly showing. By the looks on their faces they had vicariously experienced everything they'd seen. First, they were in awe of the fact we'd caught the wave so far out. Next they said, as the boat descended into its deep chasm, it looked like we'd disappeared and were swallowed by the white water. But then, they saw just the tip of the bow emerge from the white water and begin to get bigger. We all had a great time relaying that story to the rest of the guys when they reported for work. Murph had a couple of snide remarks but clearly was impressed. Catching that wave still remains one of the big thrills of my life.

Finally, the day arrived. Races are always held after work and odds of running into a nice sloppy windy southerly are about nine-to-one. That's exactly what we got.

During that time, the race was held in front of headquarters at South Carolina Avenue. Crews coming from other stretches are responsible for getting their own boats to the host beach. Some guards row to the site, while others have friends bring their boats.

Lifeguard boat racing events are very popular in South Jersey and draw many spectators. By the time Tommy and I got to South, the beaches and boardwalk were already crowded with fans and curious onlookers, ready to cheer on their favorite crew.

We talked with other crews while we waited for the judges to complete their tasks. They had us pick numbers to determine our lane. These numbers corresponded to the color flag we were required to turn. So for instance, lane number one was assigned the blue flag, etc. As I recall, we picked somewhere in the middle of the pack.

As soon as we knew what flag we were assigned, we looked for some identifying feature from a boardwalk building to line up with. This was important to avoid having to turn every few moments on the way out to see if we were lined up with our flag. Keep in mind, the weather conditions were such that they would blow you off course. Once you were half way out, and your boardwalk identifying marker became obscured, it was necessary to turn often to look for your flag. It is never easy to row and turn at the same time, but in sloppy conditions it's even harder.

The judges called us together for last-minute instructions. Basically, it was finish where you started and no dirty tricks. The boats were taken out to shin-deep water where the bow man climbed in. The stern man stood at the rear anticipating the start. Like any athletic endeavor nerves were taut as we waited for that final moment.

Suddenly, we heard the sharp crack of the starter gun and I felt the momentum of Tommy's thrust as he pushed the boat a few feet. Then, quick as a cat, he leaped in and we were rowing within seconds. Although crowd noise was not something we paid attention to, the roar was palpable and not easily ignored.

Our momentum was slowed twice from being hit by a couple of small waves. But then we hit a calm sea and in the next moment we cleared the break and settled into the competition.

There is a clear phenomenon that takes place as you move further out into the ocean. You experience a feeling of being elevated, looking down at people standing on shore. This probably has something to do with sea level.

As we saw the buildings getting further away and the noise of the crowd begin to wane I turned to check our course. Other crews were to our right and left but we were only vaguely aware of their positions. My concentration was all about staying on course. One of the worst things that can happen is getting to the turn and finding you're a block off your flag.

Tommy and I were fighting the elements while trying to keep things around us in perspective. About three quarters of the way out we realized we were separating from crews around us. This was a good sign since we would turn before the boats behind us, getting a jump on the way in.

With choppy swells constantly slapping our port bow, we continued pulling harder with our right oar, struggling to keep the boat into the wind. Regardless of your conditioning, when one arm is carrying twice the load it begins to take its toll. The arm bends with every stroke, causing exhaustion along your entire right side.

Just about the time we thought we'd never reach it, I turned to see our flag within striking distance. Now it looked much bigger and we were right on target. In the next instant it was right off our bow. We turned, as we had practiced, pushing furiously with our right oar and pulling violently with our left. This causes the boat to turn, almost literally, on a dime. Most crews get so close they run over the flag and knock it down.

That is what happened as we turned and headed for the beach. We saw a few boats turn slightly before us, but most slightly after us.

The race to the beach was on.

As mentioned earlier, where the swells acted as an impediment on the way out; they were a godsend on the way in. We could now row evenly with both oars. With every stroke, catapulted by the swells, we moved swiftly toward our destination. We found we were able to pick up our stroke, pulling even with the few crews who had turned before us.

The boat was moving swiftly beneath us and we could see the frustrated expressions on crews from whom we began to put distance. Looking to my right, I saw no one ahead of us. Turning to my left, I saw one crew leading us by a few boat lengths. I yelled for Tommy to give me some motor.

We were now about halfway to shore and suddenly I was stricken with a stomach cramp. With each stoke the pain became excruciating. I have heard cramps described as "caroming around your abdomen like a cue ball on a billiard table." I kept pulling but felt like I was going to pass out.

Finally I gasped, Tom, I've got a cramp, I don't know if I can keep going. He ignored me. I took a few more agonizing strokes and repeated myself. His answer: "Shut the fuck up!" I almost let go of the oars to reach forward and strangle him. I was so enraged, I thought, I'll finish this race if it kills me, and if it doesn't, I'll kill him when we hit the beach.

Suddenly, I heard what I thought was a distant noise. By now my body was reacting instinctively. All I could feel was pain. The noise kept getting louder and through my stupor I realized it was the beach crowd and we must be getting closer. Now with every stroke we took the noise became deafening.

The next thing I saw was a wave make up behind us and Tommy jump back to the stern. I felt the boat being propelled as I put up my oars. My next recollection was of the keel hitting the sand hard, knocking me out of my seat and onto the deck of the bow.

In a daze I felt hands grabbing and lifting me out of the boat. People were pounding me on the back. No, we didn't win but we finished second. We had not even been on the horizon as far as our chances of finishing in the top three were concerned. Tommy and I had competed with, and beaten seasoned veterans in our first race.

We were thrilled and I forgot all about killing Tommy. Truth be known, he did me a favor. To add to my joy the cramp had subsided.

We sure nuf celebrated that evening.

The next day when we got to the tent, there were congratulations and a lot of good natured-ball-busting. Murph was telling us how lucky we were. He said because we were a small crew everyone felt sorry for us and let us slip over the finish line. Underneath all that bluster he was proud as hell.

"ERT" AND FLIP

When the newspaper wrote up the race, it read thus: "Ert" (leaving out the R-o-b) McNesby and Thomas R. finished second in the Atlantic City Beach Patrol Ocean Lifeboat Rowing Race…"

A new guard named Mike had joined our stretch. Mike was of medium height muscular, fun loving, and a good athlete. He was a little cocky but not arrogant. Rather popular and liked by all the guys, Mike enjoyed the daily ball-busting routines. He loved it when the paper misprinted my name. From then on he always referred to me as "Ert." Every time he said it, he'd laugh, but not in an offensive way. He just liked the name. I got a kick out of the pleasure he derived from saying "Ert." I wasn't looking to reciprocate, but sometimes the gods on high just have other plans.

One day we came to work and the ocean was particularly nasty. It was one of those days I've described previously, with crunching hollow-back waves. It was the kind of day, if you were a bather and went out past your waist—watch out! Getting caught in one of those combers could send you crashing to the ocean's floor, rolling you along its bottom like a-tumblin' tumbleweed. During this stressful period it would not be unusual to see your life pass before you. The harder you tried getting up the less success you had. Finally, gasping for breath, you'd manage to get on your feet, giving silent thanks for your life, while making a hasty departure. After a while bathers got the message and stopped tempting the King.

Mike saw this as a good opportunity to practice his sea-shooting skills. We warned him that even if he got out, hollow-backs are not exactly the most desirable of waves for shooting seas. Being young, cocky, unafraid, and a rookie, he didn't need our advice.

Mike launched the boat, gave himself a good start, jumped in and was rowing in seconds. He was moving at an angle when a powerful midsize dumper suddenly hit him, violently flipping the boat, sending him flying. He quickly recovered, emptied water from the vessel, grabbed his oars and went back for another try. On the second attempt, as soon as his oars touched water, he got hit by a small wave and turned broad side. As he tried to straighten out he got whacked again by another hollow-back flipping and dumping him rudely into the sea.

Mike was not easily discouraged. The kid had cojones, and was determined to make it on his third attempt. His next start was his best by far. When he got in the boat there was a lull and it looked as if he would make it through the break. However hollow-backs make up very quickly and he again became the recipient of another of those sneaky bastards. He was flipped for a third time.

Mike was no dummy and didn't need a lecture from King Neptune to get the message. We were glad to see he escaped unscathed. We busted on him a little and went back to our stations.

The next morning when I got to the tent I changed and went out on the porch to shoot the breeze with the guys. Mike was first to greet me with, "mornin Ert" laughing good naturedly. Without thinking, and with no malice I responded, Hey Flip. The other guys laughed making the immediate connection. Mike, being somewhat macho, was not happy with his new nickname. Squinting one eye and curling his lip he said, "Fuck you McNesby." Hearing his reaction guaranteed the name would be a keeper, especially with me. Each time we greeted thereafter, I was "Ert" and he was "Flip," followed of course by the above noted expletive. However, there was never any rancor between us and we enjoyed lots of laughs together.

During his lifeguard career Mike would rise to the rank of lieutenant and eventually captain. Years later, whenever I visited Atlantic City, and Mike, he graciously invited me to hang out with him at his Bartram Avenue tent. I was welcome to use any facilities, or take the boat for a row in the morning. We did some serious reminiscing during those "Kodak" moments.

BISTRO NIGHTS

I was still working a second job but had left the sometimes boring, sometimes sleazy taxi business to take a bartending position. The person responsible for getting me hired was my friend Jack. The bar I'm referring to was the Senator, which you may recall was where my relationship with Mickey began. Jack had been working there for awhile and told me what a good tipping job it was. He had already graduated from Miami, and was tending bar until he figured out what he was going to do.

The Senator was still hugely popular and always filled with coeds. Now, instead of meeting girls on the outside of the bar, I was meeting them from the inside, and getting paid for it. Nice.

Tommy was also working at the Senator. We would leave the beach, get something to eat and go directly to our night job, where we worked from 7:00 pm until about 1:00 am. Because Atlantic City was/is a 24/7 open bar town, there were plenty of places to hang out. As the crowd dwindled at the Senator it would reappear at the Lafayette Lounge, about a block away. As soon as we cleaned up the bar and counted our tips we'd head over there.

The Lafayette was owned by two lifeguards, George and John. George and I had made the beach the same year, whereas John came a few years later. John and I attended the University of Miami together.

The Lafayette was more sophisticated than the Senator, the latter being more of a hangout with a jukebox. The Lafayette had a spacious dance floor and a great jukebox, with all the latest hits. It had a large, beautifully-lighted, rectangular bar. This was the first time I'd ever seen black lighting. Because of this type of lighting it was years before I discovered that a gin and tonic was not blue in color; but in the vernacular of the day it was cool.

There was a regular crowd who came often to take advantage of the dance floor, The movie, *Never On Sunday* had recently opened with the title song becoming popular quickly. The movie was filmed in Greece and featured a line dance that became fashionable in America. Some of the Lafayette crowd quickly mastered the dance and met a few nights a week to enjoy performing it. They would punch in the Percy Faith selection, lock arms, swaying and dipping, first right then left.

It was a lot of fun to watch and the group did it well, but we (the guys) were too macho to get out there and try it. Instead, we ridiculed them inferring the dance was corny and they were a bunch of girly men. We were too hung up to realize they were having a lot more fun than we were.

Working two jobs did not curtail our nightlife—it was part of our routine. Usually, we only worked four or five nights a week, so were able to get some rest on nights off. By the time we left the Lafayette we wouldn't get home until after 3:00 A.M., sometimes later. We had to be back up at 8:00 A.M. for our day job. By the way, though I haven't mentioned it before, we worked the beach seven days a week. There was no such thing as a day off and if you did take a day off you'd better have a damn good excuse. That hasn't been the case for years and guards get regular time off now.

A few days later Jack quit working the Senator bar. When I asked him why he told me he had a business deal going and might be opening his own place. I wished him luck and then didn't see him for awhile.

The next time I ran into him he told me he and a friend had purchased the old Torch Club. The Torch Club was located in the back of an alley—literally. It had been a popular nightclub featuring live entertainment in the forties and fifties. I couldn't imagine a bar making it there being so close to the Senator and Lafayette (both less than two blocks away), and in the back of an alley.

That however, was before Jack revealed his plans. He said it wouldn't take long to get open. The original bars were still intact so they only had to paint, decorate and bring in a juke box or two. To start, he and his partner would tend bar to save money. I asked him to let me know when it was ready.

Jack, being a beach lover visited us regularly. He also came to see his brother Jimmy with whom he was close. On one of his visits he told me his place was ready to open and invited me to stop around and get a preview.

A couple of days later I decided to check it out. Upon arriving, the first thing I noticed was a sign with the bar's new name: OPUS 1. When I entered, it looked like the finishing touches were being applied. Jack introduced me to his partner Don, who I liked immediately.

Don was tall, slightly overweight, with Irish good looks and a ready smile. He had the kind of distracted energy that gave you the impression he was only half listening to what you were saying. However, Don was acutely aware of things going on around him and soaked up information like a sponge. He had a razor sharp wit and winning personality, making him a hugely charismatic figure to those whose lives he touched. Don was the everyday business side of the partnership, whereas Jack was the more creative side. It was a successful complimentary alliance.

The first thing that struck me was how dark the place was. They had painted the walls black and hung colorful Picasso styled paintings. The room was L-shaped with two large rectangular bars. At the back of the room next to the smaller bar was a decent sized dance floor. Not to be outdone by the Lafayette Lounge, the guys had installed black lighting.

The feature Jack was most proud of was the two juke boxes. With the help of an electrical engineer they revised the monoral speaker and installed woofers, tweeters and amplifiers. This was the first time a juke box produced a stereophonic effect in an Atlantic City nightclub. Other speakers were installed throughout the room. This concept was ahead of its time and the company providing them began revising its boxes to conform to Jack's idea.

Upon conclusion of the tour I emerged into bright sunlight. I was left with the impression of having come from a cave like environment—that could double as an opium den. The entire experience was interesting but somewhat bizarre for that time.

The opening was scheduled for that weekend. The guys had advertised in the relevant media and had kids pass out flyers on beaches most populated by the college crowds. I told them I'd pass the word and see them opening night.

At the beginning of the summer my brother and I rented a three-story house where we would not stay for the season, due to other circumstances. Initially, four of Mick's college buddies, Jocko, Jack, Neil and Steve along with Kenny—he of banapples fame moved in. The house was huge with five bedrooms, still, seven guys made for a little overcrowding.

This was the summer the movie *Psycho* debuted. Today that film would still be among a long line of frightening movies. During our time it was piss-your-pants terrifying. In fact my brother used to tell this story. One night he was at the Lafayette Lounge during a fierce rainstorm. It was only about 9:00 P.M. but since the forecast called for clear the next day he wanted to get an early start on the other ice cream vendors. The rain was coming down so hard, instead of walking the half block to take a jitney home, he called a cab.

When he got home no one was there. As soon as you walked in the door, the first thing to greet you was a long old fashion hallway with bath and shower right at the top of the stairs. Mick said if this place was on a hill he would have called it the Bates Motel. He said as he climbed to the top of the stairs he expected to see Mother Bates come screaming at him from the bathroom, with a ten foot blade in her hand. Having survived that moment of terror he still had to climb to the third floor and his bedroom. Once he made it there and got in bed, the only thing he could hear was the howling wind and steady rain. His eyes never closed until he heard the sound of the next arrival entering the house around 2:00 A.M.

The night of the Opus 1 opening, all of us from the house, plus Tommy, headed uptown. We stopped at another regular spot first. The place was not as busy as it normally was. We hung out there for an hour then decided to see how the Opus 1 was doing. We got there about 11:00 P.M. It was bedlam.

The juke box was blaring and people were dancing all over the place, literally. If a guy was looking for a place to pick up a girl (unless he looked like Quasimodo), he was *in like Flynn*. Not only were there mobs of summer girls but all the local girls we knew were there too. Drinks were flying at both bars and people were drinking like prohibition was about to be reinstated. I ran into Jack who was socializing with everyone. He asked me what I thought about working there. He didn't have to ask twice. If Tommy and Mick were interested, he'd like to have them too.

We talked to a lot of new people that night, some we knew, some we just met. Don's crowd was among the latter. Don was from Philadelphia, having recently moved to Atlantic City. A bunch of his neighborhood crowd had come to support him and he introduced us all around. His friends were a group of good-natured hell-raisers we related to easily. They were all athletes, one having played for the Philadelphia Eagles. In time, some would also move to Atlantic City.

We left around 3:00 A.M. For the rest of the summer the Opus (we stopped using the 1) became our hangout, as well as our second work place. Actually a good part of our social life would revolve around it for a number of years.

We gave the Senator our week's notice which they didn't need. They had guys waiting in line to work there. Jack gave us the same four or five nights a week we had at the Senator. The downside was the hours were longer. The upside was we were making more money.

Because Tommy and I had finished second in the boat race we were invited to row in the annual bay race. Four crews from the boroughs of Absecon Island, including Atlantic City, Ventnor, Margate, and Longport were chosen to compete for Island bragging rights. Even though we were working two jobs and not neglecting our social life we still had to train. We kept our pre-ocean race regimen up but also added running to our schedule. Stupidly we still smoked and consumed our share of booze.

There was an after-hours bar called the Tropics. This place didn't start jumping until about 2:00 A.M. and it stayed that way until 8 or 9:00 in the morning. Most nights, after we left the Opus, we'd wind up at the Tropics. There are many mornings I left the Tropics to go straight to the beach.

The Tropics was a really cool bar. If the place wasn't busy at 2:00 A.M., it wasn't long after before it was packed. Like the Opus, it was dark inside and along with a great juke box, featured live entertainment. There was a piano player/singer named Bobby, who hailed from Philadelphia, but like Don, had recently moved to Atlantic City. Bobby was tall, dark, and as handsome as a movie star. He played a great piano, sang in a husky romantic voice and had a smile that could send women into a swoon.

Bobby was not your typical musician; he was a terrific athlete who played all sports and loved to raise hell. He was totally unaffected by his talent. If you wanted to keep your girlfriend *do not* take her to see Bobby. Not that he'd birddog you, he wouldn't, but girls would go all dreamy eyed as soon as they met him and heard him sing.

A bunch of us hung out together including Mick, Tommy, Bobby, Tommy's brother Joe, sometimes Jack, Don, and my cousin Joe. We were like a poor man's Atlantic City rat pack and even thought of ourselves that way. Every summer, Frank Sinatra, Dean Martin, Sammy Davis Jr. and Joey Bishop came to Atlantic City, and every summer we saw each of them at various times. It was not difficult to embrace their drinking, womanizing, staying up all night lifestyle. The only thing missing was the money.

The Tropics attracted an interesting melting pot of Atlantic City characters. On any given night you were likely to run into off-duty cops, hookers, criminals, celebrities, tourists, minors, troublemakers and lots of women. One group of younger guys we were friendly with, it turned out, smoked pot. Drugs were not popular at the time. The expression "dope fiend" was common to describe pot smokers. This group encouraged me to try it one night. My response was, what, and become a dope fiend like you guys? They just laughed at me.

Several nights later I started working at the Opus. Some nights I worked the big bar, and others, what was called the back bar. Once the evening got rolling pouring drinks became non-stop. About half the crowd was college kids who mostly drank beer. But there was a slightly-older crowd, a little more sophisticated, who drank other, more potent drinks. A lot of Don's crowd drank scotch or martinis.

Then there were the pseudo-sophisticates, like the two pipe-smoking mustachioed guys with dates, who appeared one night. Seagram's 7 Crown and 7 up, a.k.a. 7&7, was a popular drink of the day. This was so for two reasons; 1. There were a lot of underage drinkers who, when they ordered a 7&7 thought the bartender would think them sophisticated; actually the opposite was true. Bartenders ran into this situation every night. 2. Customers who weren't really drinkers knew about 7&7, and because the name was so popular, and they didn't know the names of other drinks, would automatically order it.

The two pipe guys were of the second variety. Also, when they came in they sat at a small table, another dead giveaway. The Opus was not a sitting-at-a-table kind of place.

Allow me another quick digression. Bars always have pouring booze, as in rye, scotch, rum, vodka and gin. They are non-name brands, purchased at a much cheaper price than the more popular brands. Jack and Don bought a pouring rye (Seagram's 7 is a rye) called Kassers 51. It was so cheap, Jack and Don stockpiled it like they were picking it up off the coast of Atlantic City.

And that brings us back to the pipes. As soon as the foursome was settled one of the guys came to the bar and ordered. He asked me for "Two 7&7's and two Seagram's 7 and 7 ups." I wasn't sure I heard correctly and repeated the order. Okay I said, Let me get this straight, you want two 7&7s and two Seagram's 7 and 7 ups. "Correct" he said. My next move was performed right in front of him. I lined up four glasses with ice, grabbed a bottle of Kasser's and a shot glass. With much exaggeration I held the bottle up, label clearly facing him. I poured shots of Kasser's in each of the four glasses. I then grabbed the squirt gun and filled each with 7 up. I picked up the first two and very deliberately said, here are the two 7&7s, and in the same manner, here are your two Seagram's 7 and 7 ups. I waited the whole time for him to say, "Is this some kind of joke?" He never did. He paid, thanked me and went back to his table. I was flabbergasted. When I told the guys they almost fell out.

On nights I worked the back bar we had a customer who came regularly. He always sat at one end by himself and was somewhat aloof. I say that because women were seemingly coming out of the woodwork. He was not an unattractive guy and by simply smiling in their direction would have had girls all over him.

Nobody and I mean nobody, ever ordered Kasser's 51 by name. If you were ordering rye without specifying a brand you were automatically getting Kasser's. However this guy's drink of choice was Kasser's 51 and ginger ale, and that's what he asked for every time he came in. Not only that, but he'd taken to calling it just 51 like he was ordering Johnny Walker Black. One night, horror of horrors, we actually ran out of Kasser's. Someone had screwed up big time. In place of Kasser's, we were pouring Imperial, a step up in quality and price from Kasser's.

I was moving pretty good when Mr. Aloof came in. I knew what he wanted but always got a kick out of hearing him order, "51 and ginger." On this night I didn't bother explaining about being out of Kasser's when he ordered, because we were so busy, and no one knew the difference anyway. I just went to the other end of the bar, grabbed the Imperial, made his drink and delivered it. When I placed it down he looked at me like I'd committed a crime. I asked him if there was a problem. In a knowing voice he said, "I saw that." Saw what, I asked. "I saw you give me Imperial instead of 51." I had to go to the end of the bar to keep from laughing in the guys face. A moment later I returned and explained to him about the Kasser's. He still looked at me like I'd stolen his favorite toy. I told him the Imperial was on the house and that seemed to satisfy him. He even ordered a couple of more after that.

Because the Opus was so busy and such a good job, Jack and Don were always getting applications for bartending jobs. During the first summer they hired a guy we'll call Tim. Tim was a friend of the two owners and was moved to the front of the hiring line.

Tim's problem was he had no experience. A further drawback; he was not a drinker and didn't much care for the bar scene. But he did like girls.

Now in working the Opus, you had to be fast and alert. The rest of us took pride in performing well and little competitions ensued. So we were somewhat disturbed by Tim's blasé attitude toward the job.

Instead of having his game face on when reporting for work and ready for the busy night ahead, his manner was that of someone on vacation. He would casually go behind the bar where he joined two other workers. His shift started at 9:00 P.M. so the place was already hopping. He would walk to the end of the bar where he'd promptly plant one foot on the beer box. If he saw a guy he knew, or a girl who looked interesting, he'd chew on a stir stick and engage them in conversation. If he had no one to converse with he'd simply gaze absent-mindedly into space.

Tim was a big man standing 6'3" and weighing about 225. Space behind the bar was limited and guys had trouble getting by him. If someone was looking for Tim to make them a drink it was necessary to seek him out; he wasn't coming to you. If someone did happen to approach him for a drink, they were likely to be met with disdain for interrupting his reverie.

Many nights the bar got so busy Don had to jump behind and help out. Customers were ordering drinks so fast even Tim was pressed into action. He hadn't developed much beyond the beer opening stage but he was a little help. When a customer requested a mixed drink he would ask another bartender how to make it.

One night when Don was pressed into service the guys were making drinks as fast as they could, barely keeping up. Tim always picked up his pace when Don was behind the bar. This of course fooled no one, least of all Don.

At the height of the evening the place was going nuts and Don was sweating bullets from the madness. With a question that couldn't come at a worse time, Tim approached Don and said, "Don, how do you make a Beefeater?" Without skipping a beat, or looking up, Don answered, "The same way you make a Tanqueray!"

It was not long after, that Tim and his short-lived bartending career parted ways.

Local girls, I mentioned earlier, came to the Opus regularly. Most of them were very attractive and had great personalities. During the winter months we all hung out as a crowd. Usually during that period some of the guys would get serious and have something going with some of the girls. But come the season all that changed. As soon as the summer girls started arriving it was c'est la vie for the locals. This really pissed them off, not that they weren't above checking out new arrivals of the opposite sex themselves.

The pickings were really good. Guys down for the summer, who came to the Opus, must have thought they'd died and gone to heaven. It was so easy to meet girls. One night I got a call from my college roommate Norm, saying he was taking a few days off from his ice cream truck to pay a visit. Being the horny guy he was, and having heard from me about the abundance of females, he was just too tempted not to check it out.

We had plenty of room at our house to put him up. As soon as he arrived he was anxious to get to the action. When we got to the Opus he was happily surprised to see what I had told him was true. Norm wasn't a drinker and wasn't interested in small talk with the boys. His mind was on one thing only. Immediately, he oiled his way around the bar, sidled up to a female, and began hitting on her with the full force of his charm.

About half hour later I saw him leave with her. About half hour later he was back. Score: Girl 1, Norm 0. But Norm was not the type who discouraged easily. He was right back at it and this continued until late in the evening. At one point I interrupted him to say he should have a sign made for his car announcing, *Norm's Taxi Service*, "We deliver if you deliver." For the three or four days he was there I didn't see much of him. I guess he was happy though because, between the beach and the Opus, he had more women than a Mormon has wives.

A couple of years earlier I worked a place called the Virginia Bar for a few weeks. There I'd met a guy named Lou, from Ambler Pennsylvania. I don't think I've ever formed a more instant friendship with anyone in my life as I did Lou. The man just exuded fun and charm. I found out right away he loved to laugh and I did everything I could to encourage it. We also found we shared a love of the Broadway Theatre, particularly musicals. After yakking through the better part of a night I invited Lou to come visit me at Michigan Avenue the next day. He started coming to our beach every weekend he was able to make it down, and we introduced him to *our* nightlife. He, Mick, Tommy and I became good friends. In fact anyone we ever introduced Lou to became an immediate friend. Lou was a first-class guy who loved to enjoy himself. He was also very generous.

Because he had his own import-export business, Lou often entertained customers from abroad. He had connections with New York ticket agencies and would arrange tickets for his clients to see the latest popular Broadway shows. One year while I was away at college, getting ready to come home for Christmas vacation, he sent me tickets for two hit Broadway shows, *How to Succeed in Business Without Really Trying*, and *Carnival*. He treated me like this on more than one occasion.

In 1960 Lou scored tickets for the championship game between the Philadelphia Eagles and Green Bay Packers. The day was freezing but Lou had arranged a flask of bourbon for each of us. We sure enjoyed that game and somehow didn't mind the frigid weather at all. After the game he somehow wangled his way to the Green Bay locker room where we met Paul Hornung and Jim Taylor. Even though he was a big Eagles fan, and knew I was a Packers fan, he went out of his way to make my day special. That's the kind of guy he was.

The big rage on the dance floor that summer was the Twist, by Chubby Checker. I always thought the Twist was a dopey vacuous dance. The only thing you had to do to master it was buy a hula hoop and go through the gyrations. However, it was extremely popular at the Opus.

We introduced Lou to the Opus. He loved the Twist, and picked it up right away. Because he was a good looking guy with a great personality he found plenty of girls to dance with. He would eventually meet his future wife Carole at the Opus.

The club that really popularized the Twist was the Peppermint Lounge in Manhattan. For awhile, all we heard about was the Peppermint Lounge and how cool it was. Supposedly they had the greatest Twist dancers on the East Coast. I recall thinking, how could they be so great? I mean, it wasn't Fred and Ginger, it was the Twist. Some of us decided to go to New York and see what all the fuss was about.

One evening we jumped in Jack's car and headed for Manhattan. It was only a two-and-a-half-hour ride and we got there about 9:30 P.M. By the time we parked and grabbed a bite to eat we'd killed an hour. The Peppermint Lounge was a short walk from where we parked.

When we arrived we were surprise to find, that from the outside, it didn't look like anything special. We were further surprised when we entered; it still didn't look like anything special. For one thing it was very narrow and decorated in red and white which reminded one of a candy cane (its intent I suppose) and didn't exactly blow you away. There were very few people and those that were there looked about as excited as someone who'd just completed a ninety six hour dance marathon.

We looked at each other and thought, we left the Opus and drove a few hours for this? The place couldn't hold a candle to the Opus. It might have been that Manhattan is quiet in the summer and the population wasn't there. Just the same, with all the major publicity it was getting, it sure turned out to be a disappointment. We stayed for about an hour and nothing ever developed. Through the years I realized a lot of bars/nightclubs in Manhattan are overrated.

We arrived back in Atlantic City around 2:30 A.M. and the Opus was packed to the rafters. People were twisting all over the place; so much for the Peppermint Lounge.

Nights Tommy and I were off we went on dinner dates or agreed to meet girls at our favorite haunts. Through all of this we were still training for the bay race. We became an oddity of sorts to the guys at the Opus, especially Don. If his Philly friends were in town and Tom and I had been out on the town we'd stop in the Opus. Don would gather his friends around telling them about our training regimen. He'd say, "These guys work every day and four or five nights a week; the rest of the time, they're out partying. They're going to be in a boat race soon. I don't know when they sleep."

We had never given that statement any thought. To us it was just the way it was. But as Don kept telling people they'd tell others. After a while we started feeling weird. I guess we were having too much fun to worry about sleep.

On the day of the race a crew came from the boatyard to transport our boat to lower Chelsea. This is at the south end of Atlantic City. Races in the bay are different than those in the ocean since there are no waves. The width of the bay where the race was being held was only about 60 yards wide. The length of the race was about an eighth of a mile. As in the ocean race, each crew had to turn a flag. We drew the flag closest to the wharf toward the ocean side.

The crowd had to assemble where the race began in order to watch it. This was the only empty area for viewing since most of the rest of the bay was lined with housing.

The other three crews we faced were all solid, so the race being shorter than in the ocean meant you had to go full-throttle all the way. One of the crews was made up of the two brothers, Charlie and Ronnie. They were not a very big crew, but because they were flawless in their rowing stroke had won several ocean races. It would be considered a feather in our cap to beat them.

The boats were in the water and judges called for us to take our places. I noticed the side we were on was very shady and dark compared to the other side which was bathed in sunshine. This was due to shadows cast by the bay housing. I should have been more attentive to those shadows.

As soon as we were lined up the gun went off.

Everyone broke together. We were close enough to hear each other's grunts and see the looks of determination. About half way there we began to ease slightly ahead. I kept turning to see if I was on target with the flag and was reassured each time. At first, I had been looking over my left shoulder but couldn't see a flag. Stupidly I looked over my right shoulder and there it was (it was so dark and shady I was unable to pick out flag colors). We had pulled ahead by three quarters of a boat length. Our abbreviated stroke was working like magic.

Usually, when you get that kind of lead on other crews and turn the flag first it's almost impossible for anyone to catch you. This is especially true in a shorter race with no impediments.

Suddenly I noticed the crew next to us was heading for the same flag, and my heart sank. I glanced over my left shoulder and to my horror there was our flag, closer to the wharf. Oh my God I shouted, I've got the wrong flag. Tommy looked around and the next words I heard were all the expletives directed at me for being such a dumb son-of-a-bitch.

We jammed our oars in the water and pushed with all we had. We made the adjustment and rowed toward our flag. Too late! By the time we got to it and made the turn the other crews were already on their way back. We rowed furiously but to no avail. Like I said, once crews turn that flag, ain't nobody catchin' em. That was particularly true for us since we had so much distance to make up. Chalk up another one for Charlie and Ronnie.

When we got to the finish and were out of the boat Tommy was furious. I couldn't blame him. He was yelling like he wanted to clobber me. All I could do was shrug and try to explain what happened. He was having none of it. That wasn't the worst of it. A lot of our friends had come, including my brother and some of Tom's family. They clearly saw we had the race won if not for my dopey mistake.

Tommy had trouble being civil to me for a few days. It may only be a boat race, but to lose like that is something you never quite get over.

Other than that, I was having a great summer working the beach and Opus and meeting plenty of girls. The initial house we'd rented was over-crowded and since we were hanging with a new bunch of guys Mick and I moved. The new place was a sprawling house on the bay, in the downtown Chelsea section of Atlantic City. It had a boat slip right underneath the house and I was able to bring the boat I'd bought in Florida, and dock it below. Several times a week, before work, I'd go downstairs jump in the boat and race through the back bays, feeling the warm sun on my back and the bay breeze caressing my face. We were joined in the house by Bobby, Tommy's brother Joe, a couple of brothers from Philly we had become friendly with, and a female named Diana, who was part of our crowd.

But then, things began to change. Tommy met a girl from West Virginia. Mick and Lou met girls from Pennsylvania. A coed Jack knew from college came for the summer and he was hooked. Don met a girl who would become his wife. Even Kenny got a date one night.

For awhile Bobby and I were the only guys who weren't involved. For me, that was about to change. Until it did Bobby and I were having a ball. We were hanging out in night clubs where he'd introduce me to other entertainers he knew.

One night, all of us went to see Sammy Davis Jr. at the Harlem Club. Because of Bobby's juice we got a table that butted right up against the stage. We could have reached out and touched Sammy. He was going through his singing, dancing and fast-draw gun routine when suddenly he stopped and threw a line to no one in particular. It was from a comedy record of that time by Mel Brooks called *The Two Thousand Year Old Man*. We had recently purchased the record, listened to it at the house almost every night, and knew it by heart.

Instantly one of us shot back the corresponding line. He hit us with another one, and we responded again. The next thing we knew we were shooting lines back and forth until the audience became a little restless. As soon as Sammy realized it he said, "Okay you guys, got to get back to the show." It was obvious he had clearly enjoyed the repartee, as had we.

A NEW ROMANCE, SORTA

There was a nightspot called the Bamboo Club on Arkansas and Pacific Avenues. It was located a block from Michigan. I had never been there, so one night when Bobby was off we decided to drop over. He knew the two entertainers there. They always stopped down the Tropics to see him on their nights off and he wanted to reciprocate.

My first thought upon entering was I should have brought a flashlight and wondered whether they'd paid their electric bill. As we drew closer to the stage there was sensual blue lighting surrounding the entertainers. I had noticed on the glass-enclosed marquee outside, the names, Nancy Lee and Sonny Dae (not their real names). The picture showed Sonny sitting at a set of drums and Nancy at the piano.

Sonny really enjoyed himself on stage. He wore a constant smile and interacted with the audience, recognizing and acknowledging all who showed appreciation for his talent.

Nancy was the opposite. She concentrated on her music. She sang in a low sultry voice and, because of the depth of feeling she conveyed, the customers were very attentive to her musical renderings. Most of her songs were ballads and she sang with a sadness that seemed born of real pain and made you feel compelled to listen.

When they saw Bobby, they nodded and indicated their set would be over soon. I saw Nancy glance toward us a couple of times and had the feeling she was wondering who I was. That thought was quickly dispelled when she and Sonny came over. The three said their hellos and Bobby introduced us. Sonny shook my hand like we were old buddies. Nancy gave me a slight sad smile continuing her conversation with Bobby.

We stayed for another set. When they came over again Sonny asked me what I did. When I told him, he said they go to the beach every day but bathe at Arkansas. He said they'd start coming to Michigan. As we were saying our goodbyes I sensed Nancy glancing my way again. I thought she was very attractive, but cold and guarded.

The next day Tommy and I were on the stand when Sonny appeared, all smiles and full of energy. I introduced him to Tommy, who he immediately engaged in conversation. While they were talking I looked behind me and there was Nancy lying on a blanket. Sonny stayed for awhile until the call of the ocean became irresistible. Like a kid he happily bounded off into the sea diving under the first wave that came his way.

Later Nancy took a walk down to the water's edge. As she passed she waved but that was it. I got the impression she didn't want to be bothered by any lifeguards. She seemed the type to be attracted to suave guys who leaned a little toward the underworld crowd. The Bamboo was full of those types. I decided I wasn't going to go out of my way to be friendly. Still, she fascinated me. I also thought she might be involved with Sonny, which she wasn't.

Tommy and I became good friends with Sonny, who we talked with every day. They continued coming daily. Sonny was always in an upbeat mood and loved to tell jokes. He was a guy who genuinely cared for others' well-being.

Often I would hang out by the boat just to get off by myself. It was such a day while I was watching bathers when I heard, "Hi!" It was Nancy. It was the first time I'd seen her up close in the daylight. This was one sexy looking woman. She had big brown eyes, full lips and dark hair highlighted with blond streaks. Her beautiful olive skin so common to those from the Mediterranean was a dead giveaway to her Italian heritage.

Still she didn't smile, and in fact seemed a little sad. I quickly engaged her in conversation. As we talked I could sense her begin to relax and loosen up. I found out she was from Pennsylvania and had signed a summer long contract to play at the Bamboo Club. We spoke for an hour until I had to go on layout.

Before she left I told her I'd like to come by the club that night. She was quite receptive and said she hoped I would. We said our goodbyes but I felt something was brewing. When I went back to the stand Tommy asked me if we had something going. I told him things seemed to be warming up.

That evening I arrived at the Bamboo about 11:00 P.M. Sonny spotted me as soon as I walked in. Nancy was deep in song and didn't see me. I took a seat at the bar, enjoying her musical renderings and having more feeling about her since we'd talked. At one point she looked down and saw me staring. She smiled so warmly I was taken aback by her silent greeting. In that moment, I knew things had changed between us for the better.

I stayed for the rest of their sets. She got off at about 1:30 A.M. and I took her for something to eat. We talked for a couple of hours and the attraction we had for each other became more obvious.

The next day, and thereafter, she and Sonny came to the beach daily. We got to know each other a lot better and our relationship grew. I reciprocated by going to see her whenever I wasn't working at the Opus. She only had one night off a week and I'd usually take her to some nice place for dinner.

Nancy's sister started coming to Atlantic City on weekends. As attractive as Nancy was her sister was a bona fide knockout. She was tall, beautiful, dark like Nancy and very shapely. She could easily have been a New York model. Lefty, the bartender at the Bamboo wasted no time getting close to her and they were together on the beach every day. Lefty was a very handsome guy who was built like a linebacker and had a quiet but likeable personality.

Soon other members of Nancy's family, including her mother, started coming to visit. The family was close knit and made me feel a part of them. When they came to the beach they always brought food and had a great time among themselves. I would have loved joining the festivities but that was out of the question. Poor Sonny, the extrovert, always felt bad that we couldn't go back on the beach and join them. Consequently, so we wouldn't feel left out (we didn't), he would stay by the stand and relay what was going on. The guy had a natural innocence and wonderful warmth about him.

Some nights, when Nancy got off work early she would come to the Opus and wait for me to get off. We had grown very close and were seeing each other exclusively.

The Opus was a large building that also contained rooms upstairs. Jack and Don rented them to friends, which brought in extra income. Sometimes, when I was particularly tired I would stay in one of the rooms instead of going all the way home.

It was that kind of night when I got off early and went upstairs to sleep. Nancy had earlier said she was tired and probably wouldn't meet me. Additionally, the weather had been inclement all day and the evening had grown worse. It was a good night to catch up on sleep.

Unwittingly, sometime during the evening, Nancy changed her mind and decided to surprise me. When she got to the bar I was already in bed for the night. She decided to sit and have a drink. She wasn't the type to be picked up, especially by rah rah college types.

Jack, who didn't know her, sensed she was there to meet someone and asked. When she mentioned my name he told her I was in bed for the night. He sat next to her and ordered a drink.

Jack had natural charm and a very easy way with women that made them feel comfortable. He and Nancy had a few drinks and the more they talked the closer they became. Later I found out they left the bar went to the Tropics and wound up together.

The next day was beautiful but neither Nancy nor Sonny came to the beach. I thought it a little odd but didn't make much of it.

That night I went to see Nancy. When I arrived she was on stage and though she gave me her usual smile it wasn't the same. I was there for about forty five minutes when Jack walked in. I was somewhat surprised until I saw the way she greeted him. He became the recipient of the smile usually reserved for me. It didn't take long to put two and two together, even to the extent that I figured she must have gone to the Opus the previous night. I said goodnight to Jack, ignored Nancy, and left.

The next day the pair arrived as usual. Sonny came to the stand trying to act like nothing had happened. It didn't take long for him to affect a sad look. He acted as if this problem had happened to him instead of me. I felt worse for him than I did for myself.

Nancy didn't come over and I made no effort to talk to her. I wished she would go to another beach. The situation was very uncomfortable. She and Jack went out for awhile but the relationship soured. Sometimes, when we caught each other's eye on the beach she would have that same sad look as when I first met her. I was unmoved.

I went back to my old ways, picking up girls on the beach. If they were interesting I would suggest we meet. If nothing happened on the beach the Opus girls were always an alternative. I hoped it bothered Nancy watching me flirt every day.

Nancy's contract ran out before summer ended and she went home. Just before I was due to go back to school for my last year she called. We talked for awhile and decided to meet for lunch, half way between Atlantic City and Pennsylvania.

Things were strained when we met. We talked about past events and tried to recapture what had looked like a promising relationship. I realized at some point that things were over between us. I think she did too. Finally, we exchanged friendly goodbyes and left.

I didn't linger long thinking about her. After my experience with Mickey I would never again allow myself to be affected in the way I had been with her.

CHAPTER 10

MOVING ON

The thing I remember most about my senior year was being anxious to graduate

Classes ended in May. If I wanted to go through all the pomp and circumstances, I'd have to wait another week for the ceremonies. Another week to put on a cap and gown with a goofy tassel hanging in my face and no one there to see how ridiculous I looked? I said to hell with that. I was outta there.

It took two days to get home because I had some trouble with my car in Georgia and had to stay overnight to wait for repairs. My final grades beat me home. I feared being greeted with a D in business statistics but hallelujah, I passed with a C. Wow! I had made it through four years.

Was I ready to go out and seek my fame and fortune? Not on your life. The day after I got home I was back on the beach. I wasn't ready to enter the world of business. I still had some oats to sew—wild or otherwise.

I believe many young guys were like me in their thinking. There was no place like Atlantic City. We thought other places boring. Philadelphia guys always thought of their city as being on the cutting edge. If that was the case, why did so many of them move to A.C.?

Don't get me wrong. Of all the guys we met from other cities Philly guys were the ones we liked best *and* with whom we had the most in common. There developed, a Philadelphia-Atlantic City connection and more than a few Philly guys married local A.C. girls.

Things were much the same at Michigan. Tommy and I were still partners, Murph still the captain. Kenny had found a home and returned every year. There were some new faces on the stretch. Roy had left to get married and start a new life. Joe R had a new partner in Bob, whom you may recall having been my partner, early on, when we were sentenced to the Inlet. Joe

247

and Bob became rowing partners. I don't recall seeing two guys who enjoyed training as much as they did.

NOT THE SAME MISTAKE TWICE

Tommy and I continued rowing together, and, I believe finished third in a couple of more ocean races. We were invited to compete again in the same bay race we'd lost the previous summer. However this time it was to be held in Atlantic City, at Albany Avenue. Earlier I described this location as one I used to row my sneak-box to as a kid. Albany Avenue Bridge was one of the bay crossing entrances into Atlantic City.

The same area crews of Atlantic City, Ventnor, Margate, and Longport would be represented. We had hoped the brothers Charlie and Ronnie, from Ventnor, would be there and we'd have a chance to get even. Unfortunately, that was not to be. Nonetheless, the crew taking their place had proven to be formidable opponents so we were still up against a force.

The bay at Albany Avenue was wider than where the race was held the previous year. Also, there were no houses casting shadows to interfere with our line of sight. Spectators had the choice to watch from either side of the bay, or from the Albany Avenue Bridge.

There were ramps on the west side of the bay making it easier to launch the boats. As each craft was lowered to the water, we climbed in and rowed to the starting line. As we took our places I turned several times to make sure I could see our flag clearly.

Judges lined up the boats as each crew nervously waited for the gun to go off. At the pistol's sharp crack, oars hit the water as we all pulled mightily to gain an advantage. *Humping your oars* is the expression used to describe the start. When everyone starts with an even chance, as we did, it is difficult to take the lead. Each crew stands up on their leg braces for the first stroke lifting their butts completely off the seat to get the boat moving from a stand-still position. The second hump gets you about a two-thirds pull. By the third hump, you should have taken a full stroke and settled into a rhythm.

Since all rowers practice this start, there is usually no clear separation between crews until the halfway mark. It is difficult not to become frustrated when you're pulling your butt off and not overtaking anyone. As you get closer to the flag things start to open up.

Later it came to our attention that a captain who was counting our strokes, reported to a colleague that we were rowing at 44 strokes a minute. He said to his friend, "They'll never keep up that pace."

As we got to the three-quarter-mark we took the lead. I turned to see that our flag was right off our bow. Just before we turned the flag we opened nearly a boat-length lead.

Making the turn, we knew no one was going to catch us. Halfway back we opened up a two boat-length lead. The captain who had clocked us on the way to the flag had us on the watch now. He sheepishly announced to his friend that we were now rowing 46 stokes a minute.

We won going away.

Something ironic happened. Neither one of our fathers had ever attended any of our races. I was surprised, after we received our trophies, to see my dad in the background. It was gratifying to know that the first race he ever saw me in—I won. He gave me the old thumbs-up sign. My dad was not an overtly expressive guy but I knew he was proud.

Tommy had no idea until he got home that his dad had been there. We were meeting all the guys at the Opus that night to celebrate (as if we needed a reason). I stopped by Tommy's to pick him up. His dad was in his usual chair watching television. When I went in Tommy was still upstairs getting ready. I said hello to Tommy's dad and instead of greeting me he said, "How could you two win that race?" I was surprised because anytime I was at their house I seldom heard him speak. I had always felt like a nonentity in his presence. Normally he was very quiet, and after his initial statement said nothing. I in turn was careful not to invade his privacy.

However, I was too curious not to ask him if he saw the race. He answered in the affirmative. Tommy's house was located less than half a block from the bay. His dad would have only had to walk a block toward the bridge to get a front row seat.

He actually uttered a few more phrases inferring how we got lucky. He just wasn't an expressive guy, but I knew he was pleased.

Besides winning the boat race, and finishing school, I was in a partying mood. I certainly didn't have to worry about company. As soon as we got to the Opus, drinks started flowing. Everyone was congratulating us for beating the other island crews. As soon as we finished one drink someone would shove another toward us.

We celebrated until late in the evening. About 3:00 A.M., Tommy announced he was going home. Stupidly, I decided to stay out and go to the Tropics, where I devoured more drinks in my quest for immortality. It's amazing, when you're out having fun how fast time goes. At 7:00 A.M., I decided, in my drunken stupor it was senseless to go home because I'd never get up for work. I started drinking water in an effort to sober up.

A LESSON LEARNED

At 9:00 A.M. I headed for the beach. I tried to avoid Murph but I had to face Tommy and he knew right away that I was still feeling no pain. To make matters worse, the ocean looked troublesome.

Actually it was a beautiful, calm, windless day but the waves were big. The tide was only a little more than half up. There was a large offset to our right that would become more dangerous as the tide got higher.

Around 11:00 A.M. we had our first run. Two kids who had wondered out too far got caught in the set. We jumped off the stand and headed for the boat, or, rather Tommy headed for the boat. As soon as I hit the sand I went straight to my knees. Tommy turned and started yelling for me to get moving. I got to my feet and made it to the boat. We launched and made for the two kids. We didn't get very far, when I turned to see a huge wave bearing down on us. I was aware of the situation but couldn't clear my head. Even in my stupor I remembered thinking what a fool I was.

We just cleared that wave and a couple of others. We got to the kids and Tommy reeled them in with the donut. Thank God they were all right and nothing serious occurred.

When we got to the beach Tommy chewed my ass out. I was aware of everything, but still functioning in an alcoholic haze. I was lucid enough to know the seriousness of the situation and kept trying to shake the cobwebs; a half hour later, a second run.

This time I jumped off the stand without falling. We ran to the boat and as I grabbed for the left tholepin to pull the boat off the rollers it wasn't there. More accurately, I wasn't there. I missed the tholepin completely. Tommy who had hold of the other tholepin was livid. I quickly recovered as we got underway.

The tide was higher now and the waves bigger. A girl, like the two kids before her, had gotten caught in the set and was struggling to swim against it. We had a few precarious moments negotiating the waves that would have flattened us, had we hesitated a few seconds. I remember thinking, don't let me screw up, we're dealing with a life here. In that moment, my head cleared and my reflexes returned. Those waves have a way of getting your attention. I gave silent thanks. Once we circumvented the break we got to the girl quickly and secured her in the boat.

Tommy lectured me as we walked to the stand. I told him I was all right now and there would be no repeats of my earlier stupidity—good thing too. The day turned out to be one in which we had a significant number of rescues. I was on my toes the rest of the day and vowed never again to repeat that kind of immature behavior.

Although I hadn't intended to stay on the beach as long as I did the attraction was too powerful. During a couple of winters, between life guarding I tried a few jobs associated with the business world but just couldn't get into the boring 9 to 5 routine. I'd rather work the beach seven days a week than any of those jobs for one hour.

The Opus stayed open during the winter months because it had become so popular. It didn't need the infusion of the summer crowd to support it. I still had my four or five shifts a week and was making good money. Additionally, my Uncle George, he of the "crabtee" cocktail debacle, had bought his own bar. It was called George's Hometown Tavern. My brother Jim was his main bartender and just about ran the place. I began working part time at George's as it grew more popular. Like the Tropics, it was a late night hangout for the younger crowd, mostly guys.

George's was located approximately halfway between the Opus and Tropics. The Opus was not open as late on weeknights as in summer, so

George's became the interim hangout until the Tropics started buzzing. George's featured something the other two didn't, namely games. There was a pool table, dart board, and shuffle board game. A lot of betting went on at the Tavern. As it got later, some of the social crowd would leave for the Tropic's while the bettors stayed at George's.

One unique thing about George's was its location, right next door to a funeral parlor called Gormley's. After family and friends had paid their respects to the dearly departed, they would come to the bar which filled up quickly. I mentioned to my brother Jim one evening that we should put a sign up announcing, When it's Dead at Gormley's, it's lively at George's. He didn't think that was such a good idea.

All three bars did very well and being located, as they were, over a well traveled route, didn't hurt. These three places made up a big part of our social life. Local girls who hung in groups, supported all three places, though not as frequently at George's, as the others. Every year, the girls, bless their hearts, forgave our summer transgressions and took us back. We in turn treated them like there were no other females around. After all, what choice did either of us have?

Tending bar at night gave us the entire day to do other things. A lot of us were golfers. When the weather was mild enough, as it often is in South Jersey, we could be found at the course. There was one course we all favored, where the pro, Bill, a special, fun loving Irishman was a good friend. If a group needed a guy he would become part of that foursome. He was not like a lot of pros who have an elitist air and treat you like you're part of their congregation.

Bill was also not indisposed to enjoying a cocktail or two. There were many nights we put him to bed, and saw he got up in the morning. Bill and our group had a perpetual home and home series. Either we'd be at the golf course, or he'd be at the Opus.

One of my fondest memories was a New Years Day when the temperature reached 70 degrees. We'd go out and play nine, come in and have a few drinks, then play another nine. We kept this up all day and hardly watched the football games—unheard of. On my last round, marking thirty six holes, I shot a forty five. I had finally discovered the secret of the game—booze!

There was a small–and I mean small–ski area about 50 miles away. It was called Pine Hill, which we promptly christened Pimple Hill. When it snowed, which was seldom, we'd jump in the car and head for the slope (singular in this case). We didn't have ski equipment and would wear the warmest clothes available.

I wish I'd gotten moving pictures of a few of those excursions. Some of the spills we took were absolutely side-splitting. A highlight of one of the trips was when one of the guys borrowed a pair of boots. As we were changing, getting ready to leave, he put them on the roof of the car. About halfway home it dawned on him that he'd forgotten to retrieve them. Oh well, someone had two new boots, or, two people had one new boot.

On nights off, we'd often go to Manhattan to catch a Broadway Show. Sometimes we'd even take a date. At other times, we'd go for a couple of days and see two or three shows. As much as I loved Atlantic City, it was always exciting, going to New York. I could be entertained just watching people walk up and down Broadway. No one ever made eye contact with you in the City. They were probably in a big hurry or too untrusting, or both.

Winters lasted a lot longer than summers but this only made you more aware of how special summers were. Holidays were always a welcome diversion and once Easter arrived, summer lay just around the bend.

EVOLVING TOWARD DINOSAUR STATUS

There is a term for lifeguards who overstay their leave–*dinosaur*. I never heard the expression until I read an article by Joe R. titled: *Who Were the Dinosaurs of Yesterday?* In it he describes the transition a guard must eventually make, when it's his time to leave the beach. "Every guard must make that decision for himself." Joe goes on to say, "The time will come to turn the reins over to the next generation. Let the dinosaurs fade into obscurity, taking with them memories of what was, and how they had replaced the dinosaurs that came before them."

I knew I should be getting on with my life but almost before I realized it, I was into my early thirties. I still couldn't come to grips with the idea of becoming an organization man. I had gotten used to being independent, not answering to anyone. The lifestyle I was leading afforded me lots of freedom and I wasn't ready to give that up. Besides, I had no obligations, was not married and had no kids.

These are things I rationalized all the time. But somewhere a little voice kept telling me I had more to do and all this procrastination was only delaying the inevitable. I was not easy to convince.

An incident occurred the following summer, when I went back to the beach that may have planted a seed that gave me pause for serious thought.

Tommy and I, embarked upon another summer with things pretty much as they had been. We were still making rescues, rowing competitively, going to dinner on payday, working at the Opus and meeting lots of girls.

We never gave much thought to a female's age as long as she was in her twenties. No women ever gave an indication they might not be interested in us because of our age. I guess we thought of ourselves as eternally young, or what might better be described as–typical men.

One week five attractive girls came to our beach and we wasted no time getting to know them. We found out they were down for the summer and working at a restaurant called Luigi's, about two blocks from our beach. They had rented rooms in a boarding house and would be bathing at Michigan every day.

Four of the five were friendly, but one, the leader always looked at us with a disdainful eye. She held back and wouldn't come to the stand like the others. We weren't concerned since she was the least attractive. Tommy and I had picked out two we liked and were getting ready to make a move on.

One day they lingered all day on the beach until we got off. We approached the two away from the others and asked them to wait while we changed and we'd take them for a drink. Arkansas Avenue sported four bars on one side of the street in the same block. One of the places was an authentic Irish pub called the Erin. It imported Irish step dancers from the old country and entertainment started in the afternoon. It was a place we went to occasionally after work. The Erin had a great Irish openness about it, making it conducive to afternoon partying. This is where we planned to take the girls.

When we got to the boardwalk, all five were still there. We saw *Attila*, motioning the two we had talked to with expressive gestures. As we got closer we heard her say, "You can't go with them, they're too old." I felt like somebody hit me in the face with an oar. We were shocked and insulted, but this little mommy figure was not to be deterred. She literally grabbed them, pulling them away. Tommy and I stood staring, dumbfounded. The two just shrugged and went with her.

To add insult to injury I ran into one of the girls in the Opus one night. I mentioned I hadn't seen them at our beach lately. She said they were going to the college beach, "The kids are younger there." As soon as the words left her mouth she sheepishly excused herself saying she'd see me later.

Up until that time, I had never thought much about age. I was still doing everything I'd always done as a lifeguard, including boat racing. Now, for the first time, I was forced to take another look. As much as I loved the beach I had always considered moving on, taking up new challenges.

There was nothing wrong with making the beach a career. For many of my fellow guards it became their choice. Being a lifeguard in Atlantic City carries a nice pension if you stay twenty consecutive years to age forty five or older. Many guards were teachers, and others had jobs that allowed them to be off summers. I had an urge to expand my horizons, to see other places. By staying on the beach I might always regret not seeking what life's adventures had in store.

Well, the seed had been sown. The question lay ahead as to when I would seriously consider making a break. I certainly wasn't dissatisfied with my present circumstances and knew nothing would excite me like my present lifestyle. However, the realization that it was soon time for a change would continue gnawing at me. Unless I faced this growing dilemma, I was destined to remain at odds with myself.

The summer months were upon us, and now was not the time to start rearranging my entire life. I mentioned things had remained status quo until now. That was not entirely true. Tommy and I had quit as rowing partners. Somewhere along the way we'd lost our coordinated rowing stroke. Where once the boat had slid smoothly over the water our oars in perfect rhythm, rowing now became an effort with every stroke. No matter what we tried, we could not recreate our earlier success. That signaled time for a change.

CHANGING PARTNERS

Russell was a guy I had grown up with in Pitney Village. He had lived in the row across from us, about eight doors away. Russell was two years younger than me so, we hung out in different crowds. However, since we were always playing sports, we'd often wind up on the same, or opposite sides of a team. Russell was also a beach and bay rat like me, so at times we hung out there together.

Apparently, as kids, we resembled each other from a distance. We were both blond, about the same height and build. Russell's grandmother often leaned out the upstairs window calling him to come home. Occasionally, she would call me, thinking I was him, and then wave me off when she realized her mistake.

After we moved from Pitney Village, I only saw Russell occasionally. When we did see each other it was as long lost friends and we'd always promise in departing to make more of an effort to get together.

Russell became a member of the beach patrol a few years after me. His true goal in life was to become a song writer (he did eventually). One of the things that kept our friendship alive was our mutual interest in theatre.

Russell had moved to Manhattan with the intention of breaking into the showbiz world. He supported himself as an instructor at Radio City's famous ice skating rink. It was there he met his future wife Juliet, who was an actress. I don't recall what Juliet was doing in New York because she was from England. Perhaps she was in a play, or visiting her sister who was also an actress. Eventually, Russell and Juliet married and moved to London.

The summer Tommy and I decided to quit as rowing partners, Russell, after being away for a couple of years came back to the beach. Juliet came with him and fit in perfectly with the beach patrol lifestyle. I loved Juliet immediately. She was a fantastic fun-loving person, with a killer sense of humor.

Russell had always been a terrific athlete, having won both the singles and doubles boat racing events. Sometime early in the season we decided to become rowing partners. We figured to be a natural crew, both tall, long of limb, with good leverage. Even though we worked different stretches we could train together, meeting alternately at each other's beach.

As soon as we began our morning training regimen I'd come to pick Russell up and Juliet would insist she make breakfast. We had a lot of laughs during those days, with Juliet poking fun at us for one reason or another. She always sent us off with some kind of encouraging message. I loved her British accent.

Whenever we trained at Russell's beach, there was a girl named Bonnie waiting to greet us. I think Bonnie was hot for Russell, but she also saw Juliet at the beach most days so she didn't act overtly toward him. Bonnie was probably about 19 or 20, attractive, with a showgirl body. Her breasts were her most outstanding feature. She had a set of knockers that would turn Dolly Parton green with envy. I don't know how we came up with the name, but we started referring to them as Lobberdoons as in, "Wow! That Bonnie sure has a nice set of Lobberdoons."

We were unaware of Juliet having any knowledge as to what we thought were secret conversations regarding Bonnie.

One morning, while having breakfast, Juliet was in her usual chipper mood having fun at our expense. As we were leaving, she gave Russell a hug and kiss followed by her usual words of wisdom spoken in her clipped English accent "Alright boys, I want you to have a good row today and work hard, but don't mess with Bonnie's lobberdoons." We looked at each other in shock, and cracked up, wondering how she knew about Bonnie's nicknamed breasts.

Because there were about sixteen boats entered in the race that year, it was decided to have row offs with eight boats in each heat. Russell and I drew the second heat so we had a chance to wait around to collect more butterflies. Juliet brought her movie camera to catch the start and finish. My brother Mick was there, as always, along with my mother who attended for the first time. Her work schedule had always prevented her coming in the past.

Russell and I went through the usual preparations as we set up our boat. Earlier in our training we had vacillated as to who should row bow, since we were generally the same size. We decided it should be me since I had more experience and knew the things to look for. Besides, with his size, Russell would make a good motor.

We maneuvered the boat into its lane. I climbed in and we waited for the gun to go off. As soon as we heard the sharp report, Russell, who had cat like movements jumped in and we were moving immediately. We cleared the break quickly and jumped off to a fast start. As usual the wind was blowing off the ocean as we rowed into a stiff southerly. We were rowing in perfect rhythm and started pulling away from crews right away. As we neared our flag we were in great position. We turned sharply and headed in, using the incoming swells to our advantage.

Getting closer to the finish line we heard the noise of the crowd getting louder. Suddenly, we saw a small swift wave approaching our stern. Russell, who was a skilled boatman, jumped to the stern to steer. He was a split-second too late. The boat sheared violently to the right. I had just enough time to see us crossing the finish line. In the next instant, the boat flipped violently, hitting me in the leg as it went over, pinning me underneath.

Within seconds, I heard voices shouting that the boat was stuck in the mud. The only thing I could think of was my mother witnessing the entire incident, knowing what her reaction would be. The next thing I heard was the sucking sound of the boat as it was pulled from the oceans floor.

The first face I saw was that of Jackie, the guard Murph had banished from Michigan. He was working the race and now took charge of freeing the boat. "We got it, Bobby, we got it," he kept repeating. The guys pulled me to my feet. I hadn't felt much pain when we went over, but now it felt like my shin was broken (it wasn't). I looked for Russell who was surrounded by Juliet and a crowd of friends.

Then I realized I was being slapped on the back. We'd won. I quickly looked for my mother and saw her standing ashen faced as my brother comforted her. I tried to hide the limp as I went to her but she knew I'd gotten hurt. I assured her I was fine and as she got caught up in the excitement of us winning, she relaxed and told me how proud she was.

I'd wondered what had happened to Russell. I found out he had been catapulted clear of the boat into a foot of water, but suffered no injuries.

Juliet had caught the whole thing on camera. I don't know how many times we scheduled getting together to watch the finish but, for one reason or another, we never did.

I will not bore you with details of the finals. Suffice it to say we got off to a bad start, were hit by a couple of waves and took some water. We couldn't get a rhythm going and started yelling at each other. The result was a distant six place finish.

That was the last boat race in which I ever competed.

I didn't know it at the time, but the following summer was to be my final one as a member of the Atlantic City Beach Patrol.

A NEW BEGINNING

Bill, he a victim of the Phantom's revenge, was now living with his new bride Jane in New York State. They had both recently completed their master's degrees and were teaching school in Poughkeepsie.

Just before Bill left New York to visit his parents, he called me to say he and Jane were bringing a friend that Jane taught with, and wanted me to meet. I was somewhat surprised. Bill and I were friendly but I wondered why I was chosen to meet their friend.

Up until now, I had never shown any inclination to meet a *nice* girl and get involved. Nonetheless, I said I'd be happy to meet her and promptly forgot about it.

On nights I didn't work the Opus, I worked my uncle's bar. It was early May, just prior to the beach opening, and I was working the early evening shift. There was hardly anyone in the bar. I was watching two guys play pool when I heard the door open. I turned to see Bill and Jane and a very pretty blonde with them. It took a moment to make the connection–this was the girl Bill had called about.

He introduced us. Her name was Charie (short for Charlotte). She had a great smile and I found her instantly attractive. They sat and ordered a drink and as the conversation got underway I was impressed with her outgoing personality and intelligence. She had a mature confidence I found appealing. She was different from many of the women I'd met on the beach or in bars.

Charie was going to spend the summer with Bill and Jane, and would leave for Washington, D.C. in September to take on a new teaching job. Before they left the bar I told Charie I'd like to see her again, while she was in town. Over the next couple of days we spent time together. I escorted her around the city pointing out places of interest. At night I took her to dinner and during the course of our lengthy conversations, we found our relationship growing.

Before they left for New York, Charie said she'd be back in a few weeks. I talked to her by phone a few times during that period. We spoke of things in general and I told her I was looking forward to seeing her again.

I was back on the beach by the time they returned. Bill brought Charie to the beach while Jane stayed behind and unpacked.

Charie and I slid unselfconsciously into easy conversation. She talked about her family and what it was like where she lived. She spoke of the mountains and how she couldn't imagine not living among them. During the winter she skied every weekend, often at different resorts. Winter sports were popular because once the first good snow fall hit it remained for the entire winter.

She generally came to the beach every day. Our conversation remained upbeat and consequential, as our feelings for each other deepened into romance. She came to influence my thinking, that there was life after Atlantic City.

As I realized I was falling in love, the beach started losing some of its allure. My boat racing days were over. I didn't try to lure girls to the stand or pick them up in bars.

Going out with the boys occurred less often because I was seeing Charie on a regular basis, whenever I wasn't working. For the first time, being a lifeguard became a *job*.

By August we had fallen deeply in love and were committed to each other. She kept encouraging me to take advantage of my education and seek a profession.

Soon our thoughts turned to marriage. Charie abandoned her plans to go to Washington, D.C. We decided I would seek steady employment after the summer and she would examine the possibility of securing a teaching position.

Naturally when she informed her parents of her plans they were concerned. Because I worked seven days a week I was not able to go to New York, so they decided to come to Atlantic City. Charie's father and I hit it off immediately. He was an excellent golfer and I took him to my course early one morning before my shift started. They stayed the weekend and by the time they left, were okay with our decision.

During that same week, Charie secured an interview at Indiana Avenue School. The principal, Mr. James Usry, (later, Mayor of Atlantic City) conducted the interview. They liked each other right away. He was happy to welcome her to his staff.

I left the beach at the end of September. By then the tourist season was long over.

There remained only a skeleton crew to watch over late season bathers. Most of the force left after Labor Day.

Unless you're a doctor, lawyer, Indian chief, or, God forbid, politician, jobs were not easy to come by. Bear in mind, Atlantic City was a town on the decline and years away from becoming a casino resort. The most decent jobs available with a livable salary were with City or County Government. A couple of friends held positions with the Atlantic County Welfare Board. They told me the work was easy and, depending on how you handled your case load, the number of hours worked was up to you. I applied for a position and was accepted.

We set a wedding date for October. Charie, with the help of Jane started attending to the details. We only invited our immediate families, along with Bill and Jane, because neither of us was interested in a big wedding.

The day dawned clear and brisk as we made our way to the church. Our families had time to meet before we went into the church. The wedding ceremony only took about twenty minutes. We emerged into the bright sunshine and went through the obligatory picture taking ritual and congratulations from our families.

A wedding dinner had been planned at one of the hotels not far from the church. It was a nice opportunity for our families to mingle and get to know each other. I was pleased to see my brothers and Charie's sister and brothers bonding. Our parents were a little more reserved but seemed to hit it off okay.

Since Charie's family had to drive back to New York, we ended the reception early. Everyone said their goodbyes and Charie and I headed for the condo we'd rented in Ventnor, overlooking the beach and boardwalk. Lack of tourists to the island in the off season made for a very affordable rent. This was a great place to spend the winter. We decided to postpone our honeymoon, since we were both starting new jobs.

It didn't take long to settle into the routine of a newly married couple. During the week we stayed busy with our respective responsibilities. Charie, always conscientious, spent a significant amount of time preparing for her students. My job was not as demanding, so I was free to read, watch the tube or practice my guitar.

As the year progressed we visited Charie's parents in New York on a regular basis. Her parents lived in the village of Millbrook, about fifteen miles east of Poughkeepsie. Things were more relaxed with her parents on this trip and I knew her dad and I would forge a close relationship. Her sister and brothers were real pranksters and wasted no time including me in their shenanigans.

Charie was an accomplished skier and suggested, one weekend, we go meet her friends at a nearby mountain called Catamount. My only skiing experience was the aforementioned Pine Hill, New Jersey. She had her own equipment and the family found an old discarded pair of wooden skis and leather boots for me to use. Charie made arrangements for her friends to meet us there.

Our ride up the Taconic State Parkway was breathtakingly beautiful. From all around us arose majestic snow-capped mountains. The rolling hills of the snow-covered countryside looked like something out of a Norman Rockwell painting. It was then that I told Charie I wanted to live there. She was ecstatic.

The lodge had a nice big open fireplace that skiers sat around while putting on their boots. Charie introduced me to her friends, Ernie and Caroline. I noticed that they, along with all the others, including Charie, had the latest shiny vinyl boots that rode high on their shins and buckled easily. Mine were leather with cowhide laces and looked like army shoes. I saw people trying to avert their eyes and wondered just how old the damn things were.

Compared to Pine Hill, these slopes looked like Mount Kilimanjaro. Actually, as mountains go, I later found out this one wasn't big at all. As we put on our skis, I observed once again that those around me had the latest flashy looking fiberglass models. They bore impressive names like Lange,

Head, Rossignol, et al. Mine were made of wood, very long, chipped and, tellingly, revealed no name. I was beginning to feel a mite insecure, to say the least.

The plan was to take me to the bunny hill where I would be given basic instructions. I knew it was going to be a long day as soon as I tried to negotiate the rope tow up the hill. I wound up on my ass five or six times before reaching what was not a very high debarking station.

Ernie did a slow motion snow plow down the hill in an effort to show me how to make a turn. I thought I'd followed his instructions to the letter but on my first attempt, wound up on my keister. This went on for several tries with the same result. Ernie told me that while going into my snow plow I was not using my edges (as it turned out, *there were no edges* on those damn barrel slats).

They eventually left me on the bunny slope and went on to the intermediate levels. I got pretty good at learning how to ski on my bum. After a while, the three came back and Ernie urged me to come and ski with them. Not wanting to look like a coward in front of the ladies, I timidly followed. At least there were chair lifts going to the intermediate slopes, so I didn't have to worry about falling.

When we got there I looked down and thought, are you out of your friggin minds? The lodge looked so small I thought it was made of legos. They told me to follow them down and took off. I gingerly pointed my skis downhill and was immediately out of control. I basically bounced down the mountain, being only able to stop by taking a dive into a snow drift. I concluded that Ernie was a freakin' sadist.

I didn't ski much more that day. I sat in the lodge trying to salvage my damaged ego, along with some tender body parts. I wondered how I, who had always picked up sports so quickly, could be such a schlep.

When we were leaving, Ernie asked me how I'd enjoyed the day. I told him I didn't think skiing was something I planned to pursue. A knowing smile crossed his lips.

Sidenote: The following year, when we were living in New York, Charie bought me the latest model skis and boots for Christmas. I took one private lesson and was paralleling in a matter of weeks. What a difference the right equipment–and *no* Ernie made.

We would like to have moved to Millbrook that first winter but Charie felt obligated to finish out her contract. I hadn't been at my job very long and felt the same sense of responsibility. But between weekends spent in Millbrook, and others spent at home with friends, the winter passed quickly.

We decided to leave the second week in June, around the time school let out. The following week was spent getting items together we were taking with us. There was no large furniture, just a television set and other smaller items that would fit in the car. Much of the rest of our time was spent saying goodbye to friends and family.

Finally, the day of departure arrived. Charie was busy with some last minute details. I told her I was going to the boardwalk and would be back soon. She flashed a sympathetic look to signal she understood.

I walked up the ramp to the boardwalk, crossed over and leaned on the railing. It was early June, the weather was chilly and overcast and there was no one on the beach. A strong uneven wind blew off the ocean. The waves crisscrossed each other as if they couldn't decide which way to go. The beach sand was gray and uninviting. The ocean looked cold.

I never envisioned myself leaving the beach for the last time and I wasn't sure this was the scene I cared to remember. Standing there, deep in thought, I flashed back to my happy childhood years and those bountiful, carefree days by the bay and ocean.

It was with pride I recalled becoming a member of the Atlantic City Beach Patrol. Working with my brother guards had established a camaraderie that would last a lifetime. I thought of those we'd rescued and hoped we had played some small part in their quest for a bright future.

Now, in conjuring those memories of the beach, I knew my happy years would not be predicated by my impression of this last day. The ability to call upon images of my choice was indelibly imprinted.

Few individuals have had the opportunity to experience the kind of fun and adventurous lifestyle I was privy to. My journey up until then was like a recipe in which all the ingredients had to be uniquely blended in order to complete the finished product.

I was fortunate to have lived a fantasy into my thirties, but was reminded of a quote from Corinthians that put things into perspective. I paraphrase:

"When I was a child I thought as a child... When I became a man I put away childish things." I turned and walked across the boardwalk. Looking back over my shoulder, I glimpsed once more the joyful memories of my youth. Then slowly, turning away, I walked down the ramp and into an uncharted future.

GLOSSARY OF TERMS

Bow the front of the boat.

Break that part of the ocean identified as the surf. Once you get out past where the waves are breaking, you have cleared the break. The break can be close to shore or farther out, depending on the condition of the ocean.

Can man or third man third man on the stand who backs up the boat crew as a can buoy man (swimmer) in the event the boat crew turns over. Can men are usually required near piers, jetties or acknowledged dangerous areas.

Can or Can Buoy a diamond shaped flotation device, with a looped shoulder rope harness, used by a "can man" for swimming rescues.

Donut a red life-preserver, two of which are kept in the lifeboat, one in the bow and one in the stern. They are attached by a long rope secured to a metal ring.

Groins man-made structures designed to trap sand as it is moved down the beach by the long-shore drift. As the long-shore drift current approaches the groin, it is force to slow down and change direction. This change in velocity causes sand suspended in the current to be deposited on the up-drift side of the groin. As the current then continues around the groin, it becomes turbulent and actually contributes to erosion on the down-drift side of the groin. Groins can present a danger to bathers.

Gunnels The port and starboard railings of the boat that run from bow to stern and to which the tholepins are secured.

Layout Each day from 2 to 4 pm guards were required to patrol the waters outside the break for the purpose of watching bathers. It was determined at some previous time that these were the busiest hours. Layout was staggered between stands, so alternating crews patrolled for one hour

Nor'easter Can be wet (rain) or dry (sunshine). Either way they are accompanied by a strong northerly wind, usually causing dangerous ocean conditions.

Offset brought about by changing tides and weather conditions that cause holes to form in certain areas of the oceans floor. As the tides rise or fall water rushes into these holes causing a whirlpool and churning effect. They are visible to the trained eye as discolored aberrations and *offset* from the rest of the ocean. Most bathers try to swim against this force instead of letting it carry them to the edge of its perimeter and out of danger. Also known as undertows, rip tides, etc.

Pitch Pole-When a lifeboat is lifted by a wave (usually a hollow-back) to a 90 degree angle it will catapult the bowman through the air with oars still in hands. The vessel will continue on over often trapping the stern man underneath.

Port left side of boat when facing the stern.

Run Run is our term (A.C.B.P.'s.) for going on a rescue.

Run whistle a series of short shrill blasts on a whistle to warn bathers to get out of the way of the boat, lest they get hit by the oars, or boat.

Scramble a term lifeguards use for a rescue that involves several or a large number of bathers and where multiple guards, sometimes from other stretches, can be involved.

Set shortened term for offset.

Shoobie during Atlantic City's early history, tourists would ride the train from Camden to Atlantic City. Since they were only coming for the day, many would pack their lunch in a shoebox. Eventually they became known as "shoobies," or "down for the dayers."

Sneakbox a small rowboat used primarily by duck hunters. They were painted olive green, as camouflage, to conform to the hunter's duck blind.

Starboard right side of the boat when facing the stern.

Stern the back of the boat.

Stretch a stretch is composed of a lifeguard beach station (tent), housing a captain, medical student and complement of lifeguards, the number varying from 8-12. There were 9-10 stretches spanning the entire Atlantic City beach. Each stretch covered approximately four blocks, Stations at each block carried a compliment of 2-3 lifeguards, a boat and lookout stand.

Tent during the early days of the A.C.B.P., late 1800's, lifeguards were housed in canvas tents where they changed and carried out other necessary duties. During the 1900's, the canvas tent gave way to a wooden structure that housed 8-10 guards in a room with lockers and a shower that took up one half of the structure. The other half had a small room for the Captain. The rest of the space was used as a medical room and housed the beach doctor. It stored equipment, such as oars, donuts, can buoy's etc. A wide hall, running the length of the structure, divided both rooms. The tent was also where lost children were kept until claimed by their parents. Even though they have been modernized several times over the years, they basically remain the same. They are now handsome wooden structures; however, guards still refer to them as "tents."

Made in the USA
Monee, IL
18 February 2021

60790572R00154